RIDING THE
HULAHULA
TO THE ARCTIC OCEAN

RIDING THE
HULAHULA
TO THE ARCTIC OCEAN
~ A GUIDE TO ~
FIFTY
EXTRAORDINARY
ADVENTURES
FOR THE
SEASONED
TRAVELER

Don Mankin and Shannon Stowell

NATIONAL GEOGRAPHIC

Washington, D.C.

Published by the National Geographic Society

Library of Congress Cataloging-in-Publication Data

Mankin, Donald A., 1942-
  Riding the Hulahula to the Arctic Ocean : a guide to fifty
extraordinary adventures for the seasoned traveler / Don Mankin and
Shannon Stowell.
     p. cm.
  ISBN 978-1-4262-0278-0 (pbk.)
  1. Adventure travel. I. Stowell, Shannon, 1968- II. Title.
G516.M36 2008
910.4'5—dc22
                          2008001068

Founded in 1888, the National Geographic Society is one of the largest nonprofit scientific and educational organizations in the world. It reaches more than 285 million people worldwide each month through its official journal, *National Geographic*, and its four other magazines; the National Geographic Channel; television documentaries; radio programs; films; books; videos and DVDs; maps; and interactive media. National Geographic has funded more than 8,000 scientific research projects and supports an education program combating geographic illiteracy.

For more information, please call 1-800-NGS LINE (647-5463) or write to the following address:

National Geographic Society
1145 17th Street N.W.
Washington, DC 20036-4688 U.S.A.

Visit us online at www.nationalgeographic.com/books

For information about special discounts for bulk purchases, please contact National Geographic Books Special Sales: ngspecsales@ngs.org.

For rights or permissions inquiries, please contact National Geographic Books Subsidiary Rights: ngbookrights@ngs.org

Interior design by Peggy Archambault and Al Morrow

Printed in U.S.A.

CONTENTS

—◦◦◦◦—

To my wife, Katherine, my partner in adventure.
—Don Mankin

To my patient wife and adventurer-in-arm, Shelly,
and my future co-adventurers Amber and Ashton.
—Shannon Stowell

FOREWORD

—◦◦◦—

I t's probably no secret that my life has been about adventure, whether starting new businesses, sailing across the Atlantic, or circling the globe in a hot air balloon. But taking on challenges, testing yourself against the elements, putting yourself in strange environments, and exploring new places is not just for the Shackletons, the Fossets, yes, even the Bransons of the world. Adventure is for everyone, not just those who are famous, rich, or willing to face extraordinary risk.

I didn't know Don or Shannon when they asked me to write the foreword for their book, but I liked what they were trying to do—spark the spirit of adventure in everyone, regardless of age and inclination, and give them some ideas for where and how to do it. I believe that inspiring that spirit of adventure and keeping it alive is the key to a happy life and a healthy planet.

While circling the globe in a hot air balloon, I could see the beauty of our world and how fragile it is. Not everyone has the opportunity to see the Earth from such lofty heights, but most people in developed countries can travel, and I think it's very difficult to understand the world's problems unless you do. How can you appreciate what damage global warming will do to our planet if you don't get out and see what we stand to lose? How can you understand other cultures and people unless you see them in the day-to-day reality of their own lives? How can you learn enough about the world to help solve its problems if you don't experience it?

What I like about this book is that it encourages readers to go outside the boundaries of the luxury resorts, get off the cruise ships, and see the world up close, on its own terms. Immerse yourself in its natural beauty, expose yourself to other cultures and their worldviews, and fight like hell to keep it and them alive. Adventure travel, with its emphasis on sustainable, low-impact tourism, intimate travel experiences, and appreciation for the natural world and diverse cultures, is the answer.

What better place to see the risks of global warming than in the glaciers of Alaska, Greenland, and Baffin Island? What better place to develop an appreciation for our historical heritage than in Scotland, Spain, or Italy? What better place to learn about different cultures than in Asia? Where else to see firsthand the benefits of wildlife conservation than in Africa? You don't have to be rich, you don't have to be unbearably uncomfortable, and you don't have to put your life in danger to learn about your world—but you do need to get out there, test your limits, and learn. Your life will be fuller and the world will be a better place if you do!

—Sir Richard Branson

Preface

REDISCOVER ADVENTURE

Y ou've toured the great cities of Europe, visited many of the popular national parks of North America, and maybe even taken a luxury cruise to Asia. Now you're ready for something different, something more exotic, challenging, and adventurous. That is what this book is about. In the next 300 pages, we will describe more than 50 unique trips for seasoned travelers who are looking to transcend the ordinary in their quest for unforgettable travel experiences—experiences that will grab your imagination, expand your horizons, and spark your sense of adventure.

The focus of the book is on "adventure travel." The very expression conjures up images of novelty and excitement, but adventure travel is also challenging. It almost always involves at least some physical activity, often in remote and exotic destinations where conditions may be unpredictable and perhaps unsettling, even for the most seasoned traveler. Most of the trips we feature pose some mix of physical and psychological challenges, combined in different ways and in different proportions to produce novel, exciting, and fun experiences.

In the words of noted travel writer Pico Iyer, we also travel "to slip through the curtain of the ordinary...to leave a sense of who we are behind...to be carried off into a sense of strangeness, and into the expanded sense of possibility that strangeness sometimes brings."* At the very least, this confrontation with "strangeness" will produce memorable experiences and great stories to tell when you return home. At its best, it can open your eyes to other cultures and lead to new insights into your own attitudes and capabilities.

These are not new ideas for the millions of baby boomers who first discovered adventure during the heady years of the late 1960s and early 1970s, backpacking in the great American wilderness, driving cross-country in their own somewhat tamer versions of *Easy Rider,* or hitchhiking through Europe. After that, they turned their attention to careers, families, and mortgages. Now they are ready to rediscover the sense of adventure that was such an

---

* Pico Iyer, *Sun After Dark: Flights into the Foreign* (New York, Alfred E. Knopf, 2004).

important part of their early lives, of that very special period when everything was new, fresh, and possible.

Whether you are a baby boomer or not, the trips described in this book will reawaken your sense of adventure, or if it has never gone to sleep, they will inspire you to kick it up a notch by giving you new ideas for places to go and things to do. The world is a fascinating place for those with a willingness to take a chance and accept the challenge.

ABOUT THE SEASONED TRAVELER:
THE UP AND DOWN SIDES OF AGE

Seasoned travelers tend to be older and are used to viewing the world through multiple lenses. With their broader perspectives, adventurous older travelers seek more complex and nuanced experiences. They also have the time and money to indulge their increasingly sophisticated tastes.

But it is also true that age and maturity can impose constraints on where we go and what we do. Despite popular, some would say delusional, claims that "60 is the new 40," it would be naïve to ignore the limitations of age. Our bodies are older and less forgiving; we have a greater need for comfort, privacy, and security than ever before; and we are more aware of our mortality in a sometimes hostile world.

This image of the seasoned traveler guided our decisions about what trips to include in our book. We have selected destinations that offer varied attractions that will appeal to readers on a number of different levels. Most offer some combination of scenic beauty, the opportunity to learn about the natural history of the destination (for example, the flora, fauna, geology, etc.), and exposure to an unfamiliar culture with all of the history, geopolitics, psychology, and everything else this implies.

The trips vary widely in terms of physical demands, comfort, and security, but all recognize the changing needs and physical realities that come with age. The emphasis throughout is on being realistic and accommodating the needs and desires of the seasoned traveler.

ABOUT THE TRIPS

For the most part, we feature off-the-beaten-track destinations or different ways to experience more familiar locations. There is something in here for most every taste and inclination. The chapters do not need to be read in order. Just dip in and move from one region to another as whim and will dictate.

Twenty-six of the trips are described in extensive first-person accounts by experienced travelers, most in their 50s or older; a few are by younger travel professionals on the cutting edge in the search for new and exciting destinations. All the narratives are personal and subjective, focusing as much on the rich, deep experiences the authors had as on the details of where they went and what they did. Our intent is to help readers imagine themselves on the trip and learn about the experience that the destination, activities, and conditions offer.

Each first-person narrative also includes information on why we recommend the trip, the special issues and challenges seasoned travelers may face, variations and options, tour operators, how to get there, places to stay (if they are not included in the itineraries provided by the tour operators), and other resources. While this information should help travelers get started in planning their own adventures, details may have changed, so readers are advised to consult with the tour operators, websites, or guidebooks for more detailed information and recent updates to itineraries, accommodations, prices, and such.

The book also offers shorter descriptions of an additional 26 trips recommended by tour operators surveyed by the Adventure Travel Trade Association in 2007. These summaries also include our reasons for recommending the trip and preview the kinds of challenges travelers may face.

REGION, TYPE, AND DIFFICULTY: The trips are organized by region—North America, Latin America, Europe, Africa, Asia, and Oceania & Antarctica. They are also roughly balanced between two types:
- *Wilderness/wildlife/natural history adventures* typically involve remote and dramatically beautiful natural environments. These are often physically challenging experiences and may require some strenuous physical activity.
- *Cultural/archaeological/anthropological adventures* take the traveler to exotic destinations with unique history, architecture, archaeology, or current economic/political/cultural situations.

Several trips offer both natural history and beauty *and* exotic, unfamiliar cultures. In addition, the adventures presented vary widely in terms of their degree of difficulty and challenge, ranging from easy and accessible "soft" adventures to some that are fairly challenging. But there are no extreme adventures in this book. While we do not rate trips for difficulty, the personal narratives provide the reader with specific information on the various challenges the trips present.

EXPERIENCES VS. ACTIVITIES: Another feature of our trips that make them especially suited for mature travelers is that they are experience based, not activity based. A lot of what passes for adventure travel these days is more appropriately described as "adventure sports." Mountain biking, rock climbing, bungee jumping, zip lines, and high-speed Zodiac trips have more to do with the adrenaline rush of the activity, not the location or environment where the activity takes place. The natural environment and culture are often secondary, serving as a gymnasium of sorts for the increasingly exotic, ultra sports invented by tour operators to keep the attention of generally younger clients.

Physical activities also feature prominently in our adventures—walking, cycling, hiking, rafting, kayaking—but the primary emphasis is on the destination; the activity is generally the means for getting to and exploring the locale. That said, the activity still plays a very important role in our adventures. Certain activities are easier than others on older bodies that are not as sturdy or resilient as they once were, so instead of carrying heavy backpacks for long distances, we feature trips where nature—in the form of mules, porters, or flowing rivers, for instance—or technology (kayaks, bicycles, cars) does the carrying and conveying. These trips are not devoid of activity or effort—where would the adventure be in that?—but the physical exertion required by most are well within the capabilities of reasonably fit and healthy readers.

"BEST" TRIPS VS. RECOMMENDED TRIPS: We have resisted the temptation to label our trips as "the *best* adventures for seasoned travelers." There are so many factors that determine whether a particular trip is worth taking—and so many of these factors are matters of individual taste and situation—that it doesn't make much sense to hype a particular trip as *the* best. Furthermore, the world is far too rich and diverse to reduce its wonders to a short list of "must-see" destinations. The adventures offered in this book represent, instead, a diverse and balanced mix that are highly recommended by those who have taken them. This does not cover all possibilities, but it is a good start.

Introduction

GET READY!

I n this chapter we offer very specific recommendations on how to prepare for adventure trips, covering everything from physical training to shoes and water filters. In the "What to Do" section, Don draws upon his considerable experience as an adventure traveler "of a certain age" to recommend how you can prepare for the physical rigors of your trip. In "What to Bring," Shannon, who has more than 15 years of experience with adventure travel products and services, addresses such issues as clothing and equipment.

WHAT TO DO

You should start preparing for your trip well before the departure date. Two of the most important aspects of trip preparation are getting in shape and buying insurance. You may need a long lead time to get yourself physically ready, and most trip insurance packages require that you purchase the insurance within a couple of days of booking the trip (to avoid exclusions for pre-existing conditions). Therefore, you should start preparing for your trip as soon as possible.

GET IN SHAPE

Besides wet feet, stolen passports, and intestinal distress, the things most likely to wreck an expensive, long-anticipated vacation are fatigue and aching joints and muscles. All the trips in this book involve at least some physical exertion—walking, paddling, climbing, cycling, etc. Even on those where you can opt for different levels of physical exertion, enjoyment of the adventure will be directly proportional to your ability to move around over rough terrain, hike up to scenic views, or walk long distances, sometimes in high heat and humidity.

How best to get in shape for potentially arduous trips?* The easy answer is to get in shape for life in general and stay in shape by exercising regularly, whether at a gym or via other frequent physical activity. Training for most

---

* The authors thank Eve Glasser, a personal trainer who frequently advises active travelers, for her help with this section. For more information, contact Eve at *lilakay2003@yahoo.com.*

trips will then involve only modest adjustments to what you already do on a regular basis. So, the best advice I can give will sound familiar, since it is the same advice you have been hearing for years from your doctor, your spouse, your friends, and the media: Develop a regular exercise routine, make it part of your everyday life (or at least every other day), and stick to it.

For many readers, it may be too late to follow this advice. Although you've been thinking about getting in shape for years, you just haven't gotten around to it. Now you've found a trip that you want to take, but you don't think that you're quite up to it. Better to go on that luxury cruise instead, or hang out on the beach like you do every year. But all is not lost. There is something you can do.

If you are one of those people who doesn't spend that much time thinking about getting and staying in shape, the following steps will explain what you can do to get fit for your adventure. These steps look simple, but some are not easy to execute. A comprehensive program of physical training requires a commitment of time, sweat, and often money, but it's well worth it.

STEP #1—TALK TO TOUR OPERATORS AND OTHER TRAVELERS. Whether you are in good shape or not, it is imperative that you talk to people who know the trip well before you sign up. If it's a guided trip, this should include someone in the company that operates the trip—a guide, if possible—or someone who has recently returned (tour operators can provide contact information). Ask these people about the demands and conditions of the trip. For example, if it's a hiking trip, how much distance will be covered each day, at what altitude and elevation gain? What are the trail conditions (e.g. groomed or muddy), climate (e.g., sweltering or frigid), and other circumstances that might affect your enjoyment? Get as comprehensive and accurate a preview as you can.

STEP #2—TALK TO YOUR PHYSICIAN. If, after getting this preview, you're still eager to go, consult with your physician to make sure your current health and conditioning are up to the demands of the trip, or can reasonably be brought up to the required level. Also ask about the potential implications of any medications you are taking. For example, beta-blockers, frequently prescribed as blood pressure medication, slow the heart rate and make users more susceptible to dehydration. Your physician can help you identify ways to compensate for these impacts.

If you exercise regularly and have had a physical examination within the last few months, and *if*—and this is a big if—the trip is similar to others you have taken in the recent past or doesn't involve any special physical demands, you might be able to skip this step. But, if you have any questions or doubts, see your physician.

STEP #3—CONSULT WITH A PERSONAL TRAINER ABOUT SETTING UP A TRAINING PROGRAM. A number of criteria can help you choose a personal trainer. Talk to several and evaluate them against the criteria listed before committing to one.

- **Professional associations and certifications:** Most trainers are members of IDEA (the International Dance and Exercise Association). This is a professional association and does not require specific expertise or experience to join, however, so you should also look for certification from a long-standing and reputable organization such as the AFAA (American Fitness and Aerobic Association), ACE (American Council for Exercise), National Council on Strength and Fitness, American College of Sports Medicine, or IFPA (International Fitness Professionals Association).
- **Experience:** Has the trainer taken similar trips him/herself or trained clients who have?
- **References:** Ask the trainer to provide references, especially clients he or she has trained for similar trips.
- **What kind of program do they propose? Does it cover what you need?** Most training programs will address strength, endurance, flexibility, balance, and mobility. Different trips require different emphases and mixes of these. Is the trainer proposing an individualized program reflecting your specific needs and the requirements of the trip, or is he or she offering you a standard, cookie-cutter program? For example, training for sea kayaking should be quite different than training for hiking over rough terrain (focusing on arm and shoulder strength and endurance rather than on the legs).

Another consideration is "functional fitness"—training that focuses on the entire body and how you move in the real world. Focusing on specific muscle groups in isolation from others may be a good approach for body builders, but it won't work as well for someone who has to carry a pack and maintain balance while walking on an uneven trail. Functional fitness is a more holistic approach that replicates how the body actually moves in multiple dimensions while carrying out daily functions and activities.

If you exercise regularly and are in good health, and if the trip is similar to ones you have taken in the recent past or doesn't involve any special physical demands, you might be able to skip the personal trainer or use an online program to help you train (for example, see *www.fitfortrips.com*).

STEP #4 — MONITOR YOUR BODY, OUTCOMES, AND TRAINER. Start the exercise program, but pay close attention to how it feels, what you are doing, and how the trainer works with you. In particular:

• **Don't let your ego get in the way.** Forget about the guy on the machine next to you who's pushing a lot more weight. It's not a competition. Besides, he may be training for a different activity or purpose and may have been doing it a lot longer. Or he may be clueless about what he is doing to his body and will one day, perhaps soon, deeply regret his macho ways.

• **Don't let the trainer push you too hard.** Monitor your body and your recovery. If you think it hurts too much, you're probably right. Give the trainer lots of immediate feedback about how you feel as you exercise, as well as how you felt after your previous session. The converse is also true—don't let the trainer be too easy on you. If you think you can work harder, let the trainer know.

• **Make sure you have the right trainer for you.** If the trainer ignores your feedback or doesn't focus all of his or her attention on you while you are working out—say, by yakking on a cell phone, schmoozing with friends, or ogling someone else working out nearby—find another trainer.

BUY PEACE OF MIND

For you and for your loved ones, you should not only purchase travelers insurance (which typically covers the cost of your trip if it gets canceled due to bad weather or other circumstances beyond your control), but also buy "rescue insurance." There are a number of companies that will transport you, should the worst occur, from a hospital anywhere in the world to the best one for you and your situation, whether you've come down with a bad case of malaria or had a misunderstanding with a bull in Pamplona. Global Rescue *(www.globalrescue .com)* takes it a step further and will actually come and rescue and/or extract you from any life-threatening situation, be it disease, famine, or war. They'll even relay messages to your family. And, amazingly, it's affordable.

Other companies that offer similar insurance include World Access *(www .worldaccess.com)*, tripinsurance.com *(www.tripinsurance.com)*, MEDEX *(www.medexassist.com)*, Travel Insurance Services *(www.travelinsure.com)*,

MedJet Assist *(www.medjetassist.com)*, Air Ambulance Card *(www.air ambulancecard.com)*, Travel Assist Network *(www.travelassistnetwork.com)*, and AIG Travel Guard *(www.travelguard.com)*. Check out *www.insuremy trip.com* to compare the plans offered by the different companies.

You should also make sure that you are properly immunized. This not only means getting all required shots but also finding out about other possible diseases you could run across where you're traveling. If your family physician is a savvy traveler, he or she may suffice for this, but also consider going to a clinic or doctor that specializes in travel medicine. While it is wise to be safe, it is also smart to not overdo the medicines. We've witnessed people taking medicines to fend off unlikely diseases (e.g., taking malaria medication where the risk of malaria is low) only to suffer from the side effects of the medication. To find a clinic and get travel health tips, start with *www.travelersvaccines.com*. Also check the Centers for Disease Control and Prevention website to see what it recommends for your destination *(www .cdc.gov/travel/destinationlist.aspx)*. This is also an entertaining, if sobering, website for tracking diseases around the world.

WHAT TO BRING

Should true adventure be somewhat unpredictable, or is adventure "just bad planning," as Roald Amundsen, a member of the first expedition to winter in Antarctica in 1897, claims? It's easier to preach than to practice, but this section will give you ideas on how to reduce some of the unknowns so that you don't have to eat sled dogs or make clothing out of fig leaves.

Traveling light does have many advantages, so the items described here tend to follow this general philosophy. If you have specific medicines, salves, spectacles, or teddy bears that you need for happiness or survival, you're on your own for those critical items. Keep in mind that I recommend only a few items and sources that I have personally investigated. Untold numbers of other options are available to you, so the goal here is to offer some guidelines for choosing among them and narrow the field dramatically to what I have found works best.

FOOTWEAR

This is one of the first items people should consider when planning an adventure travel trip. Keeping your feet comfortable will be important no matter what kind of trip you're taking. I recommend that you always have:

GOOD CASUAL WALKERS. Please don't try out shoes for the first time on your trip. You should walk in them a solid five miles beforehand. This will let you know if your feet and the shoes are meant to be involved in a long-term relationship. I often take a comfy, well-worn pair of shoes I know are on their last legs (pun intended) and leave them in the country where I traveled.

AN APPROPRIATE SHOE FOR THE CLIMATE. Traveling on rivers, lakes, or oceans? Bring Teva, Bite Footwear, Chaco, or Keen sandals. Look for the newer models that have toe guards and ridges to help keep out sand and dirt. But plan on getting dirty anyway.

Want to stay dry? Your feet release around a half cup of moisture each per day, so consider a water-repellent and breathable shoe. Gore-Tex technology is now found in many different brands of great lightweight hiking and walking shoes, including those from Salomon, Asolo, Patagonia, Merrell, North Face, and more. What makes Gore-Tex stand out is that it is both waterproof and breathable. The secret lies in the micropores in the Gore-Tex membrane, which has approximately 9 billion pores per square inch. That's more than there are mosquitoes in any square inch of Alaska! These pores are about 20,000 times smaller than a drop of water, so no liquid penetrates the membrane from the outside. (And, unlike waterproofing treatments, the effectiveness of the Gore-Tex membrane does not wear off.) However, the pores of the membrane are larger than a water vapor molecule, which allows sweat to escape. If a shoe doesn't provide enough breathability, moisture will build up inside the shoe and cause that lovely sloshy feeling (and create whole new categories of odor). The other beauty of Gore-Tex is that it has a "guaranteed to keep you dry promise," which means that if you are not completely satisfied with the waterproofness or breathability of your footwear, Gore-Tex will repair or replace the product or refund your purchase price.

GOOD ANKLE SUPPORT. Today's lightweight hiking boots have advanced light-years from 15 or 20 years ago. If you are still clodding around with an original re-re-re-soled pair of waffle-stompers from 1967, or even 1997, it's time to reboot. If you still insist on resoling or repairing that old pair of boots that you just can't break up with, go to *www.davepagecobbler.com*, a world-famous boot repair company.

HIKING SOCKS. If your socks are not up to snuff, your feet will still complain, regardless of the quality of your shoes. Forget cotton and go with Thorlo's trekking socks, which are designed with super padding and wicking capabilities (see *www.thorlo.com*). Another option is Smartwool *(www.smartwool.com).*

EQUIPMENT FOR WALKING ON ICE OR SNOW, IF APPROPRIATE. Consider some strap-on traction with a product like Yaktrax, a rubber gadget that attaches to the bottom of any shoe. The straps contain small spikes to dig into ice and packed snow. Another option is Kahtoola, a pull-on crampon that is lightweight and easy to pack.

Check the following websites for information on where to buy good outdoor footwear: *www.altrec.com*, *www.onlineshoes.com*, *www.rei.com.*

CLOTHING

After footwear, clothing is the next most critical item to consider. I recommend several principles to guide you in choosing the right clothes for your trip.

GO LOW KEY. When possible, wear clothing that doesn't scream "tourist." Hawaiian shirts outside Hawaii are neither cool nor good for you unless you plan on being a target for scammers or worse.

PICK CLOTHES THAT WILL KEEP IMPORTANT ITEMS SECURE. For a travel shirt that is specifically designed with the right features for adventurous traveling, check out ExOfficio *(www.exofficio.com)* and Patagonia *(www .patagonia.com)* for starters. I once bought a bargain travel shirt and found out after purchasing it that my passport didn't fit in the security pocket on the front—such a bargain! The nice thing about a well-designed travel shirt is that you can forgo the annoying wallet that hangs around your neck or the sweaty under-the-shirt belt around your waist. It also cuts down on fumbling for your cash in the market, which means you don't look like a money tree to the not-so-casual observer. ExOfficio also makes a couple of styles of pants with zipper pockets inside the standard pocket to help discourage pickpocketing.

PICK MULTIUSE CLOTHING. Some of the best clothing manufacturers (again, ExOfficio and Patagonia) are great at designing duds that can be worn whether at dinner or on the dhow. Add in such features as moisture wicking, bug repellent, sun protection, and odor resistance, and you've got outfits that will take your mind off your clothing and onto your experience.

LOOK FOR CLOTHES THAT REPEL INSECTS. ExOfficio produces a clothing line with a product called InsectShield *(www.insectshield.com)* that is integrated into the fabric. It's a synthetic replica of a chrysanthemum-produced chemical called pyrethrin that repels biters. This is a fantastic alternative to smearing suspected carcinogens all over your skin. The more InsectShield products you wear (pants, shirt, socks, bandanna, hat, etc.), the less likely you are to be eaten by mosquitoes, ticks, flies, ants, chiggers, and/or no-see-ums (including those that can carry West Nile virus and Lyme disease). Other retailers that carry InsectShield products include L. L. Bean and Orvis.

CUT DOWN ON STINK. Several companies have created products that eliminate, or at least reduce, odor in their fabrics. These include ExOfficio, Arc'Teryx, Mountain Hardwear, North Face, and others.

LUGGAGE

Your luggage really does matter. For a sure win, go with the grand master of the adventure travel gear game—Eagle Creek Travel Gear *(www.eaglecreek .com)*. This is one of the only companies to dedicate all three decades of its product expertise to creating bags, rollaways, and accessories for the adventurer. Although lots of companies build rollaways and duffels, there are a few key features that make products stand out—such as non-rip material and the ability to maintain balance regardless of what's inside. Some of my favorite pieces are a couple of Eagle Creek daypacks that have a SafeGuard Panel—a fairly hard-to-spot security pocket that rests against your back, ensuring that pickpockets cannot get at the goods.

If you will not be doing a lot of backpacking or trekking, consider a rollaway. I've used my large Eagle Creek rollaway in the U.S., Canada, Brazil, China, and Greenland. It's super rugged and does not tip over like the annoying cheaper models. My luggage always emerges unscathed from that gnawing beast known as baggage claim, unlike those poor souls who end up with busted suitcase zippers, ripped-off handles, or missing wheels. And Eagle Creek has a "no matter what" warranty, the most comprehensive one out there.

For organizational freaks, Eagle Creek has created a packing system that allows you to keep socks and other sundries in their own breathable, transparent mesh cubes. It's one of the few weight luxuries worth adding to your pack.

Osprey Packs, another company with more than 30 years of pack expertise, has recently entered the adventure travel market with its Meridian, Sojourn, and Vector series of bags *(www.ospreypacks.com)*. Some of the models even feature removable harnesses to convert the bag to a backpack when you can't roll along. For security, check out PacSafe *(www.pacsafe .com)*, a company that focuses on products that secure and protect your luggage, from locks to security mesh nets.

FOR YOUR HEALTH

Nobody can promise you won't occasionally get hit with something, but take the right products and precautions to reduce your chances of getting sick and the severity when you do.

WATER. Of course, the best plan is to always drink bottled. Buy labeled, brand-name products when possible—unmarked bottles might be full of untreated tap water. When reliable bottled water is not available and you don't like the flavor of water purification tablets, try these items:

- **Steri-Pen (www.steripen.com).** This is a portable water purifier that uses ultraviolet (UV) light to destroy waterborne microbes. Whether you are drinking out of a stream or a hotel tap, this product purifies water by destroying viruses, bacteria, and protozoa, including Giardia and Crypto. The only problem is that you can't use it on murky water, which tends to block UV rays. You'll need to filter it first—a coffee filter will do—before disinfecting.
- **Water filter.** If you want to make sure that everything that can wreck your intestines is mechanically removed from your drinking water, Katadyn makes the Backcountry and Ultralight series of world-class water filters *(www.katadyn.com)*.

ARE YOU A GERM-A-PHOBE? Take your obsessions and compulsions a step beyond hand sanitizer and excessive washing. Design Salt has a series of travel sheets you can take along for those hotel beds that are just a little suspect or if you have to crash in an unexpected and unsavory location *(www.designsalt.com)*.

PACK A PERSONAL FIRST AID KIT. Make sure it contains the following items:
- Hand sanitizer
- Neosporin
- Ciproflaxin (prescription) for traveler's diarrhea
- Antidiarrheal medicine such as Imodium for those moments when you really can't afford to go
- Cold and allergy medicines. Make sure you have two kinds—nondrowsy versions to take during the day and those that won't keep you awake at night.
- Band-Aids of different sizes
- A robust variety of vitamins. Give your immune system a boost before you jump on a long flight.
- And, of course, your prescription drugs in their original bottles with the labels from the pharmacy indicating medication, prescription number, and so forth on the container

MISCELLANEOUS PRODUCTS FOR TRAVEL HAPPINESS

- A few food bars (for that evening when you just can't eat all your whale blubber or jungle spiders). Clif Bar, Luna Bar, and an all-natural snack called LaraBar are great examples of healthy and edible food bars.
- Earplugs
- A small roll of toilet paper in a Ziploc bag to keep it dry
- A garbage bag for stowing dirty laundry and various other smelly items
- A color copy of your passport. Keep it separate from your passport (e.g., in a suitcase). If your passport is lost or stolen, this will help you get the replacement process going at your embassy.

You should talk to your trip provider before buying enough extra gear to sink a small pirogue. Know before you go what the critical challenges will be on your trip and you will be able to take some of the pain out of the inevitable problems that come with adventuring.

CONCLUSION

There is much more that we could add, but the recommendations in this chapter address the most critical issues and items. Most tour operators also provide extensive information and instructions on how to prepare and what to bring, plus checklists and packing lists to ensure that you do not miss anything important. If you are doing the trip on your own, we also recommend that you consult at least one of the guidebooks providing detailed information on your destination. For adventure travel, we have found Lonely Planet, Rough Guides, Moon Guides, and Bradt travel guides to be especially helpful. Also check out back issues of *Outside* and *National Geographic Adventure* magazines.

NORTH AMERICA

—⁕—

RIDING THE HULAHULA TO THE ARCTIC OCEAN (ALASKA)

DON MANKIN

No destination in North America, perhaps in the world, is more closely associated with adventure than the state of Alaska. My first visit to Alaska, in 1969, introduced me to the fjords, glaciers, and mossy rain forests of the southeastern portion of the state. Subsequent trips took me farther afield. My fantasy was to explore the farthest, most remote edges of the state—in my mind, the end of the world. I finally had the chance in the summer of 2000 to travel to the Arctic National Wildlife Refuge, about as far north as you can go in the United States, and then just a little bit beyond, into the Arctic Ocean. I almost passed on the chance because of a health scare, and it would have been a profoundly regrettable mistake if I had.

TRIP DESCRIPTION

My doctor's words were like a punch in the stomach. "Don, I think it's time we looked into this," he said while looking at the results of my latest blood test. I was leaving in a couple of weeks for my latest "trip of a lifetime" and did not want to hear about anything that might get in the way. I had been dreaming of this trip for years—an 11-day raft trip starting near the origin of the Hulahula River* deep in the Brooks mountain range in Northern Alaska and ending on a mere sliver of an island a mile or so off the coast in the portion of the

---

* The river was named by a crew of homesick Hawaiian whalers who got trapped in the ice near the mouth of the river in the late 19th century.

Arctic Ocean known as the Beaufort Sea. For most of the trip, we would float through the coastal plain of the Arctic National Wildlife Refuge (ANWR). The timing of the trip was critical—in mid-June, immediately following the breakup of the ice on the river, right before the beginning of the mosquito season, and during the height of the annual caribou migration.

I had already put this trip off for many years, most recently due to a brush with mortality the previous year when I cheated my family history by finding the clogged-up kink in my coronary artery before it found me. Then, just as I thought I might finally be able to take the trip, my frequent blood tests revealed yet another possibly threatening medical condition, and my doctor scheduled me for a bone marrow biopsy. The problem was, besides the potentially life threatening implications of the results, there was no way I would get the results back before leaving for my trip.

The doctor assured me that there was no reason I couldn't go on the trip. The worst-case scenario would be serious but not imminent, and there was little that could happen on the trip that would make the situation worse. Being a true obsessive, and a hypochondriac to boot, I couldn't imagine enjoying the trip with the test results hanging over my head until my return. Fortunately, my doctor and, most important, my wife prevailed. Several days later, I left for my trip as originally planned.

FLYING INTO THE ALASKAN BUSH

Like most Alaskan adventures, the fun began with the flight into the bush. Our first flight dropped off our group of 12—three guides and nine clients—at a Native American settlement known as Arctic Village, almost 300 miles north of Fairbanks at the southern edge of the ANWR. We unloaded our gear directly onto the airstrip and prepared for the second stage of our trip, a 45-minute flight in a four-seater specially designed to land and take off in places too small or dicey for more conventional aircraft. I would soon see why this was so important.

I was among the first group of three to be ferried to our starting point deep in the mountains of the Brooks range. Our pilot was the prototypical Alaskan bush pilot—rangy, weathered, and nonchalant. I had the good fortune to get the front passenger's seat with a view to die for. From the looks of the plane and the terrain, I wasn't all that sure that I wouldn't have to pay that price. Whether it was the weight we were carrying or just the limitations of the plane, instead of flying over the peaks in a straight line to our destination, we flew around them, following the mountain passes and river valleys that snaked through the mountains. Sometimes it seemed as if our wings almost brushed the tundra-covered slopes as we passed by. We were not that far off the ground to begin with, and the pilot would occasionally swoop even lower to give us a better view of musk oxen, moose, or a grizzly just below us.

This was one of the most memorable flights I have ever taken. Just when I thought it couldn't get any better or more breathtaking, the pilot pointed out a small gravel beach beside the river a mile or so ahead. "That's where we're landing," he calmly noted. It was a very short and uneven stretch of beach, hardly what I would call a landing strip. I gulped and replied, "I'm impressed." He smiled, "Don't be, not yet. Wait to see if we make it." I assumed he was kidding. Whether or not he was, he slowed the plane to what seemed like an aeronautical version of a crawl, hovered for a second or two before plopping down on the gravel, and came to a stop in just a few bumpy feet. It was probably the strangest airplane landing I have ever experienced.

ADAPTING TO A UNIQUE ENVIRONMENT

By early evening, everyone in our party had landed, unpacked, and set up camp for the night. Then it was time for our orientation to life in the Arctic—high rubber boots for walking on the spongy, mossy, marshy tundra; individual canisters of bear spray, also for walking on the tundra; and the ubiquitous shovel and ditty bag of toilet paper for…well, you get the picture. David, our trip leader from Arctic Wild, our tour operator, also showed us the shotgun that he would always have at the ready, just in case, and instructed us to be sure to talk, sing, and otherwise make noise whenever we wandered off for a walk or to "take care of business." Although the terrain was pretty open—bluffs, rolling hills, and streambeds—there were depressions and obstructed views that could hide a bear. The key is to avoid them when you can see them, and to make sure that you do not surprise them when you can't.

While our guides made dinner, we explored our surroundings, slogging up and down hills with the spray canisters grasped firmly in our hands, constantly scanning ahead for signs of bears. We also had to keep our eyes on the ground just ahead. Much of it was made up of tussocks of moss, lichen, and tiny yellow, white, and purple flowers. In between the tussocks were boggy depressions a foot or so deep. It was tricky going. We frequently had to walk from tussock to tussock. Miss a step and twist an ankle, or worse. There were also low woody shrubs, mats of tightly clumped plants, lots of rocks, and tufts of grass, but no trees or bushes. The views from the many bluffs, ridges, and rises up and down the valley were stunning—snowcapped peaks flanked the meandering river, its wide banks sparkling in the rays of an evening sun hanging low in the sky. The sun, which never set throughout the entire trip, cast long shadows and brought out the many and varied hues of green that make up much of the color palette of the Far North.

GETTING INTO THE FLOW OF THE TRIP

For the next two days, we drifted and paddled down the river, past huge banks of ice still remaining in the long, first few days of the Arctic summer. Mountains lined the river on both sides and waterfalls cascaded down to meet us. I thought of little else but maintaining a steady paddle stroke and the beauty that surrounded me.

In camp and on the river, we saw lots of wildlife—arctic birds, musk oxen, sheep, the occasional caribou and moose, and several grizzlies, usually and thankfully from a distance. One evening a wolf almost wandered through our camp until he (she?) noticed the strange creatures in colorful Gore-Tex gear emitting unfamiliar chattering noises.

At the end of the third day, we set up camp on a high bluff near a bend of the river. The views from this spot were particularly stunning. Looking up the river from where we had come, the view of mountain ranges and peaks was expansive. It had been a short day of paddling, so we had several hours of free time before dinner. After setting up my tent, I took off on a short hike along a ridge overlooking our camp that provided an even more dramatic view of the river, the valley, and the mountains.

Standing on the ridge surveying the Arctic landscape that stretched before me in the extended dusk of the midnight sun, I started to think about the still unknown medical test results awaiting my return. Curiously, I did not seem to care. I was aware of the potentially life-changing news waiting for me at home, but I was thoroughly immersed in the here and now. I knew that I would eventually have to deal with that other reality, but all that mattered at that particular time and in that particular place was the awesome beauty surrounding me…and the very large grizzly bear traversing the ridge across the river! For the rest of the trip, thoughts about the test results would occasionally pass through my mind, but they would quickly be pushed aside by more immediate concerns—keeping warm and dry and out of the clutches of wolves, grizzlies, and moose—and the unmatched beauty and solitude of that very special place.

We quickly fell into an efficient and congenial daily routine. Since we had 24 hours of daylight, we could raft whenever it suited us. We slept as late as we wanted, had breakfast, took down our tents, packed the rafts, and were generally on the river by early afternoon. We would paddle and drift for several hours, stop for a leisurely lunch in late afternoon, then go back on the river for a few more hours. By early evening, we would pull into a campsite for the evening, set up our tents, and then go for a hearty walk in the long shadows of the sun before it dipped behind the mountains. We frequently did not eat dinner until late evening. Then we would sit and talk, play cards, or go off to our tents and read.

Our group was older, better educated, and more ecologically sophisticated than most guided outdoor trips. That's saying a lot since these trips tend to attract travelers who are well educated and environmentally active. But this seemed to be the ultimate trip for Alaskan outdoor enthusiasts. The group included an environmental lawyer, four environmental activists, and a community college biology professor. Since our trip traversed the oil-rich and politically controversial ANWR, we had plenty to talk about in the evening. Although we were all pretty much in agreement about oil drilling in the refuge (we opposed it), we found enough areas of disagreement to keep things interesting. Most of the time, we just told stories and laughed. It's hard to muster a serious argument when you are in a place whose scale and grandeur constantly reminds you how trivial and irrelevant the things we usually argue about are.

NEW SCENERY AND
CLOSE ENCOUNTERS WITH BEARS

Over the course of our 11-day trip, the scenery and experience changed dramatically. After about three days floating through a broad, relatively level river valley, we hit a patch of faster, more turbulent water as the river dropped through a narrow canyon in the foothills before spilling out onto the coastal plain. The set of rapids in this canyon were rated an adrenaline-pumping Class IV and looked and felt every bit of it. It was quite a ride paddling in the front where I was. Just as I was about to celebrate our successful run through the hardest part of the rapids, I was slapped in the face by a standing wave. It barely dampened my enthusiasm, but did a pretty good job on my clothes.

Shortly after passing the rapids, we stopped for lunch and to dry out. We were very relaxed after our successful run through the white water. As we spread out our food, we didn't notice the large grizzly bear cresting the rise across the river, sniffing the air to find the source of the wonderful odors wafting in his direction. One of our guides drew our attention to this magnificent beast just 30 or so yards away. The bear approached the edge of the river, still sniffing and unaware of our presence just a few yards across the river. We watched in fascination, feeling secure that the river between us would keep him away.

Suddenly, the guide who had first alerted us to this prized sighting leapt up and shouted: "He's looking for a way to cross! If he gets across, we're in trouble! Grab the oars, wave them in the air, and start shouting!!!" The bear looked up, startled, not quite sure what to make of us, then retreated back up the rise. Before plunging down the other side and out of view, he stopped, turned, and squinted once more in our direction. After another burst of waving and shouting, he turned tail and got the hell out of there as fast as he could. We breathed a deep sigh of relief, took just a moment to enjoy the exhilaration of our close encounter with the king of the Arctic, and decided not to tempt fate any longer. We grabbed a few quick bites, wrapped up the leftovers, and quickly got on our way.

Soon the river took us through the foothills and down onto the wide-open coastal plain. Here the Hulahula turns into a very different kind of river— wider, slower, and very shallow, so shallow that we sometimes had to get out and guide the raft as it bumped along the bottom. It was on this section of the river only a few hours later that we had our second close encounter with a grizzly. Since the river was wider, the bear was farther away. But he was more aggressive and persistent. He paced back and forth and several times moved in our direction as if to scare us away. David speculated that he had a kill and was not about to leave it behind. We just sat alertly in the rafts at a distance and watched. David sat with the shotgun at the ready on his lap just in case. We must have spent close to an hour watching. Finally, we had our fill and it was time to move on and find a place to camp for the night, hopefully far away from our new ursine friend on the opposite side of the river.

THROUGH THE COASTAL PLAIN

For the next couple of days we rafted through the coastal plain. The scenery here was quite different than in the mountains. To the east and west, the views went on forever and, to the north, a misty haze hung over the pack ice a few miles off in the Arctic Ocean. To the south, the mountains and deeply carved valleys of the Brooks Range, where we had been just a day or two before, framed the unbroken expanse of the coastal plain. I have rarely felt so insignificant and small, nor so exhilarated by such dramatic, untouched beauty.

The wildlife viewing was also exceptional. The trip overlapped with the annual migration of the porcupine caribou herd from Canada to their calving grounds on the coastal plain of the refuge. In good years, thousands of caribou would be scattered over the tundra as far as the eye could see. This year, a heavy snowfall late in the year had trapped most of the caribou herd in Canada, so we saw fewer of them, and therefore fewer grizzlies than usual. Nonetheless, we did see more caribou than I have ever seen before, plus musk oxen, arctic birds, and enough bears to keep us on our toes and the shotgun and bear spray canisters close at hand.

As we neared the coast, we entered the river delta and the river broke up into a series of very shallow braided channels. Not all of the channels reach the sea, and picking the wrong one would mean ending up in a dead end and having to retrace our "steps" or portage to a more promising channel. Since the pattern of braids changes from one year to the next, choosing the right one is pretty much an educated guess. There are no elevated vantage points from which to scan for the most promising path.

Given the potential for so many bad choices, it is pretty amazing that we only had to portage once. But that was more than enough. It was grueling labor, carrying the rafts and all of our equipment for half a mile or more over very soggy ground. It took several trips and several hours. By the time we were done, we were finished! Most of us set up our tents and crawled in, exhausted, for a short nap before dinner.

TO THE END OF THE CONTINENT AND BEYOND
The last day of the trip was what I most looked forward to, not because I badly needed a bath—which I did—nor because I was anxious to get my test results, which were still part of a very distant reality. The reason for my excitement was that our trip was scheduled to end on a small island, little more than a gravel bar, about a mile off the coast in the Beaufort Sea. It would be as close to the end of the world as I had ever been. Then, in a mirror image of how our trip began, a four-seat Cessna would ferry us from the island to the Inupiat township of Kaktovik just a 30-minute flight away, from where we would all fly back to Fairbanks on a regularly scheduled commercial airline.

After a short paddle down the last channel of the river, we poked our way into the Arctic Ocean. As impressive as that sounds, the water from the edge of the continent to the island is only a few inches deep. We could have walked most of the way without getting our knees wet. The water was too shallow to paddle, so we pushed the raft along by digging our paddles into the sand on the bottom. The guides often had to get out of the rafts and pull them through especially shallow sections.

The view from the island south, back in the direction from which we came, was incredible, with the Brooks Range framing the horizon as far as the eye could see. But just as incredible was the view in the other direction from the north side of the island. Just a couple of feet offshore was the edge of the polar ice pack, which stretched into the distance until it met the sky. That is where we spent the last few hours of our trip, walking on the pack ice, as far out as we dared, keeping our eyes open for seals sunning on the ice or, most important, a polar bear looking for his next meal. In fact, we spent the summer solstice walking on the ice casting long shadows in the midnight sun. This was the high point of a trip that was filled with high points, a fitting end to a long-delayed adventure that I almost did not take.

Oh yes, about those test results. I checked my phone messages from the lodge in Kaktovik where we cleaned up before our flight to Fairbanks. They were negative! It would have been a shame if I had postponed this trip yet again for what turned out to be no good reason. The lesson—carpe diem—is obvious and almost trite, but this ride of a lifetime down the Hulahula River to the Arctic Ocean made this lesson real, transforming the cliché into something much more personal.

WHY GO: The spectacular scenery and wildlife, the unsurpassed opportunity for solitude and reflection, and the intimate connection with nature would be reason enough to take this trip. But the area is also the focal point for one of the defining issues of our age: the trade-off between cheap energy and the societal costs of acquiring that energy. As almost everyone who follows the news knows, oil drilling in the ANWR is a controversial topic and a political hot potato. It is hard for me to imagine that anyone who has ever been fortunate enough to experience such a place would ever advocate defacing its beauty and solitude by our insatiable hunger for cheap energy, especially when other options are possible. Go there while you still have the chance to experience this very special place in its wild, pristine state.

SPECIAL ISSUES AND CHALLENGES: This trip is not as arduous as a backpacking trip would be in the same region. Clients do not have to carry heavy packs or even walk that much. There are plenty of opportunities for long hikes, especially in the first few days in the mountains, but they are optional and you can always turn back and return to camp when you have had enough. The paddling does require some upper body strength and conditioning, but not as much as a long kayak trip. You will also have to carry a lot of gear to and from the rafts and up and down riverbanks. And the portages are a bear and could require significant exertion for a couple of hours at a time. The bottom line is that you do need to be in decent shape, but you do not have to be in great shape. The fitter you are, the more you'll enjoy the trip.

VARIATIONS AND OPTIONS: The tour operator I used, Arctic Wild, offers a number of different trips in northern Alaska, including rafting trips on other rivers, backpacking trips, and canoe trips. Although I have not done any other trips in the region, I imagine that the overall experience is similar, although the backpacking ones would be more strenuous and the details of the itinerary would vary depending on the specific location. Other operators also offer similar trips or variations.

If you are going to go to the trouble and expense of visiting Alaska, you should try to schedule some time before or after your trip to visit some of the state's other attractions. Denali, for example, is only a two- or three-hour drive from Fairbanks, the jumping-off point for most trips into the Arctic. I followed my ANWR trip with a five-day sea kayak trip in Prince William Sound—featuring spectacular tidal glaciers and icebergs, plus lots of marine wildlife—and several days of driving around the Kenai Peninsula.

RESOURCES AND INFORMATION: Information on our tour operator, Arctic Wild, can be found on its website at *www.arcticwild.com*. The approximate cost for the trip is $4,000, which includes all costs north of Fairbanks except for personal camping gear (tents, sleeping bags, etc.). Contact Arctic Wild at 888-577-8203 or *info@arcticwild.com*.

Other operators offering trips on the Hulahula and other rivers in the region include Arctic Treks *(www.arctictreksadventures.com)*, Kaktovik Arctic Adventures *(www.kaktovikarcticadventures.com)*, and Mountain Travel Sobek *(www.mtsobek.com)*. OARS *(www.oars.com)* runs a similar trip on the Firth River just across the border in Canada.

TOURING THE ISLANDS OF THE GULF OF ST. LAWRENCE (CANADA)

DON MANKIN

A wedding gift inspired this adventure—an exploration via car, boat, and foot of the unique cultures and scenery of several islands in the Gulf of St. Lawrence: Quebec's Îles de la Madeleine (Magdalene Islands), Nova Scotia's Cape Breton Island, and Newfoundland. The gift consisted of three nights and a lobster dinner at a B&B on one of the islands of the Magdalene archipelago in the heart of the gulf. We had never even heard of the Magdalene Islands until our friends—the sister and brother-in-law of the owners of the B&B—showed us pictures from their trip several months earlier. My soon-to-be-wife, Katherine, fell in love with the place just from the pictures, and that inspired our friends to give the gift that inspired the trip.

I had also been intrigued with Newfoundland since I was a teenager growing up in Philadelphia. It seemed very far away, yet still reachable from the small world defined by the neighborhoods I could reach by public transportation and on foot. So we added Newfoundland to our itinerary, as well as Cape Breton Island, which lies in between the two. It was not the usual honeymoon in a tropical paradise but a trip to a unique destination, with some of the most beautiful scenery and diverse cultures to be found within a day's travel of the major cities of the northeastern United States.

TRIP DESCRIPTION

I wasn't expecting all that much from the Magdalene Islands. From the pictures and descriptions, they seemed pleasant enough, but they didn't score high on my personal strange/exotic/adventure scale. But it was our honeymoon and Katherine was charmed by the idea of going some place "French." I guess French Canadian was close enough. For me, it seemed like a good place to chill out for a few days before embarking on the real adventure, driving to the far north of Newfoundland.

The islands, part of the province of Quebec but 130 miles away from its closest border, are a five-hour ferry ride from Prince Edward Island.

Of the dozen or so islands in the Magdalene archipelago, only seven are inhabited. Six of these are connected in the shape of a fishhook by long, narrow dunes and a two-lane road that runs from one end of the islands to the other. The seventh island is a one-hour boat ride away from the main island, Cap-aux-Meules.

My initial indifference quickly melted among the sand dunes, red sea cliffs, quaint lighthouses, windswept vistas, colorfully painted houses, artsy cafés, and incredibly delicious lobster meals. We were there in mid-May, several weeks before the beginning of the tourist season, so we had the islands pretty much to ourselves. For three days we just wandered, driving and stopping wherever we wanted and walking for hours on the beaches, which extended for miles in all directions. We rarely saw anyone else on the beaches—hundreds of seabirds, but no people. Since the islands are small, there are sweeping ocean views from almost everywhere.

One day we drove to the very end of the archipelago, to the tip of the "fishhook," to watch the lobster boats return to port with their catch. During the short ten-week season that begins in early May, the lobster boats go out hours before sunrise to bring back what aficionados consider to be the best lobster in the world. We took every opportunity to test their opinion and were never disappointed. One night we had our lobster dinner at the Factory, a modest cafeteria-style restaurant overlooking the factory floor where live, freshly caught lobsters were prepared for shipment around the world. The no-frills lobster dinner was excellent, the best lobster I had ever eaten, and cost only a fifth of what a comparable dinner would have cost back home in Los Angeles. In fact, wherever we ate in the Magdalenes, the food was excellent, reflecting the fortunate convergence of French cuisine and incomparably fresh seafood.

At the end of our three-day gift, I was sold on the islands and had become a Francophile to boot. We decided to stay for another couple of days at our own expense. We made very good use of those extra days.

The highlight was the day-trip to Île d'Entrée, the only inhabited island that cannot be reached by road. There was only one other passenger and the crew with us on the small boat that carried us across the sea. (The ferry runs only during the summer months and takes only pedestrians and cyclists.) About 130 people live on this isolated outpost. Unlike those on the other Magdalene islands, the residents of Île d'Entrée are primarily of Scotch and Irish descent. As isolated as the other islands are from the rest of the world, Île d'Entrée made them seem almost like the boroughs of New York City.

This island is also different in other ways. Instead of beaches, it is ringed by high red cliffs that rise steeply above the surf. There are only a couple of roads, some houses, a church or two, treeless valleys, and open fields dotted with cows and horses that sweep down to the edge of the cliffs. In the middle of the island is Big Hill, at 530 feet the highest point in the archipelago. From the top of this hill, we had a 360-degree view of the island and could see Île du Havre-Aubert, the island on which we were staying and the vast, empty beach we walked on every day.

We walked wherever we wanted for the next several hours, stopping occasionally to admire the view or to eat the huge and very French lunch our hosts at the B&B had packed for us—wine, cheese, sausage, bread, and pastries. At first I hesitated to climb over the fences that ringed the fields until I realized that they were intended to keep the cows from getting out rather than tourists from getting in. I took some ribbing from a few locals about this later that afternoon as we waited for the boat back to Cap-aux-Meules. "You Yanks probably thought that you would get shot if you climbed over those fences, right?" In fact, that was exactly what I thought, I had to admit, somewhat embarrassed.

That was our last day in the Magdalenes. Our hosts, Louie and Michilene, capped off this perfect and surprisingly enjoyable first leg of our honeymoon by preparing a lobster dinner, with typical French panache, that was the best of all. We were now ready to move on to the next leg of our unlikely honeymoon adventure.

CLOGGING AND HIKING ON CAPE BRETON ISLAND

After a day of ferries and driving, we arrived at Cape Breton Island at the northeastern tip of the province of Nova Scotia. Although Cape Breton was originally settled by the French in the early years of the 17th century, after almost a century of conflict it became a British colony in 1763. Later in the century thousands of Highland Scots, attracted by the region's resemblance to their homeland, settled here. This heritage is suitably reflected in the name of the province, which in Latin means "New Scotland." This history is also reflected in the many old churches and cemeteries we passed, with old gravestones dating as far back as the early years of the 19th century.

The mixed heritage of French, Scottish, English, and Irish was particularly prominent in Chéticamp, a gateway to Cape Breton Highlands National Park at the northern end of the island. Unlike the rest of Nova Scotia, the culture of Chéticamp is primarily French, or "Acadian" as the descendants of the early French settlers are known. Chéticamp is also known for its music, that lively blend of Irish, Scottish, and French music known throughout the world as Cape Breton music. We spent several hours one Sunday afternoon at Doryman's Pub, a world-famous showcase for Cape Breton music, watching the musicians play fiddles and spoons and members of the audience spontaneously jump to their feet to clog in time to the music.

But the primary attraction of Cape Breton Island is the scenery and hiking trails in the national park. The Cabot Trail, a two-lane road, encircles the island, much of it hugging the coast, soaring over hills to provide dramatic views of the ocean, then dipping down into valleys and rocky coves. The scenery is reminiscent of California's Pacific Coast Highway through Big Sur.

There are numerous hikes long the way, from steady climbs ending in panoramic views of the coastline (a hike referred to as "L'Acadien" on the map available at the park) to leaf-strewn paths through lush forests and along streams framed by moss-covered rocks ("Le Chemin du Buttereau" on the hiking map). One of our favorite hikes was along the beach, past headlands and through sections where we had to pick our way over large rocks that looked like dinosaur eggs (the "Coastal" on the map, but I prefer my wife's name for the trail, "Eggland").

At one stop along the Cabot Trail, we looked out over a sunny beach at Cabot's Landing, where the famed English explorer John Cabot supposedly landed in 1497. We drove around the hills behind us to a fishing village on the Bay of St. Lawrence, which was enshrouded in fog. We spent our last night on Cape Breton in a cabin just a few feet from the rocky beach in Ingonish. Our departure from the Cabot Trail seemed appropriate, via a tiny cable ferry that pulled us across a narrow inlet. We were soon on the road to North Sydney, Nova Scotia, to catch the overnight ferry to Newfoundland.

DODGING MOOSE ON THE
NORTHERN PENINSULA

Despite its proximity to Cape Breton and the Magdalenes, Newfoundland is quite different. The cultural influences are more homogenous, primarily

English and Scottish, and unlike the tiny Magdalenes and the somewhat larger Cape Breton Island, Newfoundland is huge. The bilateral province of Newfoundland and Labrador is three times larger than the other three Atlantic provinces combined. As a result, there is a lot more to see and the variety of scenery and wildlife is much greater. In the eight days we spent on the island, we barely scratched the surface.

We spent all of our time on the Northern Peninsula, the home of two UNESCO World Heritage sites. The first, near the bottom of the peninsula, is Gros Morne National Park, about a three-hour drive from the ferry landing at Port-aux-Basques. The first thing we learned as we entered the park is to drive carefully, especially at dusk, to avoid hitting the many moose that can be seen on the sides of the roads—and sometimes on the roads, ergo the warnings. Despite their almost comical appearance, with snouts that would do a burlesque comic proud, this is not a laughing matter. Many moose get killed every year by cars, and the drivers often do not fare much better. At first I wondered why anyone would want to speed by these magnificent beasts. We slowed down at every sighting and often stopped on the side of the road to gawk. But they are so plentiful that after three days, the novelty wore off. Still, we kept our eyes open and tried to plan our days so that we were off the road by dark. We also saw caribou from time to time, but they weren't as bold as the moose, so we had to keep our eyes open to spot them.

The scenery is as beautiful and varied as anything I have ever seen in one destination—forests, fjords, snow-dotted tabletop mountains, and lobster traps stacked against weathered barns in scenes reminiscent of Winslow Homer. One day we hiked through a lush forest to a roaring multitiered waterfall (this hike is called "Baker Brooks Falls"); another day through a barren rock-strewn volcanic landscape (the "Table Lands") that looked like it came straight out of the high desert of the southwestern U.S.; a third hike took us along a ridge overlooking a long, fjord-like lake ("Trout River Pond"). The best hike was the "Green Gardens Trail," which descends steeply to cliffs overlooking a hidden, rocky beach and sea stacks pounded by wild surf. We hardly ran into anybody on any of our hikes, although as we sat on the grass at the bottom of the Green Gardens trail eating our lunch, a flock of sheep wandered by, gave us a quizzical look, then went on their way.

The only disappointment in this portion of our trip was that we were a week too early for the boat ride through the narrow fjord at Western Brook

Pond. The ice was still blocking the flow of water into the fjord, and as a result, the water level was too low for the boat. It is supposed to be a spectacular ride as the boat glides between the sheer walls of granite on each side. Next time we will plan a later visit to make sure that we have the chance to take this excursion.

THE LAND OF VIKINGS AND ICEBERGS

After several days in Gros Morne, we drove up the officially designated Viking Trail to visit the second World Heritage site at L'anse aux Meadows, the site of the first Viking settlement in North America. To those familiar with Annie Proulx's novel, this is *Shipping News* country—rocky coves, hearty people, hardscrabble country, and many, many icebergs. L'anse aux Meadows is almost at the very tip of the Northern Peninsula, where the strait that separates Newfoundland from Labrador, unofficially known as "Iceberg Alley," meets the Atlantic Ocean. L'anse aux Meadows dates back nearly 1,000 years. There is not much left of the original settlement, just some stones outlining where buildings used to stand, but the Canadian government has reconstructed the sod huts to give the visitor a good idea of what it was like to live in these smoky structures. There is also a small but very informative museum in the visitors center.

I explored the walking trail that meandered through and around the site and stood at the edge of the windswept beach trying to imagine what it must have been like to live there. The setting hasn't changed very much, and there were few other visitors when we were there, so it was not hard to imagine myself as one of the settlers, very far from home in a place that was even more inhospitable. It was easy to see why the Vikings abandoned L'anse aux Meadows after only a few years.

Wherever we saw ocean, we saw icebergs. We saw them in "Iceberg Alley," we saw them stuck just off the beach in Hays Cove where we stayed for two nights, and we saw them drifting en masse into the harbor in the town of St. Anthony, quickly turning a warm spring day into winter.

The most impressive sighting was from a small former fishing boat that had been turned into a tour boat for whale watching and iceberg viewing. Paul, the captain, was the last generation in his family to fish commercially. Large factory fishing vessels have overfished the area, so government regulations now restrict cod fishing to allow time for the stock to regenerate. As a result, the local, family-based cod fishing industry has been decimated. Paul had seen the handwriting on the wall after graduating from college and convinced his father and uncle, his partners in the fishing boat, to apply their knowledge, assets, and work ethic to this new business venture. We had read about the devastating changes in the fishing industry in Newfoundland, but our two hours with Paul placed much of what we had seen and heard for the last several days into context and put a human face on the statistics. We were very touched by his story and impressed by his commitment to help his family move beyond one of their most cherished traditions into this new and highly uncertain venture (more about the results of their efforts shortly).

We rode out from the harbor for at least half an hour to see a huge iceberg stuck on the bottom of the ocean in about 300 feet of water. It was enormous! The part of the iceberg that jutted out of the water was about 100 feet high. It looked like a giant piece of whipped meringue with peaks, swirls, swoops, and arches. It was so huge that it had its own waterfalls. Paul pointed to the veil of fog that circled the highest swirl and told us that the iceberg was so large that it created its own microclimate. After circling at a respectful distance several times, we motored on to the next iceberg, then to a few others after that. Each was distinctive and incredibly beautiful. They took my breath away. Even now, years later, I look at the dozens of pictures I took that afternoon and still think that those icebergs are the single most beautiful objects I have ever seen.

The icebergs also serve as an apt metaphor for the entire trip—unexpected, majestic, and a symbol for the courage and exceptional strength of the people who every day face the challenges of this rugged land. This may not be everyone's idea of a romantic honeymoon, but I believe that few people have as many great pictures, memories, and stories as we do or had as interesting a time.

WHY GO: Besides the obvious reasons—beautiful scenery, interesting wildlife, and unique culture—one of the best reasons to go is the accessibility of the region. It's essentially two to three days away by car from most of the Eastern Seaboard, a day or so less if you use the ferry from Maine to Nova Scotia—or even less if you fly into Halifax, Nova Scotia's capital (see Getting There, p. 44). Most everyone speaks English, including the residents of the Magdalene Islands, though the heavy, distinctive accent of the "Newfies" might suggest otherwise.

Another advantage of this trip is that you can easily do it on your own and be fairly spontaneous about where you go and stay. If you travel there any time other than the peak tourist season from mid-June through early September, you should be able to find reasonable accommodations without planning ahead.

SPECIAL ISSUES AND CHALLENGES: This trip can be as easy or challenging as you like, depending on how much hiking you do and where you go. You can also rent kayaks or sign up for half- or full-day kayak tours on most of the islands.

VARIATIONS AND OPTIONS: The trip described in this chapter took about 18 days, not counting travel time to and from the region. With more time, we could have visited a number of other places in Newfoundland, including the very cosmopolitan capital city of St. John; crossed the Strait of Belle Isle to Labrador; or spent a couple of days exploring Prince Edward Island. Halifax is also well worth a visit of at least a couple of days. The city is very picturesque and historic and has excellent restaurants and shopping.

RESOURCES AND INFORMATION:

Getting There: You can take a six-hour high-speed ferry from Portland, Maine, or a three-hour ferry from Bar Harbor, Maine, to Yarmouth, Nova Scotia, or you can fly to Halifax on several major airlines. There is a daily five-hour ferry to and from the Magdalenes from Souris, Prince Edward Island, and a daily overnight ferry from North Sydney, Nova Scotia, to Port-aux-Basques, Newfoundland.

Where to Stay: The charming B&B where we stayed in the Magdalenes is unfortunately no longer open for guests. See *www.tourismeilesdela madeleine.com* for a listing of other accommodations on the islands. For the Cottages by the Sea in Ingonish, Nova Scotia, see *www.thepointcottages .com* or call 902-285-2804. Prices range from $80 to $110 CDN during high season. The Gros Morne Cabins are roomy and rustic and have great views (*www.grosmornecabins.com/index.htm*, 709-458-2020). The Vikings Nest in Hays Cove, Newfoundland, was comfortable and homey; rates start at $35 CDN for a single (709-623-2238).

Tours: I am pleased to report that the family-owned business that conducted our tour of the icebergs, Northland Discovery Tours, is still flourishing (*www.discovernorthland.com*; 709-454-3092). Peak season for icebergs is late May to early July; for dolphins, mid-July; and for whales, end of June through early August.

SEA KAYAKING BAFFIN ISLAND (CANADA)

DON MANKIN

This trip had been at or near the top of my "must" list for a number of years. But I had put it off for numerous reasons, including cost and, yes, apprehension about taking such a long and arduous trip in one of the harshest and most remote regions of the world. From the descriptions and pictures on the tour operator's website, as well as from my previous trips to the Far North, I knew that the scenery would be spectacular and the intrusions of modern civilization would be few and far between. I was not disappointed. I also expected bad weather, scary conditions, and more than a few periods of abject misery, but as the following pages demonstrate, I was pleasantly surprised. Nonetheless, this is one of the most challenging and difficult trips in the book, but also one of the most rewarding.

TRIP DESCRIPTION

I sat in my camp chair, basking in the sun on the sandy beach, watching several of my fellow travelers play a lively game of beach paddleball while others tossed a Frisbee. A typical sunny Southern California beach scene… except that it was 10:30 at night in the far reaches of northern Canada several hundred miles above the Arctic Circle.

For several days, we had been kayaking through one of the most spectacular and harshest wilderness areas on Earth on a 14-day guided expedition offered by Black Feather, one of Canada's most respected wilderness adventure travel companies. The trip started in the town of Pond Inlet on Baffin Island. Since the mid-19th century, American, Canadian, and European explorers and traders have passed by and often landed on Baffin Island on their way through the famed Northwest Passage across the top of the world. For two weeks, our small but diverse band of kayakers—three Americans and five Canadians, three women and five men, ranging in age from 27 to 63—were like a family of Inuit, the traditional name for the Eskimos who have inhabited this part of the world for thousands of years. Like the Inuit of "old" (as recent as the previous generation), we glided slowly and deliberately in our sea kayaks through this primitive wonderland of ice, water, and rock massifs from one epic setting to another.

Only a week before our trip, the waterways had been frozen solid. When our trip began in early August, the remnants of the ice pack and the cruel Arctic winter were still visible. Snow flurries greeted us in Iqaluit, where we changed planes for our flight north to Pond Inlet. Fierce winds kept us awake in our hotel in Pond Inlet the night before the trip started. Ice floes choked the bay that was supposed to be our starting point and delayed the beginning of the trip by a day. Massive icebergs marked our way as two boats took us deep into the wilderness to our new dropoff point.

Our first morning started off well—sunny, light winds, and hardly any ice floes blocking our way. Soon, however, the winds picked up and drove the ice floes into the bay in front of our camp. We were trapped on land for yet another day.

Our guides—Katja, a congenial but no-nonsense Swiss national who had emigrated to Canada years earlier; Sally, a 56-year-old with boundless energy; and Scott, a young but seasoned wilderness guide who couldn't have looked more the part if he had been cast for the role by a Hollywood producer— decided that we had to get a very early start the next morning before the wind picked up. The first day of paddling would be long and difficult, they warned, and would include an extended paddle through the turbulent waters around Cape Hatt. But when the wake-up call came at 4 a.m., the sun was shining, the winds were light, and the sea was calm. We were finally on our way.

The waters around Cape Hatt were less treacherous than we expected, but still lively enough to raise our heart rates. After this, the waters were more protected, so we were able to relax and enjoy the spectacular scenery. Imagine Yosemite with dozens of Half Domes and El Capitans laced together by long fjords, wide bays, and dramatic views that seemed to go on forever. Between the huge granite cliffs plunging to the sea were beaches and lagoons straight from the tropics. Taking advantage of the break in the weather, we paddled for almost eight hours and covered more than 18 miles to make up for lost time. As this very long day wore on, the sun grew warmer and the waters even more placid.

EASING INTO A DAILY ROUTINE
After that long first day of paddling, our days took on a familiar tempo—an early wake-up call, usually around 6:30, a very hearty hot breakfast that included excellent coffee, followed by an intense hour or so of packing up our tents and

gear. Then we would carry the kayaks down to the water's edge and try to stuff everything into every available nook and cranny. Finally, we would launch the kayaks and paddle for the next four to six hours, stopping once or twice for lunch or a much-needed "pee" break behind a large rock—or as the days passed and modesty went the way of personal cleanliness, just a few feet away with our backs turned discretely to our companions (for the men; the women continued as before, though they didn't go quite as far in their search for suitable rocks).

By early to mid-afternoon on most days, we would start looking for a likely campsite for the night—one with a freshwater stream, level tent sites, and, if possible, a sandy beach for landing the kayaks. Then the order of the morning's tasks would essentially reverse—unloading the kayaks, pulling them farther up on land to secure them against the rising tide, setting up our tents, and changing into warm, dry clothes. Some of us would then go on exploratory hikes over tundra that alternated between soft and spongy, marshy and uneven, and rocky and more uneven. These hikes would take us along streams you could drink from to pristine lakes, or up hills and cliffs to reveal breathtaking views of the towering cliffs across from the lagoons and fjords where we camped.

The guides would typically prepare a hearty and very tasty dinner out of our supply of freeze-dried food and—surprise!—the fresh vegetables that we were able to squeeze into the kayaks (less fresh as the trip unfolded). There always seemed to be time for just sitting and contemplating the majestic land-scape, listening to the silence, writing in journals, or watching the rosy light and long shadows cast by a sun that never set. And there was always Frisbee and paddleball for those who still had energy to burn.

The weather was our ally in what otherwise would have been an alien and hostile place. It was the summer, so some good weather was to be expected, but 11 straight days of it was unheard of in this part of the world. The daytime temperatures were in the 50s and 60s, I estimate (we didn't have a thermom-eter with us), although we did get some periods of wind and fog that chilled us to the bone and reminded us of where we were. At "night," after the sun dipped behind the cliffs overlooking our campsites (the sun didn't actually set until the last few days of the trip), it would get very cold. Several morn-ings there was frost on our tents.

Early in the trip, I put my watch in one of my bags and rarely checked it thereafter. I depended on the guides to tell us when to eat and my body to tell me when to go to sleep and when to wake up. Despite sharing a tent with someone I barely knew, sleeping with only a Thermarest to cushion me from the gravel underneath our tent, and putting up with the pungent odors that accumulate over a trip of many days where water temperatures are too cold for bathing, I slept better than I had in months.

WHAT HAPPENED TO THE WILDLIFE?

The only disappointment was the lack of visible wildlife. Whales and narwhal (large sea mammals with a single tusk like a unicorn) are supposedly plentiful in the area, but they remained well hidden from us. The problem, the guides explained, was that the bay in which they were most abundant was the one that was ice-blocked at the start of our trip. We did see several seals and lots of birds, including ducks and geese. Some people saw an arctic fox, and I and several others spotted an ermine (a member of the weasel family) that peeked around the corner of a rock on which I was sitting during our lunch break one day, no doubt attracted by the gaudy colors of my dry suit (a breathable, insulated suit that I paddled in to protect me from the cold water in case our kayak capsized—which, gratefully, it did not).

We also did not see any polar bears, but we were prepared in case we did. Scott had a pump-action shotgun to scare any threatening bears away or, if necessary, to stop one in its tracks if it charged. As magnificent as they are, and as excited we would have been to spot one, we were relieved that we did not run into any. Polar bears are very aggressive and purportedly the only animal that views humans as prey. I guess that we are at least as tasty as the arctic char that filled the waters and streams that surrounded us. This fish, a member of the salmon family, is a gourmet treat, especially when it is fresh from the water, as it almost always is in this part of the world. (First Air, the airline that serves the north, offers fresh arctic char on many of its flights.) Anyone with a fishing line and a license can catch this fish directly from the waters we paddled in every day or from many of the streams along which we camped.

THE PEOPLE OF THE ARCTIC

Although we saw few animals, their bones were scattered all over our camp-sites, especially whale bones and caribou antlers. The Inuit use these sites as fishing and hunting camps year-round, and the Arctic cold helps preserve the detritus of their efforts.

Some of our campsites even included the remnants and foundations of dwellings that dated back to the Thule people, the ancient Eskimo culture that spread across the Arctic from Alaska to Greenland from A.D. 500 to 1400. The occasional gravesite, including one with a visible and well-preserved skeleton, was a reminder of just how compelling this wild land has been over the years to a wide assortment of explorers, traders, and the indigenous people who subsisted on its rich bounty. One grave was for a John Mitchell, chief engineer on the S.S. *Esquimaux,* who apparently died on a voyage to the area in 1885.

We ran into very few people while we were kayaking, but at the beginning and end of the trip we had the opportunity to interact with the local Inuit. Given the harshness of their environment and their not unexpected difficulty in adapting their traditional culture to the modern world, it is striking how good-natured and fun-loving they are.

On the last day of the trip, while waiting for our plane back to Ottawa, we sat in on a show put on by the local people for the passengers of a "cruise ship" (a Russian icebreaker that had been converted into a very Spartan passenger ship), one of the very few cruises that make it this far north. I guess that the performers do not perform frequently enough to get jaded, since they seemed to enjoy putting on the show as much as we enjoyed watching it.

The show featured dances, ceremonies, singing (including their own version of throat-singing, an art found in Northern cultures throughout the world), and games and athletic competitions especially suited to living in small, confined spaces during the long Arctic winter. The one that made the biggest impression on me involved two young men standing next to each other, draping an arm over the other's shoulder, hooking a finger in the corner of the opponent's mouth and pulling until one of them yielded in pain.

It may not have been the most polished or professional of performances, but their smiles and laughter as they sang, danced, wrestled, kicked, and pulled were infectious. The show was not part of our itinerary but was, instead, an unplanned treat that provided a welcome conclusion to this surprising adventure in a most unlikely place!

WHY GO: While the cold climate and stark environment of Baffin Island may not be everyone's cup of tea, dramatic vistas at every turn await those who are willing to make the effort and take a chance on some bad weather. As the trip description illustrates, horrible weather is not inevitable, especially in August, the only time of year that tour operators schedule this trip. Global warming may also be having an impact (no surprise!)—the locals and tour operators have noted that in recent years the ice has been breaking up earlier than usual. That said, it is important to remember that this is not the tropics and the Arctic sun is a lot brighter than it is warm.

Another reason for taking this trip is the wildlife. The dearth of animals described above is the exception to the rule. The area is not teeming with visible wildlife—most of it is underwater or busy looking for food at the edge of the ice—but the possibility of seeing creatures that you are not likely to see anywhere else is worth the effort, expense, and potential discomfort. Black Feather guides say that they see narwhals and other whales on most trips. Polar bear sightings are very rare, thankfully!

Besides the weather, the historical and cultural value of the trip was the biggest surprise. For this writer, the gravesites and remnants of old hunting and fishing camps were a bonus. From our contact with the local people, we also learned a great deal about the realities of modern Inuit life, which unfortunately includes widespread poverty, drug use and alcoholism, and unemployment. Despite these problems, our interactions with the local people and observations of how good-naturedly they deal with their hard lives attest to their indomitable spirit.

SPECIAL ISSUES AND CHALLENGES: This is one of the most difficult trips in this book. There are good reasons why Black Feather notes in its trip brochures that this is not a trip for novices. Fourteen days is a long time to go without showers, toilets, and beds, even under the best of circumstances. And the distances covered each day—more than 12 miles on average—significantly exceed the daily averages on most guided kayak trips. That can be a daunting distance to cover day after day, and on the trip described above we had only one layover day to rest.

Long days sitting and paddling in a kayak means that your shoulders and arms will ache, your butt will get sore, and your back and knees will get stiff. It's hard to stretch your legs and wiggle around as you're sitting in the kayak, especially the first few days with food and gear stuffed between your legs, under your knees, and behind your back.

The stresses and strains do not begin and end with the long days in the kayak. Carrying gear back and forth between campsite and kayak, loading and unloading the kayaks, and lifting and carrying them over frequently rocky beaches can further stress aging bodies. Tents also have to be anchored to heavy rocks to make sure they do not blow away in the fierce winds that frequently funnel through the fjords and inlets and sweep over the exposed beaches. Low-impact camping, which most tour operators in the area practice, means carrying these rocks to the campsite to set up and returning them to their original location the next day.

Then there are the hikes over uneven Arctic tundra (no trails) to explore the incredible setting—rushing streams, hidden lakes, and vistas from atop ridges and hills. Of course, just sitting on the beach with a good book or staring at the view can sometimes be the wisest option, especially for seasoned adventurers who know better than to try to keep up with their younger companions. Regardless of what you choose to do once you have set up your tent and settled in, it all adds up. No one should consider this trip unless they are willing to spend hours at the gym to get in shape for it. Following the recommendations on physical training in our introduction (see p. 15) is especially important for this trip.

Getting the right equipment is also crucial to enjoying, tolerating, or even surviving this trip. Like most tour operators, Black Feather provides a detailed equipment list, so there is no need to go into much detail here, but there are a few items that bear special mention or emphasis. One is a good set of paddling gloves. I had a pair, but after a few days they started to fall apart. After several days of paddling in super-cold salt water (about 35°F), my hands were a mess. Lugging rocks, setting up tents, etc., didn't help, either. My hands were so sore and chapped only a few days into the trip that even simple things like tying my shoes made me wince. Splurging on high-quality gloves is worth the money. Hand lotion also helps. Bring plenty and use it liberally.

Another piece of indispensable but easily overlooked equipment is a folding camp chair with no legs. It didn't fit in the cargo hatch, but it did fit nicely under the bungee straps on top of the kayaks, wrapped in a garbage bag to keep it dry. Since sitting and gazing at the views is such an important part of this trip, having something comfortable to sit on is essential, especially for older travelers who need back support and something more comfortable than a rock. It was a simple thing that brought me a great deal of pleasure.

VARIATIONS AND OPTIONS: Given the remoteness of Baffin Island and the difficulty of the trip, there are few tour operators offering this trip and, therefore, few variations from which to choose. The two companies that operate here—Black Feather and Pacific Rim Paddling Company—offer pretty much the same itinerary with similar features at approximately the same cost.

One option for experienced kayakers with some familiarity with polar climates is to do it yourself. A local outfitter, Polar Sea Adventures, can rent equipment, including kayaks, make local arrangements (e.g., dropoffs) and even organize and guide custom trips. They can also arrange add-on or alternative trips in the area—hiking, helicopter trips to the edge of the ice floes to view wildlife (especially polar bears), and for the especially adventurous, winter trips as well, including dogsledding, skiing, and snowmobiling.

An alternative way to experience Baffin Island is via a guided backpacking trip in the interior in Auyuittuq National Park. These trips are long (10–16 days), very arduous, and suited only for the most fit and experienced adventurers, mature or otherwise. Black Feather offers these, as well as trips that range even farther north, to Devon and Ellesmere islands.

RESOURCES AND INFORMATION:

Getting There: From Ottawa, connecting service (with change of planes) to Pond Inlet is available on First Air *(www.firstair.ca)*. Fares to the Arctic can be quite high, ranging from $2,500 to $3,500 CDN for a round-trip.

How to Do It: Black Feather offers only one kayak trip each year in the region, costing approximately $4,000 CDN for the full 14 days, including kayaks, tents, group equipment, guides, food, and boat dropoff *(www.blackfeather* *.com*; 705-746-1372). Black Feather also offers kayak, canoe, and hiking trips throughout the Canadian north, Iceland, and Greenland and kayak trips in the Sea of Cortez. Pacific Rim Paddling offers essentially the same trip *(www.pacificrimpaddling.com;* 250-384-6103). If you are especially adventuresome and want to do it on your own, you can rent kayaks from Polar Sea Adventures or have the proprietor put together a custom trip for you *(www.polarseaadventures.com*; 867-899-8870).

PACKING INTO THE HIGH SIERRA BACKCOUNTRY, THE EASY WAY (CALIFORNIA)

DON MANKIN

L ike many of my peers, I cut my wilderness teeth on backpacking trips into California's Sierra Nevada mountains in the late 1960s. I returned often in the years that followed, then expanded my range of destinations to include the mountains and rain forests of the Pacific Northwest and the canyon country of Utah. But like most first loves, the Sierra Nevada continued to hold a special place in my heart. At some point, I stopped taking these trips because the effort of carrying a heavy pack up primitive trails made them more work than fun. Then I discovered an alternative that enabled me to return to the Sierras and explore this incredible area with fresh legs and undepleted energy and in the company of good friends.

TRIP DESCRIPTION

Thwack! The crisp sound of the pitching wedge hitting the Day-Glo orange golf ball echoed through the thin high Sierra air. The ball sailed a hundred or so yards and landed in a lush green meadow just a few yards from its target, a large granite boulder by a gurgling mountain stream. The first annual High Sierras Target Golf Tournament was under way. For the next couple of hours, we wandered around in the meadow surrounded by the sharp, snowcapped, white granite peaks of the Sierras, over 13,000 feet high.

Of course the sky was deep blue, as were the lake where we camped and the streams cascading off the peaks and winding through the meadow. We were high enough in the mountains to feel safe from parasites as we dipped our Sierra cups (a classic stainless-steel cup first used by mountaineers in the 19th century) into the clear streams for a cool drink. Several cans of beer were tucked behind some submerged rocks waiting for our late-afternoon cocktail hour. With only a few puffy clouds bumping up against the mountains, the peaks glistened in the sun. The air was typical for midsummer in the

The author would like to thank Charles and Rafe Furst for their help with this chapter.

High Sierras—comfortably warm and dry, with a light breeze to cool us down from our "exertions." We all agreed, life couldn't get any better than this.

Charlie, Bill, and Ed were old friends from their graduate school days in California; I was an honorary member of this circle through my friendship with Bill. The ostensible reason for the trip was to mark our rapidly approaching transition into the sixth decade of our lives by returning to an old haunt, the John Muir Wilderness in the Sierra Nevada mountains. We were joined by Charlie's 20-something son, Rafe. Charlie and Rafe had done father-son backpacking trips since Rafe was seven. Despite his relative youth, Rafe fit in well with his father's geezer friends.

The plan was to take the "equine escalator" up to Lake Ediza in the heart of the Minarets section of the John Muir Wilderness—that is, to ride horses to the lake while mules carried our packs. At the end of the trip, we would do it the old-fashioned way, hiking down with the packs on our back. We could still hump it up the trail with packs like we used to, we told ourselves, but why bother? It would take us a good day or two to recover from the uphill 10-mile hike at high altitude with 50+ pounds on our backs. By riding horses, we would be ready to hike and explore from the moment we arrived. We could afford the cost of hiring a packer with his horses and mules, and we couldn't afford the time not to. We all had jobs to get back to, or spouses, or concert tickets, or golf games or any of the other accoutrements that accompany maturity.

Speaking of golf, Charlie and Ed had another bright idea. Avid golfers, they decided to bring along a golf club and soon had invented the game of "target golf." The idea was to hit the ball as close as possible to a designated target, usually a large boulder or tree in the meadow, rather than into a hole. The winner of the hole got to pick out the next target. And as avid environmentalists, they also brought along Day-Glo golf balls that could be easily found in the green Sierra meadows, as well as wooden tees to minimize divots—environmentally friendly golf at 11,000 feet! I don't remember how we kept score, or if we even bothered, but like most golf games among old friends, who won was less important than the laughs.

THE BOYS RIDE THE EQUINE ESCALATOR TO ANOTHER WORLD

Our trip began early morning at the Red's Meadow Pack Station, a short drive over the ski mountain past Mammoth Lakes, about 4–5 hours by car from Los Angeles. As the gear for our five-night stay was being packed on the mules, we were introduced to the horses that would carry us up the trail to our campsite. My horse didn't look that happy to see me—I was a bit of a porker in those days—and I felt likewise. I wasn't crazy about the idea of sitting on a horse for several hours while he made his way up a narrow winding trail cut into the side of a very steep mountain. I was a city boy whose only contact with animals of the equine persuasion was atop one of those little ponies in the park that my dad made me ride when I was a kid, plus a couple of misadventures at the track during my undergraduate years.

The instructions from our packer didn't help. He warned us to get off the horse as quickly as possible if he fell, or he might roll his several-hundred-pound body over the rider and break his leg or worse. Our packer showed us the handgun he would carry with him in case he had to "put down" a horse with a broken leg or, I imagined, an overweight camper with a busted gut.

Despite my trepidations, most of the ride up the trail was uneventful. The scenery was stunning—long vistas down steep valleys, craggy mountain peaks, clear streams winding down from the melting glaciers above us into sparkling, pristine lakes surrounded by a green necklace of grass, trees, and mossy meadows.

We were just a quarter-mile from our campsite alongside Lake Ediza, one of the many jewels of the John Muir Wilderness, when my biggest fear came to pass. As my horse struggled up a very muddy and steep section of the trail, he buckled under my weight. In a moment forever frozen in my memory, he and I were poised in a precarious balance before he sank in the mud, lost his footing, and started to roll over. In a proprioceptive flash from my younger days scurrying through grass drills on all fours during football practice and later as a rugby player rooting around in the heart of the scrum, I scrambled off the horse as he rolled over and quickly scurried out of the way. It all happened so fast, yet seemed to unfold in slow motion. Fortunately, the horse was OK and so was I. As the packer put his gun back in the holster (only kidding), my horse and I warily eyed each other. He was visibly relieved when I decided to finish on foot, but probably not as much as I.

The rest of the day went better. The packer unloaded our gear and set off with his horses and mules down the trail back to the pack station. We were now on our own. Reasonably rested, albeit with sore butts, we quickly set up our tents and took off on a long hike to explore the neighborhood. Our campsite was on a ledge by a mossy meadow and overlooked the lake, with a view of the long valley through which we had ridden earlier that day in the distance. Behind us were lush green meadows with dozens of streams cascading down from the lake above us, the next in a series of lakes tiered like steps up the side of the mountain. Each lake rested at the base of a caldera formed by jagged semi-circles of granite ridges and gargantuan fields of fallen boulders. We climbed up a trail following a stream to the next lake, then moved on to the lake above that. The views grew more expansive and distant the higher we climbed.

After a few hours, we headed back. As we walked through the meadow to our camp, I noticed a spring in my step. I wouldn't have been "springing"— or even walking for that matter—if we had spent the day schlepping a heavy pack up the trail. I would probably be passed out in my tent. I also noted how the moss added to the spring. It was soft and spongy, almost sensual to the step, and felt much better than the rocks that jarred my toes and rubbed my heels with every step as we descended the trail.

When I took off my boots, I saw the result of all of that jarring and rubbing and was reminded of just how long it had been since my last Sierras trip and what a "tenderfoot," literally, I was. My feet were covered with angry red spots that would soon erupt as full-blown, painful blisters! If I hadn't been so carried away by the beauty of the place and how good it was to be there, I would have felt the hotspots and put on some moleskin. As it was, I would not be able to participate in the ultimate adventure, the nontechnical ascent of 13,000-foot Banner Peak that was planned for the next couple of days.

The following day, Ed, Charlie, and Rafe packed up their tents and headed up one of the streams to set up their base camp for the ascent. Bill stayed behind with me. So, while the three intrepid adventurers spent the next two days preparing for, then climbing up, moraine and ice fields with little more than crampons, ice axes, and a rope to use in emergencies, Bill and I slept late, read, and explored—I wearing sneakers instead of the now unbearable boots. I was of mixed mind about missing out on the climb. From their accounts, it sounded like a great adventure. On the other hand, I really enjoyed the two days of relaxation surrounded by some of the most beautiful scenery in the world. It was also a great opportunity to hang out with Bill, my oldest friend from my postgraduate days, who lived a continent away on the East Coast.

Two days later, the others returned. After a final round of target golf, we took down our tents, hefted our packs on our backs, and headed down the trail. Still in my sneakers, I stepped gingerly but was able to walk without too much trouble. On the way down we met a small group of backpackers on their way up, an encounter that reminded me why we head into the wilderness to spend days out of touch with radio, TV, and, these days, cell phones. After exchanging a few pleasantries, one of us asked, "Did anything important happen while we were gone?" "Yeah," one replied. "We're at war. Iraq invaded Kuwait." It was a sobering conclusion to our trip. I was glad to have been away from that world and in this one, even for just a few days.

THE BOYS BOND IN THE BACKCOUNTRY

It was almost a decade before I had the chance to return to the Sierras with my friends. This time it was just Charlie, Rafe, and me. I was now married, for the second time, 30 pounds lighter and in better shape. The plan was to enter on the western side of the Sierras, a more gradual climb but one that was just as scenic. The trip would start at the High Sierra Pack Station at Edison Lake, only a four- or five-hour drive from Los Angeles or San Francisco. But what a drive! The last 25 miles is breathtaking, a rough single-lane road with blind curves and turnouts to get out of the way of oncoming vehicles—usually large pickups and SUVs hauling boats on trailers.

This time, my horse managed to stay upright. I guess losing those 30 pounds helped. After an easy four-hour ride, the packer dropped us off at the first lake, at 10,000 feet in the Graveyard Lakes area, also part of the John Muir Wilderness. Like those on the eastern side of the Sierras, these glassy lakes sit in granite bowls surrounded by ridges and peaks. The lakes are tiered one above the other, separated by climbs of a few hundred feet along trails and over rock falls. For the next day or so, we hiked up to those lakes and fished. Rafe caught several medium-size trout, which we pan-fried with some garlic for dinner.

The peak experience of the trip—literally and figuratively—was a hike that took us from one lake to the next, finally leading us up a long steep trail out of the large bowl surrounding the topmost lake. At the top of the pass, we looked down into the valley a couple hundred feet below on the other side of the divide. A huge boulder field covered the slope; it would be a real ankle turner as we picked our way through it down to the valley. But we could see the rewards if we made the effort: a very wide green meadow dotted with large rocks and evergreens and a string of lakes—and not another soul in sight. We couldn't resist.

We slowly made our way down through the boulders, trying not to think what it would be like climbing back up, wandered around in the meadow for a while, then settled down on the bank of the largest lake (on our topo map, it was called Peter Pande Lake) for lunch. After almost an hour of food and rest, thunderclouds started to build up in the distance. Not wanting to get caught at the top of the pass in a thunderstorm, we ended our idyll and headed back.

In a couple of hours, we were back in our camp with our boots off and cold beers in our hands. My feet were fine this time—new boots and the prophylactic application of moleskin apparently did the trick. It was one of the most memorable days of hiking I have ever had. We didn't see another person the entire day, and the weather, the views, and the company were just perfect.

Another highlight was the opportunity to hang out with Rafe. I had known him since he was a kid, but this was the first time we had had the chance to spend extended time together in a small group since he turned into an adult. I was fascinated by his stories as a successful Internet entrepreneur and a good-looking Venice Beach volleyball player—and also just a little bit envious. The three of us had a lot to talk about besides the usual during our several days together—such as women (mostly of Rafe's acquaintance), how to keep our food away from the bears, and the best place to "go to the bathroom" (though that wasn't exactly the vernacular we used).

A "FAMILY" TRIP, DOG INCLUDED

The vernacular of our next trip a few years later changed quite a bit when the boys trip morphed into a boys' and girls' trip. Charlie's wife, Hazel, my wife, Katherine, and Rafe's girlfriend, Laura, were now part of the group, along with our friend Carol from New York and Kazwell, Charlie and Hazel's dog. We returned to the eastern escarpment of the mountains for this trip, going out of the Cottonwoods Pack Station, a scenic 45-minute ride from Lone Pine. We also varied our mode—while mules carried our equipment and supplies, all but one of us hiked the five miles up the trail, a relatively easy, gradual incline through the woods to our campsite in a meadow on South Fork Creek, just below the Cottonwood Lakes. Hazel, who is susceptible to altitude sickness, rode a horse. Kazwell scampered along ahead of us, careful to stay out of the way of the mules and horses.

For the next three days we hiked, fished, read, took afternoon naps, and ate elaborate meals, laughed, and told stories around a roaring campfire. The trip provided a great opportunity to get to know a new member of the extended family (Laura) and reconnect with an old member who lived far away (Carol). I have to admit that the conversations around the campfire were much more sophisticated than on our earlier trips—movies, theater, politics, families—and a lot less scatological.

The scenery, of course, was just as spectacular as on our earlier trips. With more people, we were able to create subgroups to match different interests and different levels of skill and conditioning. One day, Katherine, Laura, Rafe, Carol, and I hiked to a lake above our campsite. While Laura and Rafe stayed at the lake to fish, the three of us took off on another hike to find the next lake. We were unsuccessful, so we headed down the trail back to camp, only to cross paths with Charlie, Rafe, and Laura on the way up.

I then peeled off to explore on my own, while Katherine and Carol returned to camp for an afternoon nap. I poked around for a while before finding a spot on a wide ledge above a waterfall overlooking a long valley. I sat there for an hour meditating on the view, on life, and on the upcoming NFL season. Such was the rhythm of our days.

This was a different kind of adventure trip for me—in effect, a family trip, or at least the very contemporary version of "family" that comes with age, a version that includes friends as well as relatives. The size of the group and the easy familiarity of long-term relationships made for a freeform and spontaneous trip. We pushed ourselves only as far as we wanted, hung out in small groups or all together as circumstances and wishes dictated, or just went off on our own. It was a wilderness trip, but an especially relaxed and comfortable one.

Around the campfire one night we talked about how we could make these trips even better. Next time, we agreed, we would also hire a cook to prepare meals and clean up. Since we took as much advantage of the daylight as we could, we usually ended up cooking our dinners by the light of headlamps, lanterns, and our campfire. Cleaning up was even more of a challenge, and it had to be done right or we risked having black bears poking around for morsels outside our tents as we slept. But it wasn't just about being lazy or careless. It also had to do with snatching a few more hours of precious time to have fun with family and friends or by ourselves in a setting unlike any other.

The High Sierras are not just beautiful, they are also familiar, iconic, and accessible to aging baby boomers willing to let go of old ideas about "roughing it" and to try new ways of getting there. But just as important, they offer a great setting for periodically reinforcing the bonds that keep good friends and family together.

WHY GO: Besides distinctive scenery that rivals anything found in much more exotic and remote corners of the world, the Sierra Nevada mountains also have the added advantage of accessibility. Most trailheads and pack stations are no more than a five-hour drive by car from Los Angeles or

San Francisco, and it doesn't take long on the trail before you get into the backcountry. The Sierras also encompass a huge area, which means you'll have many choices about where to go, and also means you probably won't run into lots of other people in the backcountry (the Yosemite Valley, on the other hand is very crowded).

You can pack a lot of stuff on mules, so it's possible to bring along things that will turn the idea of "roughing it" into a yuppie irony—coolers with beer and steaks, comfortable folding chairs with built-in cup holders, etc. But please leave the stereo systems behind! You can also bring your dog along if you stay within the boundaries of the national forest (not in a national park, though).

SPECIAL ISSUES AND CHALLENGES: High altitude can be a problem for some people, since most campsites in the Sierras are above 8,000 feet. Get in shape, acclimate by spending a night or two before the trip in a nearby motel or campground, and ride a horse up if you have problems.

Most trails are well groomed, but they still can be rough, especially when you are working your way through a boulder field. I recommend hiking poles for those with bad knees, or anyone with good knees who wants to keep them that way.

There are lots of black bears in the Sierras. They rarely attack people, but can be very aggressive about getting to your food. Special bear canisters for storing food are now required for anyone going into the backcountry. Acquaint yourself with bear "dos and don'ts" before embarking on a trip. Most park ranger stations will provide that information.

VARIATIONS AND OPTIONS: Muir Trail Ranch, on the western side of the Sierras at 7,600 feet, provides a comfortable, hassle free option. Sleep in a real bed in a log or tent cabin, eat in a rustic dining room or on a terrace, read in the lounge by a fireplace, soak in the hot springs, ride a horse, take a hike, go fishing, swim in a warm lake, take an overnight pack trip, or do nothing. Getting to the ranch requires a drive and a boat ride across a lake, followed by a 5.5-mile hike. For more information, see *www.muirtrailranch.com*.

RESOURCES AND INFORMATION: Different areas of the Sierras are serviced by different pack stations. For the western Sierras, go to *www.high sierrapackstations.com/destinations.html*; for the eastern, *www.owensvalley history.com/pack_stations/page54.html*. Packers can customize your trip almost any way you want—for example, you can ride horses up, down, or both ways; hike and have mules carry your packs up, down, or just up; or take the full-service option, where the packers provide the animals, packer, cook, food, and group camping equipment for the duration of the trip. They will do all of the planning, preparation, cooking, and cleanup. The current rates are about $200 per person for five or more riding horses both up and down, or $170 for hikers.

FLOATING THROUGH TIME IN DINOSAUR NATIONAL MONUMENT (UTAH)

DON MANKIN

The southwestern U.S. was the site of some of my earliest wilderness experiences. For several years, I returned almost every spring or summer to explore the sculpted canyons, colorful rock formations, pine-forested high desert plateaus, and unique cultures and history in and around such magical places as Zion, Bryce, Monument Valley, Canyon de Chelly, Canyonlands, and Capitol Reef. These were the sites for many of my most memorable backpacking trips.

In recent years, my attention has shifted to other places and other adventures, but the lure of the Southwest has endured. In the late spring of 2007, I decided to return with my wife, Katherine, to visit a place I managed to miss in my earlier trips to the region, and to do it in a new way better suited to a body and mind matured by time and experience—floating down a river between soaring walls of layered sandstone with a geologist to explain the millions of years of history unfolding in the walls of rock as we drifted past.

TRIP DESCRIPTION

On paper, or at least on the website, the trip sounded great: a five-day rafting and camping trip down the Yampa River through Dinosaur National Monument with a professional geologist. The trip offered a unique combination of geology, archaeology, paleontology, natural beauty, and excitement. The Yampa is the last free-flowing major tributary in the Colorado River system. As we floated down the river, we would travel back in geological time, from the age of the dinosaurs to the Precambrian era more than a billion years ago. The ancient history of the region would be displayed in the colors, folds, layers, and uplifted faults in the cliffs and canyons along the river. The rocks

The author would like to thank Holly Godsey, director of the WEST (Water, Environment, Science, and Teaching) Program, University of Utah Department of Geology and Geophysics, for her help with this chapter.

would not only reveal the passage of geological time, they would also seduce us with their majestic beauty.

At first, the trip was disappointing. The group was larger than I was used to—ten guests, four guides, the geologist, and a photographer hired by the trip operator, OARS, to take pictures for the company's marketing materials. In addition, when I saw our boats—three rafts and a dory, all powered by a single oarsman—I also realized that we would not be paddling the boats ourselves and that the trip would be less active than I thought. The two inflatable, one-person kayaks offered the only possibility for significant activity on the river.

My interest in the inflatable kayaks, or IKs, was soon tempered by the obligatory safety lecture that preceded our launch. I had heard most of this in my first and only white-water rafting trip many years earlier: Don't panic if you fall out of the boat, keep your feet up and facing downstream, and don't get caught between the boat and a rock. But the danger of getting your feet trapped by a rock just a few feet below the surface I had not heard before, and the warning was delivered with an earnestness that grabbed my attention. This was the inaugural trip of the season so the water was running high and fast. For the first time since signing up for the trip, I realized that the risks were tangible and consequential. I felt a slight pang of fear. I was no longer so sure about hopping into one of those IKs anytime soon.

I spent the rest of the day sitting in the dory trying to pick up a few pointers by observing two of our group as they made their way in the IKs through a few easy rapids. I didn't learn much from watching Sarai—she was an experienced white-water kayaker and was in her element. There was no way that I could do what she was doing…if I could even figure out exactly what it was that she was doing. From watching Scott, a seasoned adventure traveler in his mid-60s, I learned that even the easy Class I white water we passed through that first day can present a challenge. His IK seemed to bounce around precariously, and it looked like it could tip over at any moment.

I dozed off several times over the next few hours as we drifted down the river. The mostly flat scenery didn't grab me at first and when it finally yielded to the more majestic, colorfully striated cliffs that I usually associate with the American Southwest I had grown lethargic. The lack of activity had dulled my senses and dampened my enthusiasm. Unless I screwed up my courage and got into the IK, this trip would be a dud, I feared.

At least the dinner was great—grilled salmon, fresh broccoli, and a white chocolate fondue with strawberries for dessert. Katherine and I retired early to our tent. The murmur of voices of the other campers swapping jokes and telling stories around the nonexistent campfire only irritated me. They were clearly having more fun that I was. I just didn't feel the usual magic of the Southwest and spent a restless night tossing in my sleeping bag.

GREAT HIKES SAVE THE DAY

Things changed dramatically on day 2. The scenery improved—the canyon walls were higher and more colorful, looming directly overhead at the water's edge. The layers of rock started to tilt, hinting at the geological forces that shaped this place hundreds of millions of years before. Most important for me was the opportunity for physical activity that didn't require hurtling through churning water in what seemed like little more than a plastic backyard kiddie pool.

Our first hike of the day was at lunchtime. It wasn't long, but it did involve a relatively steep climb up a drainage past colorfully eroded rocks, ledges, and overhangs to a trickling small stream that disappeared after a few feet in the dry streambed. Holly, our geologist, pointed out plant and animal fossils in the rock. I'm not sure that I always saw what she pointed out or understood everything she said, but it did reinforce the sense that we were merely an inconsequential blip in a very ancient landscape.

After lunch, we faced the first significant white water of the trip. To the surprise of most everyone, Sandy, another member of our group, volunteered to run the rapids in one of the IKs (Sarai would be the other, but that was no surprise). In terms of their appearance and experience, Sandy and her husband Charlie—who hail from the City of Broad Shoulders, Chicago, and look it— would seem to be the least likely candidates for such vigorous, risky activity. But as we would see in the days that followed, appearances can be deceiving. Sandy rode through the rapids like a champ and seemed to enjoy every second! How could I wimp out after a gutty display like that? I vowed to myself that before this trip was over, I would take the challenge—but just not yet.

The second hike of the day was the turning point of the trip for me. After pulling into our campsite and setting up our tents on the sandy beach, several of us hiked and climbed two miles (it seemed a lot longer) up a steep trail to an overlook 800 feet above the river. This was not an easy hike. The narrow trail was washed out in spots, and for much of the way it snaked between a steep slope on one side and a steep dropoff on the other.

Speaking of snakes, as we got closer to the overlook, we heard the chilling rattle of a very pissed-off rattlesnake. Charlie, who was just in front of me, turned around abruptly and tried to beat a hasty retreat. Charlie looks like a smaller—but not much smaller—version of former Bears linebacker Dick Butkus, so I tried to get out of his way. But there was nowhere to go. Fortunately, Deb, one of our guides who was leading the hike, quieted us down and slowly backed us up a few feet until the angry reptile slithered off.

A few minutes later, we reached the top. The brief scare and sustained effort were well worth it. The overlook offered unobstructed views up and down the river. Upstream we could see the winding, narrow canyon we had drifted through just an hour or so earlier; downstream we could see the curves, canyons, and rapids that awaited us in the morning. We stood for several minutes marveling at the views and taking in the long shadows, white rock, and graceful cottonwoods on the shore. We were just able to make out our campsite 800 feet below and watched the guides scurry about preparing dinner.

We hustled back down the trail, keeping a watchful eye out for our reptilian friend, and arrived back in camp about 45 minutes later, sweaty, tired, and hungry. After another fantastic meal—BBQ chicken, cheesy potatoes, mixed fresh vegetables, and brownies—we all sat around telling stories and praising Sandy for her courage and skill. Everyone seemed funnier and smarter than they had the night before. After dragging my weary body back to our tent and crawling into my sleeping bag, I fell fast asleep and didn't wake up until the morning.

THRILLS, CHILLS, AND SPILLS IN THE KAYAKS

Day 3: I was now ready to try out the IK. So was Charlie. The morning should be pretty tame, we were assured. We would hit the biggest rapids of the entire trip in late afternoon, but until then it was all easy Class I with only a few bounces to negotiate along the way.

In just a few minutes in the kayak, I felt like an old hand. Paddling the IK wasn't all that different than paddling a sea kayak, a watercraft with which I have a lot more experience. As long as I didn't try to paddle into or across the current, it was pretty easy to control. I turned right, I turned left, I spun around, I even sat up on top of the back rest, like I had seen Sarai do, to get my wet butt out of the cold water in the bottom of the kayak. The kayak was described as "self-bailing," but a more apt description would have been "self-leaking."

I could see Charlie a few yards away, approaching the dory to talk to Ben, our trip leader. Charlie turned his head to look over at me, then back to Ben, and said, "I think I'll sit up on the back rest like Don." Ben replied, "Good idea, you'll be more comfortable, but be careful…" Charlie pushed himself

up with his arms braced on the sides of the kayak, "…because it's not as sta—"
Before Ben could get out the second syllable, "…ble," Charlie plopped down
a little too far back on the back rest and the kayak shot up like a rocket on the
pad at Cape Canaveral, dumping him into the cold water.

I wish I had a picture of the yellow kayak sticking straight up in the water
and Charlie's burly body flipping backwards into the drink. I didn't know
whether to laugh or launch a rescue mission, so I did both. I paddled alongside
his overturned kayak and could see that he thought it was as funny as I did.
As he laughed heartily in that Butkus-like voice, I helped him turn the kayak
over and hauled him in. The air was warm and dry, so there was no cause for
concern, especially for a hearty native of the Windy City like Charlie.

The rest of the morning passed without further incident. It was idyllic, watching the red cliffs glide silently by as I drifted and turned in the
current. Having successfully managed the few ripples of white water that
popped up from time to time, I was getting a little cocky and even considered taking a shot at the mighty Warm Springs rapids later that day. Warm
Springs, the Yampa's biggest rapids, is bona fide Class III white water that
was formed in 1965 when a flash flood picked up huge boulders, some
as big as houses, from the side canyons and deposited them in the river.
Soon, however, the wind picked up and I found myself paddling harder
than expected against the wind. By lunch I had had enough for the day and
decided to switch to the dory.

Before reaching Warm Springs, we floated by Tiger Wall, a sheer cliff of
slickrock sandstone lined by bold vertical stripes of black "desert varnish,"
the distinct manganese oxide coatings found throughout the deserts of the
Southwest. Kissing Tiger Wall is an old tradition on the Yampa—as the oars-
men row the boats to within inches of the wall, the more foolhardy lean over
and literally kiss the wall while others take photos. Several succeeded until
the wall slapped back when the wind shifted and blew us too close too fast.

Then we reached Warm Springs. I couldn't believe that earlier that day
I had actually thought that I might give it a try. It was awesome! The river
churned as it squeezed through the narrow canyon, over and around the huge
boulders, then took an abrupt left turn around a bend into a "rock garden" at
the end. We all got out of the boats to scope it out and look for the safest route
through. Much of our discussion was drowned out by the roar of the rapids.
The mood shifted from lighthearted to serious, almost somber, as Ben gave us
directions about what to do if the dory got hung up on a rock.

We all made it through without incident, even Sarai, the only one brave enough to attempt it in an IK. Ben guided the dory through the rapids without so much as brushing a rock, at least not that I could tell, but the waves slapped us silly and I got very wet. It was exciting, it was exhilarating, and I didn't mind the soaking, especially since I was still sitting in the boat, not swimming in the water.

That evening at camp the conversation and food—shrimp cocktail, three kinds of pasta, and cheesecake—were even better. After a short but intense burst of wind, rain, and blowing sand—the first inclement weather of the trip—we went to bed, and I slept like a rock.

THROUGH WHIRLPOOL CANYON

The next morning I was ready for more. I just didn't realize how much more. I opted once more for the IK. At first, the river was calm. I drifted and turned like the day before, gaping at the towers of rock all around me. All was silent save for the drops of water trickling off my paddle and the frogs croaking on the shore. After close to an hour of this sublime meandering, we reached the confluence of the Yampa and the Green River. A few minutes later, I began to hear the telltale roar of white water as we approached the entrance to the appropriately named Whirlpool Canyon.

The canyon was strikingly beautiful, even more beautiful than the scenery we had been gliding through for the last few days. The cliffs were higher, the colors were richer, and the rocks looked even more rugged. But I didn't get much of a chance to admire the scene as the sound of the rapids grew louder. I plunged ahead. The first set was turbulent enough to provide some thrills, but nothing I hadn't seen the day before. The next set was another story.

I watched as the big yellow raft in front of me rose up on the crest of a big standing wave and almost dropped out of sight down the other side. I gulped. This was much bigger water than anything I had yet encountered in my tiny craft. What looked easy in a big raft was considerably more intimidating in the IK as it rushed faster than I would have liked into the maelstrom just a few yards ahead. Despite my misgivings, I took a deep breath and followed.

In a few seconds, I was sucked into the middle of the waves rushing through the rapids. "Keep the nose pointing straight ahead," I repeated to myself like a mantra. I also remembered to "stay in the V," where the waves converged (the momentum of the water made that easy), to keep paddling (that was also easy in my pumped-up state), and to stay away from the rocks (not so easy, if the current happened to take me in their direction). I bobbed like a cork in the waves. A huge (that's the way it looked to me) standing wave loomed just a few feet ahead. I met it head on. It lifted the front of the kayak and suddenly I was looking up at my feet, which were now well above my head. I dropped down with a thump onto the water, paddled like hell, and let out a loud whoop. The kayak was still upright, and I was still in it. I bounced ungracefully but triumphantly through the waves onto the next set of rapids.

THE TRIP ENDS WITH SHEEP, FLOWERS, PICTOGRAPHS, AND WOMEN'S CLOTHES

That lift, thump, and whoop were the highlight of the trip for me. But the fun wasn't over; we still had several more hours to go that day and half the next. I figured that I wouldn't press my luck any further and chose to sit back and relax in the dory for the rest of the trip.

A bighorn ewe with a couple of kids joined us for lunch, or at least they came down to the river's edge within just a few feet of Katherine, who was looking for a private place to pee. That was the best, but not the only, wildlife sighting of the trip. In addition to the aforementioned rattler, over the course of the trip we also saw a family of mule deer on the bank as we floated by and lots of birds, including hummingbirds, Merganser ducks, great blue herons, ospreys, swallows, canyon wrens, turkey vultures, and a woodpecker.

After lunch, we also went on a great hike along a creek, through fields of pink, red, white, yellow, and purple wildflowers and blooming thistles and cactuses. The hike took us to some of the most accessible and well-preserved pictographs and petroglyphs I have ever seen. During the trip, we had seen other traces of the prehistoric Native Americans that used to live in the area, including a granary from the Fremont Indian era dating back to the years before Columbus.

At dinner on our last night—grilled steaks, mashed potatoes, corn, and chocolate cake—we honored an old river-rafting tradition by dressing up in gaudy, ill-fitting (at least for the larger men among us) women's clothes. We looked like refugees from the West Hollywood Halloween Parade. I must say that brawny Bruce, one of our guides with biceps as big as my head, looked particularly fetching in his dress and bustier.

The river on our last day was anything but placid. We rafted through some surprisingly energetic rapids that made my turbulent run the day before look like a piece of cake. Scott and Sandy were in the IKs for one last run, no doubt lulled by my success, and the looks on their faces alternated between exhilaration and abject terror. But they managed to stay in the kayaks and out of the water, except for the several inches in the bottom of the kayaks that failed to self-bail. The trip ended on a surprising and sweet note, with the call of "Mommy" from our geologist's four-year-old son, who was waiting patiently on the bank of the river as the rafts pulled into shore.

WHY GO: The main attraction for me was the incredible beauty. According to James, our OARS photographer, this was the best scenery he had seen on any trip—and as a wilderness photographer, he takes many trips of this sort.

Besides the beauty and intimacy of the place and the thrills of river rafting, especially in the kayak, I learned more on this trip about how the Earth was formed and fossils created than I ever learned in school. With one glance at the canyon walls, I could look back 500 million years and see the history of the Earth embedded in the layers of rock formed by advancing and receding seas and thrust up into view by tectonic forces. Of course, without our geologist present, I probably wouldn't have known what I was looking at, surely not at the same level of detail. Her explanations, as she pointed out the visible evidence of the phenomena that shaped these canyons, brought it all to life better than a textbook ever could.

SPECIAL ISSUES AND CHALLENGES: The trip is not physically demanding unless you choose to go on all of the hikes and spend a fair amount of time in the IK (when the wind picks up, the paddling can be hard work). You can make the trip as active as you like. Other than sleeping on the ground (most of the campsites are on soft, sandy beaches) and using a portable privy, there are no special challenges for reasonably healthy, fit, and adventurous travelers.

VARIATIONS AND OPTIONS: Make sure that you visit the Utah Field House of Natural History State Park Museum in Vernal, Utah, where the trip begins, and also the Dinosaur Quarry a few miles away just within the boundaries of the national monument. The former has informative exhibits on the geological forces that shaped the area and life-size replicas of prehistoric animals. Unfortunately, the Visitor Center at the quarry, which contains a display of impressive dinosaur fossils still embedded in their original excavation site in a wall of rock, has been closed since July 2006 because of building instability. However, there is a short trail outside the center where you can see unexcavated fossils partially buried in the earth.

I recommend visiting these places before the trip so that you can better understand what you will be looking at as you drift down the river.

RESOURCES AND INFORMATION: In summer 2007, OARS, a pioneer in the river-rafting business, offered this trip for $922. A four-day trip and a trip without the geologist are also available for less, but I would strongly recommend the trip described here. OARS also offers river and other kinds of trips all over the world (see *www.oars.com*). Holiday Expeditions runs similar four- and five-day trips down the Yampa *(www.bikeraft.com)*.

SEA KAYAKING GWAII HAANAS IN THE QUEEN CHARLOTTE ISLANDS (CANADA)

DON MANKIN

I first heard about the Queen Charlotte Islands in 1969, two years after the summer of love. The Vietnam War was still raging, the country was in upheaval, and I was vaguely dissatisfied with my life and career. The most recent issue of the Whole Earth Catalog, the "tools for living" bible of the hippie era, featured an article about homesteading in the Queen Charlotte Islands—free land in the wilds of British Columbia for those willing to work it. The article did warn that it rained a lot there. Nonetheless, the area offered the promise of a different life in an exotic place, a sanctuary from the turmoil of the times. Wisely, perhaps, I never took advantage of this opportunity. But the iconic images of islands covered by rain forests, surrounded by pristine waters with flocks of eagles soaring overhead, sparked my fantasies of escape for many years to come.

A few years ago, I finally had the chance to check out what I had passed up when I signed up for a one-week kayak trip through the Gwaii Haanas National Park Reserve in the Queen Charlotte archipelago. It takes two weeks to paddle the reserve from end to end, but most kayak trips are broken down into one-week segments. I chose the first week, which included the multilevel hot springs on Hot Springs Island overlooking the vast Juan Perez Sound. The trip also took us through Burnaby Narrows, a channel sandwiched between two islands with some of the most colorful displays of marine life I have ever seen.

What I didn't get to see were the rugged windswept islands at the southern tip of the reserve at the edge of the Pacific Ocean, and the UNESCO World Heritage site of Ninstints, the remains of a Haida settlement with the largest collection of totem poles in their original location in the world (the Haida are a First Nations tribe, the Canadian equivalent of Native Americans). So, when the opportunity came up in the summer of 2007 to return to the Queen Charlottes and kayak the portion that I had missed years before, I jumped at the chance.

The author would like to thank Hamish Kerr for his contributions to this chapter.

TRIP DESCRIPTION

We battle the wind and waves for every inch as we try to paddle our way out of the bay. I feather my paddle, turning the blade at an angle on the upstroke to slice the wind rather than catch its full force, but it barely makes a difference. As we near the point at the end of the bay, almost breathless from the effort, we're blasted by a gust of wind that stops us dead in our watery tracks. Derek, our guide, decides that it is futile to continue. We turn as quickly as we can to keep the wind and waves from pounding us broadside and flipping the kayaks. With the wind now at our backs, it takes us 20 minutes to retrace the hard-fought mile it took an hour to cover on the way out. We pull up on the beach, relieved, and stretch out on the sand to wait out the unpredictable but always interesting weather of the Queen Charlotte Islands.

Gwaii Haanas National Park Reserve and Haida Heritage Site, to give it its full name, comprises the bottom third of the Queen Charlotte archipelago. It stretches almost 400 miles from north to south and encompasses more than 400 islands. The reserve is rich in natural beauty, ecological diversity, and cultural heritage—it is the home of the Haida First Nations people who populated the islands and ruled the region long before the arrival of Europeans. In recognition of all that is has to offer, the July/August 2005 issue of *National Geographic Traveler* magazine selected Gwaii Haanas as the number one national park in North America.

The adventure began as we boarded the Dehavilland Twin Otter floatplane in Sandspit, the jumping-off point for most trips to the reserve. Floatplanes are a special treat for me. It's not only the soft, graceful water landings; they are also a personal symbol of adventure, since I only take floatplanes when I am heading someplace wild and remote.

Besides the pilot and co-pilot, there were 11 of us boarding the plane— a family of four, including a teenage son and daughter; a 24-year-old woman; a woman in her early 60s; a couple in their late 60s or early 70s; my 50-something friend Hamish; one of the guides; and me—a diverse mix of outdoor adventurers. As the pilot revved the engines for takeoff, he turned around to look at his passengers and asked a question rarely heard on commercial flights: "Which way do you want to go?" We had two choices—the usual way through the heart of the islands or the more scenic route along the west coast. The center route is also scenic, with views of emerald islands and blue water on both sides of the plane, but the west coast route is incredible, flying over the rugged fingers of barren rock reaching into the sea on the one side and the uninterrupted expanse of the Pacific Ocean—next stop Japan—on the other. The choice was easy: We took the west coast route, flying low, under the clouds, and through the wispy, patchy mist that usually covers the islands.

As we approached our destination, an island tucked into a fjord just around the corner from where the ocean pounded the shore, we saw our camp. The kayakers from the trip that was just ending huddled on shore in the drizzle waiting for their flight back to Sandspit and to hot showers, dry clothes, soft beds, and cheeseburgers at the local pub. In the ritual common to trips where one group gets picked up at the same time a new group is dropped off, we checked each other out. They looked wet and tired, but not particularly rugged. "We'll do fine," I thought. They probably thought that we looked like wimps in our dry clothes and clean boots.

After switching places with the other group and unloading and loading gear, we stood on the shore and watched the plane taxi across the bay before it lifted off into the mist. Now the only way for us to get out was to paddle. And that we did for the next several days, starting with a brief orientation trip around the island under the soft gray skies and past the rich green fringes of the rain forest.

THE WORLD OF THE HAIDA

The next day was our first big day of paddling, through some of the most exposed water of the trip, to Anthony Island at the edge of the Pacific Ocean. This can be one of the most difficult days of the trip; kayakers often have to wait out the weather to make the relatively short but frequently turbulent crossing. The big attraction of Anthony Island is Ninstints, the ancestral village of the Haida.

The Haida call their settlement SGang Gwaay (that's the way they spell it; don't ask how they pronounce it). Ninstints was the name used by European traders in the 1800s, a mispronunciation of the name of the village chief, Nan Sdins. From a spiritual and cultural perspective, the Haida consider this to be their most important ancient site. Early contacts with Europeans led to epidemics of smallpox and other diseases and almost wiped out the Haida population. Many hundreds died and were buried in caves, in the earth, and at the top of the majestic mortuary poles that still stand proudly throughout the village site. No one lives here anymore except for the "watchmen," guides designated to oversee the site and educate visitors, but the Haida believe that the spirits of their ancestors are still present. Walking among the standing poles, midden sites, and remains of massive cedar longhouses and through the hushed rain forest, it is easy to believe that they are right.[*]

Normally, I prefer that an experience like this comes at the end of a trip rather than at the beginning, as a sort of climax that builds up over several days. But that wasn't the way this particular trip was structured. Besides, it also gave us some flexibility in case we had to wait for better weather to get to the island. But most important, I soon realized that starting our trip with a visit to SGang Gwaay provided the lens through which I would view the rest of the experience. This was Haida country, and the history and culture of this proud people are inextricably connected to the natural setting. The seas and land provided a bounty of food, materials, and supplies, and the sheltered bays offered protection against the elements and enemies. After our visit to this revered place, we felt as if we had passed into the emerald, gray, and blue world of the Haida. It was easy to pretend that we were a band of Haida explorers scouting out new places to fish and build villages. Overly romantic and naïve, to be sure, but a deeply satisfying delusion that further enhanced an experience that was already unique and very special.

Camping is not allowed at SGang Gwaay, so after a tour of the site led by a watchman, we set out for our next campsite across the open waters on a protected beach and bay just 45 minutes away. The paddle was short but exciting. As Morgan, one of our guides, described it, the water was very "lumpy"—big swells and waves coming from different directions, crashing against each other to create a rough, bouncing, twisting ride. It was the "lumpiest" water I have ever kayaked. As much as I enjoyed the ride, I was very happy to pull into the bay and stretch out on the beach to catch the rays of the setting sun peeking through the clouds.

THE WEATHER IMPROVES

The third day was sublime. The morning overcast soon gave way to sunny skies dotted with a few puffs of clouds. We headed east, away from the turbulent coast and toward the protected bays and coves in the interior. The rolling swells lifted and pushed us gently on our way. We paddled leisurely

---

[*] Adapted from the booklet "SGang Gwaay: UNESCO World Heritage Site," produced by the Gwaii Haanas National Park Reserve and Haida Heritage Site.

along the shore, gazing at the jagged rocks covered in barnacles, the kelp forests, and the hushed forests of spruce, hemlock, and cedar carpeted in moss. We deeply inhaled the fecund fragrance of intertidal life.

We stopped for several hours at Rose Harbour, the site of a historic whaling station from the early 1900s, now a thriving guesthouse with a distinctly counterculture air. I wondered if this was where the few remaining hippies from the U.S. had finally settled, but the proprietors were too busy serving their guests—tourists in for a day or so, kayakers and sailors passing through—to satisfy my curiosity. But from the looks of one of the proprietors, with his beaded gray beard and pigtails, it was probably a good guess. Hippies turned entrepreneurs! "Good for them," I thought, and settled instead for a shower heated by a wood-burning stove.

Later that afternoon, we headed across the bay to a beach a couple of miles away that would serve as our campsite for the night. The day ended with views of Rose Harbour in the distance and the soft rustle of pebbles at the water's edge clinking against each other as the waves rolled back into the sea.

The next day was supposed to be our most difficult. Our route would take us out into Hecate Strait on the eastern side of the islands. The strait is 60 nautical miles wide from the Queen Charlottes to the B.C. mainland. It is a shallow, stormy stretch of water that often produces some of the wildest seas in North America. Rounding Point Benjamin can be especially hairy: The currents of the strait often converge here and create aquatic chaos. Our guides feared the worst, so they told us about Plan B...and Plans C and D, places where we could pull out and spend the night if the wind and currents acted up. We went for it. We were soon rounding the feared point and, much to our surprise and delight, encountered some of the most placid water of the trip.

We were now committed to covering the full distance—11 nautical miles (almost 13 statute miles)—to the next campsite, one of the longest days of the entire trip. The high point of the afternoon, besides the almost perfect conditions, was the family of black bears playing on a beach as we passed by. The calm, the sun, the views lulled us into an abiding sense of peace.

Then, just as we were about to begin the last big crossing of the day, about an hour across the mouth of a wide bay to our campsite for the next two nights, all hell broke loose. The winds picked up and slammed us. It was one of the most difficult hours of sustained, hard-fought paddling of my life (soon to be topped a couple of days later).

After we finally pulled in on the beach, ate a late lunch, and set up our tents, a few people went swimming in the cold sea, others bathed in the even colder freshwater stream that ran alongside our campsite, and some did both. I did neither, but collapsed instead on the beach with a cold beer (chilled in the stream) and stayed pretty much in that position for the rest of the day.

After that excitement, the next day was especially welcome, a layover day to relax, organize our clothes and gear, or take another swim or bath. I woke early to catch the sunrise. From my tent, I could see a band of orange growing on the horizon. It expanded and turned to rose. The crescent moon hung in the sky until the last minute. Sea lions croaked on the rocks a few hundred yards offshore.

After a sumptuous breakfast of eggs Benedict with smoked salmon, one of the many advantages of a layover day, several of us took off for a short paddle to explore the shore around the bend on the other side of our camp-site. We drifted over gardens of rock and kelp, spotting purple and orange sea stars, schools of tiny fish, and delicate jellyfish along the way. And the wonders were not just under water. Eagles swooped and dived over the sea, and another bear roamed the beach next to the one where we ate our lunch. The day couldn't have been better.

THE TRIP ENDS

The weather did change…and change again. The next day was very windy and the seas were even lumpier than they were on the day we left SGang Gwaay. They were also "snotty," an expression used by the guide on my previous trip to the Charlottes to describe whitecaps. Definitely not paddling weather. But, as described at the beginning of this chapter, we did give it a try. We paddled for an hour into the blasting wind, covering barely a mile before reversing course and returning to the beach to wait it out.

Our guides "read" the weather and listened to the marine forecast on their shortwave radio. They figured that the winds would turn around by late after-noon or early evening and we would be able to get out and at least cover a few miles before dark. Otherwise we might not be able to get to Swan Island, our last stop, in time for our scheduled pickup two days later.

So we lounged on the beach waiting for the winds to change, reading, nap-ping, or exploring the edges of the rain forest. I fully expected that we would eventually have to unload the kayaks, set up our tents, and spend a third night at this campsite. But the winds did shift just as the guides expected and the choppy seas settled down. It was 5:30 p.m. when we finally left the beach.

We would have to haul butt to get to Swan Island by nightfall. We had other options, of course, but everyone wanted to go all the way so we could kick back the next day and be in place for the plane the day after. We wouldn't get there until close to 10, even if everything went OK. The sun would have set, but the sky would still be light enough to put up our tents, we hoped.

I have never kayaked so late in the day. For the last couple of hours, we were surrounded by soft, darkening sky and water. Hamish called it the "sweet light" of the Canadian dusk—dark clouds framed against the gray-blue sky, long shadows on the water, islands and mountains in silhouette in the distance, fog hugging the peaks, sounds as muted as the surroundings, and the outlines of the kayaks ahead frozen in time in the fading light.

If I hadn't been so tired, I could have paddled in that light for hours. Dozens of eagles took flight as we passed by the appropriately named Eagle Island and entered the vast Skincuttle Inlet. The first couple of islands of the Swan Island group were just visible across the inlet, at least an hour away. It had been a very long day, and this last hour was tough going. It was a very strange experience—excruciating beauty and excruciating weariness. But we made it to our destination before the sky turned completely dark. We had just enough light to set up our tents. Then, much to the surprise of our guides, we returned to the beach for an impromptu celebration of our accomplishment. We drank wine, told stories and jokes, and laughed for a good hour before we stumbled very carefully through the dark back to our tents.

The trip wasn't over, but that day felt like the climax for me. After a night of thunderstorms, a rarity in the Charlottes, we slept late, then had a huge breakfast of pancakes with yogurt and Saskatoon berry sauce. We spent the day poking around the nearby islands. On our last morning, we woke up early to catch the low tide and made our way to Burnaby Narrows, one of the highlights of my earlier trip. As we picked our way through the narrows, we floated above a colorful display of red and orange sea stars, gold anemones, purple crabs, green kelp, and white clam shells. We were back in camp in plenty of time to finish packing, have lunch, and wait for the arrival of the floatplane to take us back to Sandspit. It would soon be our turn for hot showers, dry clothes, soft beds, and cheeseburgers at the local pub.

WHY GO: As mentioned, Gwaii Haanas, which includes the National Park Reserve and the Haida Heritage Site, was identified by *National Geographic Traveler* magazine as the number one national park destination in North

America (based on their 2005 survey of 300 experts in park management, archaeology, and historic preservation). The reasons for its high rating included light traffic (about 3,000 visitors per year), the pristine environment, and the "unique partnership between [the Canadian government] and the native Haida people." According to one survey respondent, this partnership has helped the park retain its "wilderness character and cultural significance," and another described it as "beautiful and intact."[*]

SPECIAL ISSUES AND CHALLENGES: Because of the potential combination of long days of difficult paddling, inclement weather, and hazardous conditions, this is a not a trip for the faint of heart or for novices with little kayaking and wilderness experience. That said, it is doable by anyone in good health with some experience, an adventurous spirit, a high tolerance for uncertainty, and reasonable upper body strength. Even the latter is not essential, since it is often possible to compensate for weak paddlers by pairing them with stronger ones.

VARIATIONS AND OPTIONS: Many options are available. Kayakers can choose either or both of the two weeks: the northern section, which includes Hot Springs Island, or the southern section described here. For those looking for more comfort, Butterfly Tours offers base camp and mother ship trips in the area *(www.butterflytours.bc.ca)*.

I strongly recommend visiting the excellent Haida Heritage Center in Skidegate, a short ferry ride from Sandspit, before the kayak trip or at least the day following the trip. The center is an excellent introduction to Haida culture and includes an impressive collection of recently carved totem poles and canoes.

RESOURCES AND INFORMATION:

Getting There: Air Canada *(www.aircanada.com)* flies at least once each day to Sandspit from Vancouver.

How to Do It: The tour operator for our trip was Pacific Rim Paddling *(www .pacificrimpaddling.com)*, which conducts seven trips in Gwaii Haanas from

---

[*] Jonathan B. Tourtellot, "Destination Scorecard: How Do 55 National Park Regions Rate?," *National Geographic Traveler*, July/August 2005; Hope Hamashige, "Surprise Finds Top List of Best National Parks," *National Geographic News,* June 2005.

late June through late July. The 2007 cost for these trips was approximately $1,500 US. Other companies that offer similar trips include Tofino Expeditions *(www.tofino.com)* and Ecosummer Expeditions *(www.ecosummer.com)*.

For more information on Rose Harbour, see *www.roseharbour.com.*

LATIN AMERICA

———∞∞∞———

COPPER CANYON BY RAIL, VAN, AND FOOT (MEXICO)

JOAN MERRICK

J oan is a nurse practitioner and native New Yorker who has lived for 37 years in the Pacific Northwest. She currently lives in Alaska on the Kenai Peninsula with her husband, Mike, a physician in general practice. Joan is an intrepid traveler, having visited such countries as Laos, Vietnam, Ecuador, and India over the years. In these travels and in her earlier work with refugee populations in Seattle, she has been fascinated by people's stories, cultures, and experiences. Like most Alaskans, Joan and Mike take a vacation every February or March to escape the relentless darkness and cold of the long northern winter, usually to someplace with a beach to bask in the warm sun. This past year, she wanted something more exciting, so she chose the Copper Canyon in the Sierra Madre mountains in northern Mexico. —Don Mankin

TRIP DESCRIPTION

The ride to the bottom of Copper Canyon was breathtaking, in more ways than I would have liked. The information packet from our tour operator had warned us that the ride was not for the faint of heart, but I had no idea just how hair-raising it would be! I am usually afraid of heights—I won't ride a camel or even a horse—but I can be stubborn. I was determined to get to the bottom of the canyon, a remote corner of Mexico with dramatic scenery, lost history, and exposure to a unique culture. To get there, we had to ride in a van for five hours with 12 other people over 40 miles of winding, steep, one-lane gravel roads. When other vehicles needed to pass us, we pulled over almost to the edge of the cliff and somehow they squeezed by. After a few hours of switchbacks, I had to move to the front seat to keep from getting sick.

Why was I subjecting myself to this torture? Because this year for our winter vacation, I wanted a destination that offered more than just sand and sun and sweet alcoholic drinks with funny umbrellas. Copper Canyon in Mexico seemed to fit the bill.

Copper Canyon is actually a series of canyons that all together are four times larger than the Grand Canyon and almost 300 feet deeper. The system of canyons is traversed by the Chihuahua al Pacífico railroad, which runs through 86 tunnels and over 37 bridges and offers spectacular views of the canyons, riverbeds, villages, and pine forests along the way. The canyon is also the home of the indigenous Tarahumara people, who are well known as artisans for their baskets and weavings and as long-distance runners. I was drawn by the majestic canyons, the remoteness of the area, and the isolation of the Tarahumara.

The train ride also appealed to me. We had taken train trips all over the world and found to be them both fascinating and relaxing. We especially like local trains for the view they offer into people's everyday lives. Also, as a native New Yorker who did not get a driver's license until turning 30, I prefer to let someone else drive so I can look at the scenery and take pictures at my leisure.

THE UP AND DOWN SIDES OF GROUP TRAVEL

After deciding on Copper Canyon, the next big decision was whether to do it on our own or as part of a tour group. Usually I plan our trips and make all the arrangements myself. Doing the research, finding wonderful out-of-the-way places to stay and visit, and negotiating the transportation, currency, and customs are all part of the adventure for me. I also prefer the spontaneity and flexibility of independent travel. Or maybe, as my husband and friends note, I just like to be in control.

A recent trip to Eastern Europe led me to reconsider my travel preferences. Dealing with five different countries, languages, and currencies had left me exhausted. I have also learned over the years that my husband, Mike, is more likely to go on the hike or to the cathedral or whatever if it's part of an itinerary that we have already paid for. So, I researched various options and signed up for an 11-day tour offered by a company called The California Native. This was a big step for me. I had my concerns about the constraints imposed by group travel and a fixed itinerary, but I was willing to give it a try.

Our group of 11 ranged in age from 55 to 75 and consisted of retired and semi-retired Americans and Canadians, plus our 27-year-old guide Jessica, a former social worker. This was an active bunch of travelers. The group included hikers, golfers, glider pilots, and seasoned travelers. We were all energetic adults, with different backgrounds and different cultural and political perspectives. This was a mixed blessing for us. Sometimes our companions would make comments during dinner or on a hike that we found offensive, leading us to wonder how we could survive the dinner or the hike, much less the next several days.

On the other hand, we met several lovely people we would not have met on our own. Some had interests similar to ours in gardening or health care, and others were full of information about glider airplanes and other obscure and exotic (to us) interests. There were some in our group we wanted to keep in touch with in the future. While taking a tour meant I lost some control over the itinerary and perhaps missing out on the adventure of finding an out-of-the-way place or getting on the wrong train, I gained companionship, for better or worse, the expertise of our guide and travel company, and the ease of pre-made arrangements. Throughout the trip, I weighed the pros and cons of group travel, sometimes coming down in favor of the herd, sometimes for a small group of friends, or perhaps just the two of us. Each had its positives and negatives that may add up differently for different travelers.

BEARS (?), HORSES, AND A SWINGING BRIDGE

For the next several days, we rode the train, traveled in vans, and hiked through this remote corner of Mexico with its rich blend of natural beauty and exotic culture. One of our first stops was the Paraiso del Oso (bear's paradise) named for a Yogi Bear–shaped rock overlooking the hotel where we stayed, halfway between the town of Bahuichivo and the farming village of Cerocahui. It is a wonderfully rustic and tranquil spot, seemingly in the middle of nowhere. Hiking and biking trails abound, but the big attractions are the horses and rugged riding trails. My husband, who grew up with horses but hadn't been on one in years, was reluctant to ride at first, but with some encouragement he rode off with a small group to look at caves and old bones—and had a blast.

I doubt that we could we have found the "Oso" on our own. It's listed in the guidebooks, but they don't tell you how incredibly out of the way it is. I also doubt that Mike would have gotten on that horse—clearly the highlight of the trip for him—if there hadn't been a handful of others to join him on the ride.

The next day, we traveled by train and van to Urique at the bottom of one of the canyons. Part of the trip was over a private road through communal land with beautiful views of the steep Urique River valley. Our long, dusty, and hot ride in the van ended at a picturesque restaurant decorated with local art, painted in bright tropical colors, and filled with palms and lush tropical plants, many of which were hanging from the trellis that covered the patio where we ate. The meal was delicious, featuring fresh fish from the river cooked with complex but not overly hot spices.

After lunch, we took a short walk on a swaying wood-slat suspension bridge over the river. You don't see many bridges like that anymore, so I enjoyed every swing as we made our way across. It didn't seem like there was much going on in the town, but I was curious and wanted to look around a bit more. However, the rest of the group was already heading back to the van. That day I experienced my first serious regrets about the lack of spontaneity and the constraints of the group tour.

THE TARAHUMARA INDIANS

Back on the train we headed for Divisadero, where we could see the most incredible views of the canyons and really get a feel for their size and depth. Divisadero itself isn't a town, only a tourist railroad stop with hotels and walks on easy trails and dirt roads. Tarahumara Indians stand along the tracks here and at other similar railroad stops, selling their baskets to the tourists. The train stops are only minutes long, and tourists crowd the area between cars to look and buy baskets in what can only be described as a frenzy.

The Tarahumara Indians were the highlight of the trip for me. They remain a unique people in this modern age of technology and urbanization. They still live remotely in the canyons, far from each other in isolated family groups. Many still live in caves or small cabins without electricity or running water. Until recently, when tourism in the area increased, they had very limited contact with the outside world. They are a shy, gentle people who have to travel great distances on foot to get to villages or interact with other Tarahumara groups. That probably explains their world-renowned skill as long-distance runners.

Their baskets and weavings are beautiful, accounting for the buying frenzy at almost every train stop. Through Jessica's efforts, we had the good fortune to visit the home of a Tarahumara weaver, little more than a simple house plus a couple of outbuildings in the middle of nowhere. Since I am a weaver, I wanted to see her loom. She was shy and reluctant at first, but when Jessica told her that I was also a weaver, she opened her small back room with a dirt floor for me to view the loom. It was very basic, little more than a frame, but in her hands it performed wonders, making very intricate belts from surprisingly high-tech materials. I thanked her for opening up her workshop to me and gave her a small sewing box brought from home as a gift. I also bought one of her belts.

Jessica also arranged a dance and game demonstration by the local Tarahumara and took us to the home of a violin maker, who very graciously demonstrated his instrument for us by playing a few simple American folk tunes. He also showed us how he made the violins, using several pieces in various stages of construction as examples, and told us about the different kinds of wood he used in the process.

These are just two examples of the several times during the trip that Jessica's language skills and the goodwill that she and the company had built up over the years led to a unique experience. She made it possible for us to enter the Tarahumaras' homes, ask questions, and see their lives in a way that we would have missed if we were doing the trip on our own. These experiences convinced me of the advantages of visiting this area with a guide who has already established personal relationships with these very special people.

THE TOWNS AND VILLAGES
OF THE SIERRA MADRE

Our last train ride was the most interesting. Instead of a straight climb out of the canyon, the train executed a slow, 360-degree upward spiral, giving us lingering, heart-pounding views of the steep cliffs and the majestic sweep of the canyon. This area of track doubles back on itself and is fittingly called *el lazo,* the rope. We were on our way to Creel, the largest town in the area, and at 7,600 feet one of the highest. After days in tiny towns and villages, we were glad to get to Creel and the Best Western Hotel and our first television in a week. This was also our first chance to shop for souvenirs in small local shops.

As health care professionals, we were anxious to see the Santa Teresita Clinic, which cares for Tarahumara children and some adults, primarily for malnutrition-related problems. Lucy, a retired nurse in our group, was also interested in seeing the facility. The clinic is run by just a few nuns, but the children and their parents participate in their own care and help keep the clinic operating smoothly. Everyone, children and their families included, has assigned chores to keep the clinic clean. The results were impressive—the clinic was spotless, especially in comparison with the town.

Again, this was an opportunity arranged by our guide. The clinic usually doesn't allow tourists in, but agreed to our visit because we were health care professionals. They didn't ask for a donation and seemed very surprised when we gave them one. The experience touched me deeply and made me realize that this is the kind of work I want to do someday—maybe after we retire and are looking for something meaningful to do, in a warmer climate.

The visit to the clinic was followed by our hair-raising drive to Batopilas at the bottom of the canyon, 5,000 feet down. After plunging down that one-lane gravel road, we finally reached Juanita's, a little hotel in Batopilas along the river of the same name, where we would spend a few days. The town has 1,500 people, one main street, a small sleepy town square, and a sprinkling of businesses, including a sandal maker who uses pieces of old tires for soles and an American woman who runs a little jewelry shop. A small store sells mango ices dusted with chili powder. The town was charming, a step back into the past and well worth a little discomfort and anxiety to get there.

We all wanted to see the "lost cathedral," a church about 4 miles from town built sometime around the 17th century (who built it and precisely when is subject to some dispute). We were told that the wooden cross in front of the church was placed there to honor the architect who fell to his death putting the last brick in place in the tower. This was our longest hike, along dirt roads in fairly hot weather, but the entire group completed the walk. Then we were ferried back to town in pickup trucks with sofas in the truck bed, a fun and comfortable trip that had been arranged by Jessica.

It was hot enough to swim in the Batopilas River, but sewage and trash in the portion of the river that went through town caused us to look for another option. Jessica led several of us through some brush a few miles upriver to a clear swimming hole where we spent a refreshing, idyllic few hours splashing among the rocks and talking to young backpackers who were camped along the river. This was the only time the main group split up, and it was nice to be with a smaller group for a while. On the way back, we stopped at a shop run by a German watercolor artist who has lived there for many years and paints local scenes. He also sells drums of wasema wood and goatskin made by a Tarahumara Indian from La Bufa who happened to be in the shop that day.

ANOTHER HAIR-RAISING DRIVE!

After a few days at the bottom of the canyon, we were ready to head back to Creel. I was sitting up front again to avoid motion sickness. Poncho, our driver, looked sleepy to me, and I asked him how he was doing. He said he was fine, but I was already anxious from the winding, narrow roads, and I kept a watchful eye on him. After we finally got off the dirt road onto the good paved road to Creel, the van drifted onto the shoulder. Poncho was asleep! A tree loomed into view just feet from the windshield. I screamed, then everyone screamed. Poncho woke up and swerved back on the road, but not before clipping a pine tree and snapping off the side-view mirror.

I remained shaken for the rest of the ride and refused to sit in the front seat again. We changed drivers in Creel, and that night at dinner Jessica conducted a debriefing with the group, asking people how they felt and if anyone needed to talk to her privately. She calmed us down and helped us put the close call behind us, so we could enjoy the rest of our trip.

While this may have been the most dramatic demonstration of her inter-personal skills, it wasn't the only time that her social worker training came in handy on the trip. Had she been less skilled, the entire tour would not have been as pleasant. Jessica remained impressively calm and effectively managed the tensions that arose from the heated political discussions, inter-personal difficulties, or changes in itinerary that are inevitable in group tours. Jessica was decisive, clear, and unapologetic regarding decisions she felt were in the best interest of the group. She would listen to input, explain her reasons for leaving out a place that was on the written itinerary, and then continue on with her well-thought-out plans.

THE TRIP CONCLUDES

One of the last sites on our itinerary was Basaseachic Falls. The falls, the second highest in Mexico, are more than 800 feet high. The surrounding park has a beautiful man-made reservoir, hiking and horse trails, fishing, and boating. Unfortunately, the recent drought in the area had reduced the usually thundering falls to a mere dribble. We were all disappointed. Some grumbled, others grew cranky, still others complained loudly. Ever resourceful, Jessica made alternate plans.

We hiked through the windy valley to the reservoir near the falls. This hike was very steep at first, and the rocky terrain made it difficult to keep my foot-ing. For someone as afraid of heights as I, this was very frightening. I was tempted to turn back and spend the rest of the afternoon in the van, but with the help of a walking stick, encouragement from others, and their helping hands, I continued on. My reward for overcoming my fear and not turning back was beautiful views of rugged cliffs and deep canyons. But the best thing was that I was standing in a place that an hour before I hadn't thought I would be able to reach.

We spent the night at a lodge called Noritari, meaning Place above the Clouds. Our accommodations consisted of rustic cabins with fireplaces and kerosene lamps. The proprietors, Lauro and Soledad, let me watch them make dinner in their tiled kitchen—soup made from fresh, organically grown vegetables, chicken, and tortillas. As they chopped vegetables on a huge table and stirred the soup in an equally huge pot, they told me of their dream to build an eco-resort that would use local resources and food grown or raised in the area.

They were well on their way to realizing their dream. Their resort has none of the usual tourist attractions—for example, no shopping—but is just a comfortable, attractive place in this cool, windy, breathtakingly beautiful setting. The cabins and main buildings are decorated with local art and pottery, and colorful jars of locally grown, preserved fruits and vegetables are displayed in the dining room. Lauro, an engineer, designed the cabins, and Soledad did much of the decorating and artwork. We spent most of our stay sitting on rocking chairs on the hillside overlooking a lake. In the morning, their ten-year-old daughter helped serve us *pinole* (pine nut) cereal with *amaranth* (a grain that dates back to the Aztec) sprinkled on top before leaving for school.

This was a perfect finish to the trip. It convinced me that I had made the right decision to travel with a group. Although I missed the sense of adventure to be had by making my way through mishaps, language confusion, and wrong turns, I really appreciated the guide's expertise and the way the tour afforded us easy companionship and limited responsibility. We had lots of time to visit with old friends who had joined us for the trip, without the hassle of bad hotels and missed connections.

But most important of all were those special personal encounters with the people, encounters that might not have been possible if we had done the trip on our own. Jessica and the goodwill and connections of the tour company literally opened up doors into the real lives of the people of Copper Canyon.

WHY GO: Copper Canyon is one of the most picturesque and remote spots in North America. The Tarahumara Indians, who have resisted modernization, are unique and well worth the limited interaction to see their simple and peaceful lifestyle. And if you like trains, this is a great ride.

SPECIAL ISSUES AND CHALLENGES: Copper Canyon is isolated, with poor roads in many areas. Driving can be hazardous. Some places do not have reliable electricity, and consumer goods are minimal. I lost my camera charger and could not replace it. Medical care is also minimal, and the distances to hospitals or even rural clinics can be long. Transportation to the bottom of the canyon is via vans, cars, or local buses, so pack light. There are few banks, and exchanging money can be a challenge, although many places will take dollars.

VARIATIONS AND OPTIONS: We signed up for an 11-day tour. Seven- or 14-day tours were also available, but the 14-day itinerary seemed like it contained redundant elements, and the seven-day tour didn't go to the bottom of the canyon.

RESOURCES AND INFORMATION: Of the many companies that offer tours of Copper Canyon, I chose The California Native group for its interest in the local Indian population *(www.calnative.com)*. The company supports the local schools and clinics by bringing occasional supplies and supply-laden clients. It suggested that we bring contributions of school, sewing, and medical supplies to donate to the communities. The tour was comprehensive, well planned, and thoughtful.

Other operators offering similar tours include S&S Tours *(www.ss-tours .com)* and Canyon Travel *(www.canyontravel.com)*.

HIKING THE INCA TRAIL
TO MACHU PICCHU
(PERU)

DON MANKIN

S everal years ago, I was invited to speak at a professional conference in Lima, Peru. Since the university sponsoring the conference was covering my expenses and paying me a generous honorarium, I invited my then girlfriend, Katherine, to accompany me on the trip. The plan was for her to hang out with me while I was at the conference, then we would fly to Cusco and hike the Inca Trail to Machu Picchu, the famous "lost city of the Incas," a stunning archeological gem in an equally stunning setting in the Andes Mountains. Machu Picchu not only lived up to our highest expectations, the trip changed our lives in a very surprising and profound way.

TRIP DESCRIPTION

The bus pulled up to the curb outside our hotel in Cusco. As I climbed on board, I checked out the passengers, the ten other people with whom we would be hiking the Inca Trail for the next four days. I turned to Katherine, who was still on the steps of the bus behind me, and said ominously, "I think we're in a lot of trouble." We were older by decades than anyone else on the bus. Maybe this adventure was going to be more difficult than we thought!

We really hadn't spent much time preparing for this trip. Katherine had taken the California Bar exam a few days before we left, and I had spent most of the prior several weeks working on my presentation for the conference in Lima.

Visiting Machu Picchu was a lifelong desire for both of us, and doing it via a four-day hike at high altitude was a middle-age conceit. We were devout gym rats, though, so we figured, how difficult could it be? What we weren't figuring on were the effects of altitude, age, and the erosion of our gym time in the face of two very demanding work schedules.

While I attended the conference and prepared for my presentation, Katherine caught up on her sleep, shopped, and visited the Lima office of the South American Explorers Club to find a reliable tour operator for our Inca Trail trek. She also ate some bad ceviche for lunch one afternoon and suffered the consequences for the rest of the trip. After a few days, however, she had recovered enough to fly to Cusco with me as planned after the conference ended.

We took the next two days to acclimate to the altitude (about 11,000 feet) and explore the impressive archaeological and historical sites in and around Cusco: the massive stone walls built by the Incas that still line the streets in the center of the city, the 16th-century cathedral on the Plaza de Armas, and the Inca ruins at Sacsayhuaman and Ollantaytambo. We also visited the Sunday market in the colonial town of Pisac and gawked at the stunning scenery of the Urubamba Valley. Upon hearing that we would soon be hiking the Inca Trail to Machu Picchu, one of our guides grinned and told us that by the time we got to the ruins, we would be able to see them "through Inca eyes." All of this only whetted our appetite for what was to come.

It was only when we climbed on the bus and surveyed our fellow hikers that I began to have my doubts. After two days in Cusco, we were still sucking wind at the slightest exertion, and Katherine was still feeling the effects of her recent run-in with the bad fish. Besides, what could we possibly have in common with this group of post-adolescents? Not only were we old enough to be their parents—or even grandparents, in some cases—we were the only people from the U.S. on the trip and the only native English speakers. Three of the youngest, ages 19–21 were French; the two from Germany and the Mexican graduate student were in their early 20s. Our two guides were also in their 20s. We quickly bonded with the couple from Belgium. At 28 and 30, they were closest in age to us and she was the only other woman guest on the trip.

ON THE TRAIL

It took a couple of hours to drive to the trailhead. By the time we arrived, some of my apprehension had begun to melt away. Despite our generational, national, and linguistic differences, it was a friendly and lively group. Most of the group spoke some English and several were fluent, so we were able to communicate reasonably well with each other.

We began the hike in midafternoon by crossing a footbridge over the Urubamba River. The river was still swollen and churning from the heavy rains the week before, rains that had caused deadly mudslides just a few miles away. It was the middle of the rainy season, but the sun shining through the puffy white clouds was a good omen for the beginning of our trek.

From a starting elevation of about 7,200 feet, the trail followed the river for a few miles, then rose gradually to provide sweeping views down long, emerald valleys framed by steep, snow-covered peaks. Despite the dramatic views, this was not a wilderness area. Rustic cottages and farms marked our way along the trail. The plan was to hike a few miles and spend the first night at about 9,000 feet. "This is not so bad," I thought, breathing deeply in the thin air. But I knew that this would be our easiest day.

At our campsite, in the schoolyard of a small village, we quickly slid into our respective roles. There was the jester, the brooding intellectuals, and the world wanderers, among others. Our parts, not surprisingly, were a cross between surrogate parents and favorite aunt and uncle. The others could not believe that someone as old as their parents would be on a trip like this—hiking, camping, and even using a funky group latrine.

The latter was a particular problem for Katherine. She still wasn't feeling well, so she spent more time than she (or anyone) would have liked in that facility. She was also struggling on the trail. That first night, we seriously considered turning around and heading back. But she didn't want to spoil the trip for me and was determined to stick it out. Her perseverance would serve us well when things really got tough over the next couple of days.

The next day was the most difficult of the trek. It was all uphill, and steep uphill at that, taking us from our campsite at 9,000 feet to the highest point of the trail, a mountain pass at almost 13,800 feet, ominously named "Dead Woman's Pass." To make things even worse, this was only the first of three passes above 13,000 feet we would cross that day.

We did have a few things in our favor. Unlike the youngsters, we had hired porters to carry most of our gear, except for the rain shell and pants, fleece top, water, and other essentials that we carried in our day packs. In addition, we all had an ample supply of coca leaves to chew (yes, the same leaf that is the source of cocaine) to help push us along the trail when our spirits and bodies flagged.

As we got higher and higher—I'm talking about altitude here—the air got thinner, our hearts pounded, and the short rest breaks to catch our breath grew more frequent. The coca leaves no longer had any noticeable effect. I resorted to counting my steps and stopping after every five to gasp and pant until I felt ready to take another five steps. Despite my regular visits to the gym, I was barely able to keep up with the younger members of our party, who annoyed me no end by taking frequent cigarette breaks to give me time to catch up.

Katherine had an even more difficult time than I did. Her shorter legs, months studying for the bar, and recent food poisoning in Lima took its toll. We all waited patiently at the crest of the pass while she doggedly made her way up the trail. She had little time for celebration, however, since it was time for us to descend down the other side and make our way to the next pass, which was at an elevation of only (!) 13,100 feet.

For the next day and a half, we passed through some of the most beautiful scenery I have ever seen—deep-cut, misty valleys, thundering waterfalls, cascading streams, green meadows and hillsides, and fingers of clouds drifting between the steep, snowcapped peaks. Much of the trail took us through the cloud forest, which lay along the highest ridges. I can't think of a more appropriate and romantic description for this hushed hike through mist and rain.

Along the way, we passed by several Inca ruins, dwellings and villages dating back to the pre-Columbian era, each one more impressive than the last. An hour or so beyond the first pass was Runkuraqay, an oval-shaped ruin that commands a sweeping view over the steep river valley plunging before it. Another hour or so beyond that brought us to Sayacmarca, which also overlooks a valley, and a couple of hours beyond that was Puyupatamarca, a beautiful ruin arrayed on several different levels along the trail. The name means "cloud-level town," a fitting description since the lower levels were lost in the clouds that enveloped the trail. I thought we would disappear in the mist as we descended, and we did. The trail turned into a long granite staircase at this point and dove steeply into the mist. We made our way carefully down the slick stairs. The steps were so high and slick that Katherine had to turn around and face them and descend on all fours. It was the longest staircase I have ever seen. It seemed to go on forever.

At the end of a very long day, we finally arrived at our final campsite just as it was growing dark. After the splendor of the last three days, the visitor center and hotel at this final site were a disappointment. To call them nondescript would be generous. And they were also very crowded, since every group on the trail ends up here on the last night of their trek. But you can get a cold beer and dry off by the fire, so it did have its "charms." After a hot meal, a cold beer, and a few laughs, we returned to our tent to get a few hours sleep before our 4 a.m. wake-up call the next morning.

SEEING MACHU PICCHU THROUGH INCA EYES

The point of getting up so early was to view the first rays of the rising sun striking the vertical face of Huayna Picchu, the mountain peak that looms over Machu Picchu like a sentinel. After an hour or so making our way single-file along a narrow, rough trail through the dark, we reached a steep flight of stairs. At the top of the stairs is a ruined gateway. This is Intipunku, the Sun Gate, which marks the final pathway into Machu Picchu and the first point along the trail where you can actually see the city. I am sure that it is a stunning view, but we couldn't tell because of the fog.

We started down the trail toward the city, carefully picking our way around the llamas lounging nonchalantly across the narrow path, leaving just a foot or two between them and the sharp dropoff over the edge. The fog, the llamas, and what little of the view we could see enhanced the overall sense of mystery that seeped up from this enchanted place. For the most part, I kept my eyes on my feet to make sure I did not slip over the side. Then, as I looked up to see where I was heading, the fog lifted for an instant and I got my first glimpse of the lost city of the Incas, spread out like a miniature before me. It took my breath away. Everything I had heard didn't do justice to the moment or to the raw beauty of the ruins and their setting.

We arrived at the edge of the ruins dirty, tired, and breathless, but also exhilarated in anticipation. It was still early, so the buses of tourists had not yet arrived. Perhaps it was the time of year, well off peak season, or the scale of the ruins, but even after the tour buses arrived, it never felt crowded.

We spent the next few hours walking in hushed reverence through Machu Picchu. The engineering was impressive: sturdy doorways framing views of mountains in the distance; walls of carefully shaped and fitted stones; waterways and fountains cut into the rock; stairways and terraces arrayed along the slopes; and precision-built astronomical observatories. The scenery was awesome—misty mountains, deep valleys, and the sun streaming through undulating clouds.

By midafternoon, it was time for the group to break up and move on. Our companions piled onto one of the buses to ride down to Agua Caliente, the town on the river at the bottom of the hill. Some were planning to take the train back to Cusco, others were staying the night in one of the spare but reasonably priced guesthouses in town.

In one of the few consolations of age on this trip, we treated ourselves to a night at the much more expensive but basic hotel adjacent to the ruins. By staying there, we would have the ruins almost to ourselves from the time most of the tourist buses left in midafternoon until they returned at midmorning the next day. We saw this as a personal payback and reward for our struggles along the trail.

After a well-deserved shower and nap, we took a walk through the ruins at dusk. We climbed up and down the stairs and terraces, strolled through the ancient plaza, and poked around partially intact rooms in the last, long rays of the setting sun. As we walked, we could see a white llama across the plaza at the center of the ruins. As we tracked the mysterious animal through the maze of rooms, the physical setting, the otherworldly glow cast by the fading daylight, the memory of our days of intense effort, and our state of mind seemed to open me up to sensations and thoughts that could only be described as mystical. I finally understood in my gut what our guide had meant several days earlier when he said that hiking the Inca Trail to Machu Picchu would enable us to see the ruins through Inca eyes.

While we were walking, Katherine related a story from her childhood about a pact she had made with a close friend to "meet in Machu Picchu" if they ever lost track of each other while growing up (they didn't know very much about the place, but the name had intrigued them). She then turned to me and said, "Mankin, if we ever lose each other, let's meet in Machu Picchu." I inexplicably started to cry.

The thought of losing her was too much to bear. Her perseverance, spirit, and good humor through the trip had touched me in ways I had managed to overlook back home. The support we had given each other throughout the trip, our common perspectives about this incredible place, and most of all, the fun we had shared—I did not want that to end after our adventure was over. I knew then, unequivocally, that I wanted to spend the rest of my life with her, to share the peaks and valleys of my life just as we had shared the peaks and valleys of this adventure.

After exploring the ruins again the next morning at dawn and, following that, climbing Huayna Picchu, we returned to Cusco. A few days later, we were back home in Los Angeles. We married the next year and have been together ever since.

WHY GO: The trip description says it all. Everyone has heard of Machu Picchu, and it is probably on most "must-see" lists. A World Heritage site since 1983, its historic role and function—royal retreat, spiritual center, or final stronghold against the incursions of the Spaniards—are still a subject of argument and controversy in the archeological community. The issue is whether to visit Machu Picchu the hard way via the Inca Trail or to do it the easy way via train from Cusco and the bus from the train to the ruins. These are two very different experiences. It should be clear which one I recommend, as long as—and this is a very important qualifier—one is healthy, physically fit, and willing to put up with the challenges of an arduous group trip (although there are alternatives; see below.)

For us, doing this trip with a group was a plus. We learned a great deal from our young, multinational friends. They were spirited, smart, funny, worldly, and friendly. Most of all, their reactions to us were very affirming. Their respect for us for taking on the challenges of this trip helped reinforce our own sense of adventure.

SPECIAL ISSUES AND CHALLENGES: This is one of the most difficult trips in the book, not so much for the distances covered each day, which are significant but reasonable (the entire hike is only about 25 miles), but for the elevation gain and altitude. One should never underestimate the impact of high altitude on the human body. There is often no way to tell how you will do, unless you already have some experience at high altitude. If you have a history of problems, you probably should not take this trip, at least not the Inca Trail portion. The potential consequences of making the wrong decision can be very serious, especially for people with other medical problems such as cardiovascular disease, a history of heart failure, or sleep apnea. Regardless of your previous experiences at high altitude, the state of your health, or level of fitness, you should consult your doctor before signing up. You should also know the signs of altitude sickness (headache, nausea, and fatigue), understand how to prevent or mitigate its effects, monitor your body for signs of sickness, and not be embarrassed to turn back if necessary. Expect to acclimatize for at least two days (preferably three) in Cusco before starting the trek.

Other issues for mature travelers are the same as you would expect in any group trip in a rustic environment—lack of privacy, primitive toilet facilities, sleeping in a tent with nothing more than a sleeping bag and pad, and the like. This trip has also become very popular in recent years and the trail can get crowded, so don't expect to find much solitude.

It is important to note that several things have changed since we took this trip several years ago. First, because of concerns about conservation, crowding, and overuse, the Peruvian government now strictly limits the number of hiking permits for the Inca Trail. The only way to ensure that you will actually get on the trail, short of booking very far ahead, is to do it through a tour operator.

The second change is that it is no longer possible to get into the ruins at Machu Picchu before it opens at 6 a.m. or after it closes at 5 p.m. But most tourists do not arrive until midmorning and leave by 3:30 so it is still possible to have the ruins pretty much to yourself if you get there early enough and stay until the gates close.

VARIATIONS AND OPTIONS: A less crowded alternative to the Inca Trail is the increasingly popular Camino Salcantay. The route is even more scenic than the Inca Trail, though there are few ruins along the way. It is also a shorter but higher altitude route, with one pass as high as 15,000 feet. Probably the most important difference for seasoned travelers, besides that 15,000-foot pass, is that it is possible to stay in comfortable mountain lodges along the way through the company, Mountain Lodges of Peru (*www.mountainlodgesofperu .com*; also see the article "Machu Picchu the Cool Way" in the November 2007 issue of *National Geographic Adventure).*

If you want to see more of South America, you can take World Expeditions 23-day tour, "The Best of South America," which includes the Inca Trail and Machu Picchu, as well as Iguazu Falls in Argentina, sites in and around Cusco, and Lake Titicaca in Bolivia *(www.worldexpeditions.com)*.

RESOURCES AND INFORMATION:

Getting There: Several airlines operate regular flights between Cusco and Lima, including Lan Peru *(www.lanperu.com)*, TACA *(www.taca.com)*, and Aero Condor *(www.aerocondor.com.pe)*, among others.

How to Do It: The tour operator we used is no longer in business. Most major adventure travel companies offer this trip, as do many companies operating out of Cusco. For further information, go to *www.andeantravelweb.com/peru /treks*. The South American Explorers Club *(www.saexplorers.org)* is also an excellent source of candid information on tour operators.

Trips booked through a tour operator can vary in cost from less than $1,000 to as much as $4,000, depending on whether you wait until you get to Cusco to sign up with a local operator or book ahead of time through a well-known company like Wilderness Travel *(www.wildernesstravel.com)*. What is included will also affect the price (e.g., Wilderness Travel includes tours and five-star accommodations in and around Cusco as well as accommodations at the hotel at the ruins).

Where to Stay: The only hotel at the ruins is the Machu Picchu Sanctuary Lodge *(www.machupicchuorient-express.com).* Rates for two are more than $600 per night. The Inkaterra Machu Picchu is a luxurious alternative located at the bottom of the hill below the ruins near the town of Agua Caliente, the terminus for daily buses to and from the ancient site. Rates start at more than $400 per person per day for a double room.

SLOWING DOWN ON ISLA DE OMETEPE (NICARAGUA)

DEBORAH ("KOALA") VANDRUFF

Koala has had the travel bug since traveling with her parents in the summers as a kid and taking a whirlwind trip to Europe while she was in high school. As an adult, her flexible work schedule—she is a nurse in Alaska—has enabled her to travel widely in South and Central America, Mexico, and Asia. In her travels, she usually looks for what she calls "real" places—no McDonalds, no Wal-Marts, no ReMax Realty signs, not even postcards. She also likes to find ways to be part of the places she visits—for example, in 2006 she and her partner, Susan, worked for three weeks on an organic farm near San Blas, Mexico. Since her brother and his family live in Costa Rica, her travels frequently take her to Central America. It was on one of these trips that she discovered the laid-back charms of Isla de Ometepe in central Nicaragua. —Don Mankin

TRIP DESCRIPTION

The island floats seductively in the middle of the lake. Two volcanic cones rise up, leaving a small isthmus of land between them. From the mainland, it draws my eye and I gaze at it from the bus as we zoom by on the Interamericana Highway, as the Pan American Highway is known in Nicaragua. People living in small ranches and homes along the windy shore may think nothing of it, but I am mesmerized by the sharp lines on the horizon and the wispy cloud that wafts around the northern cone. Some travelers from Italy, just returned from the island, board the bus and tell exciting tales of climbing one of the volcanoes and seeing an abundance of monkeys and birds. This first glimpse of Isla de Ometepe many years ago on my first trip to Nicaragua etched the image into my memory. I knew then that I would one day return to the lake and explore this mysterious island.

If the name Nicaragua evokes memories of civil war and contras, it is time to update your travel consciousness. I almost hesitate to sing the praises of this fascinating country, but I am afraid the secret is out. Stories about the amazing undiscovered beaches regularly show up in the travel media along with articles on how to retire in this "new Costa Rica." The irony is that some of the best things about Nicaragua are just how much it is not like its increasingly popular and well-explored neighbor to the south.

For travelers, Nicaragua has lots to offer. It is full of adventure, wildlife, and history, plus lots of opportunities to relax in a hammock on a tranquil beach. It is also a great place to work on your Spanish. The people are welcoming, friendly, and glad to chat with visitors. Perhaps because of this friendliness and the rural nature of the country, it is one of the safest countries in Central America. Best of all, there are still lots of out-of-the-way places where you won't find any American fast food joints or real estate signs offering luxury condos for sale. One of the most special of these places is Isla de Ometepe.

Isla de Ometepe is the largest island in Lake Nicaragua. In fact, it is the largest lake island in the world. The lake itself, also known as Lago Cocibolca, measures almost 90 by 35 miles. It has the odd distinction of being a freshwater lake inhabited by saltwater fish, which swim up the Río San Juan from the Caribbean and eventually return. It is also the home of the world's only freshwater sharks. Thirty-five thousand people live on the 100+ square miles of the island. The nearly perfect-shaped northern cone, Concepción, at almost 5,600 feet high, is still active; a small eruption occurred most recently in February 2007. The southern cone, Maderas, is not as tall (4,600 feet) and is somewhat tamer. It is considered to be dormant, and there is a clear, cool lake inside the crater that rewards climbers who make it to the top after hiking for hours over steep, rough terrain in the muggy, unpredictable weather that often swirls around the peak.

ON TO OMETEPE

After several more sightings of the island on subsequent trips through Central America, I finally made it to this fascinating place at the end of a visit to Costa Rica and Panama. My partner, Susan, and I crossed the border from Costa Rica at Peñas Blancas and took a taxi to the ferry dock at San Jorge on the western shore of the lake. We usually travel by bus, but taxis in Nicaragua are often only slightly more expensive and a lot more convenient. Taxi drivers are also full of local information they are happy to share (of course, you may end up at their brother-in-law's restaurant or hotel, but this can work out well in the end).

While we sipped cold Victorias (a local beer) at a restaurant within sight of the ferry, we met two women from the U.S. One of them had been working as a volunteer at an orphanage on the island for the last year with her husband.

They had visited Ometepe on vacation a few years earlier and decided to return after they retired to teach computer skills at the school. She said they were having a great time and felt they were doing something for the kids that could really help them get ahead in life.

The woman was returning to the orphanage with her vacationing sister after meeting up with her in Managua. The sister looked a bit skeptical about her vacation choice as the ancient, rusty ferry was loaded with livestock, trucks, and all manner of goods bound for the island. When it was our turn to board, the veteran ferry traveler sized up the swells in the lake and evaluated our chances of a smooth crossing. Not too bad, she assessed. A stiff wind pushed impressive waves toward the beach for the kids swimming next to the dock. It was a Sunday afternoon and quite a few families were enjoying the last of their day off from work.

The old vessel actually did well riding the wind-whipped swells, though it was a bit of a challenge maintaining balance as we walked around the deck to watch the sun set and the lights from San Jorge fade in the distance.

An hour or so after leaving the dock, the lights of Moyogalpa, the largest town on the island, came into view. Travelers don't find much of interest in this port town, whose name means "place of mosquitoes" in the Nahuatl language, so we decided to go on to Altagracia, a charming old town in the shadow of Volcán Concepción, just an hour or so away by local bus.

We arrived after dark and found the Hotel Castillo to be as we had been told; friendly, family run, and comfortable. Our room was medium-size and the showerhead kept falling off, but it was clean and quiet and cost only about $10. This hotel has a nice tropical courtyard, a good restaurant, and my favorite, hammocks! We enjoyed a nice home-cooked fish dinner featuring *gallo pinto,* a mixture of black beans and rice served with most meals (including breakfast) in both Nicaragua and Costa Rica.

Altagracia is a great walking town. We spent the next morning exploring the picaresque central plaza and the bright yellow and white church with well-maintained pre-Columbian stone carvings in the front. After that, we just wandered around under the lush trees that offer much-appreciated protection from the scorching Nicaraguan sun. The cooling breezes off the lake also helped.

Here, as everywhere we went on the island, people were friendly and cheerfully greeted all passersby, be they locals or travelers. They often gather and sit on their porches or in the plaza in the late afternoon, sometimes listening to music, sometimes making their own. Oxcarts are still a staple of transportation, along with bikes, horses, and old trucks. Like the rest of the country, people here are generally very poor, but despite (or perhaps because of) the troubles of the recent past, the people seem hopeful about the future. It is easy to get "Nicas" to talk passionately about politics and their country. Graffiti on the walls often include the word "Sandanista" as a prominent part of the slogan.

During our walk, Susan said she was feeling a bit shaggy after a month or so of traveling and decided that this would be a good place to get a haircut. Usually, she looks for a sign with the word "unisex" or *salon de belleza* and some scissors, but we wandered all over town and found no such telltale signs. We finally returned to our hotel and asked one of the owners' sons where to go for a haircut. He gave us fairly understandable instructions, which brought us at last to an unsigned house that met his description. Inside was a young man in a big wooden chair getting a cut in a very hip style from another youngish man in a barber's smock. There were some well-worn copies of styling magazines for both men and women, so we figured the proprietor knew what he was doing. We waited awhile under a tree, watching the clouds float around the top of Volcán Concepción. Soon, the barber was finished and gave us a thumbs-up. It was now Susan's turn. If the guy was surprised to see a mostly white-haired gringa wanting a cut, he concealed it like a pro. He gave her a nice trim and charged only 75 cents.

Besides getting a haircut, a good thing to do in Altagracia is to visit El Museo de Ometepe, where various examples of pre-Columbian ceramics, statues, and petroglyphs are displayed, all found on the island. This little museum also sells interesting ceramics with indigenous designs that are made locally and has lots of information about things to do in the area. It was definitely worth the visit.

EXPLORING THE ISLAND

A traveler who likes to explore could spend a month and not run out of things to do here. Horseback riding, kayaking, bird watching, a zipline through the forest canopy, and of course volcano climbing are all available on Ometepe. One of my favorite activities when visiting countries that are very different from the U.S. is to do things that show what life is like for the local people. I have found that one of the best ways to do that is to travel by bus. On this island with only one actual paved road (between Altagracia and Moyogalpa), the bus was a slow, bumpy ride, but it gave us lots of time to see what's out there and connect with fellow riders. The slow bus was also good for getting photos of the lush countryside.

It takes at least two hours, depending on the time of year and road conditions, to travel from one side of the figure eight–shaped island around to the base of the volcano on the other side. Knowing some Spanish really came in handy on this trip. We traveled with farmers carrying machetes, women with baskets and bags of produce, and students coming from and going to school. From cobbled-together homes by the side of the road, the kids would emerge looking immaculate and starched and board the bus to go to school. Uniforms are required, and it must take quite an effort to send kids off to school every day looking so nice with such basic living facilities. Nicaragua is one of the poorest countries in Central America and out in the countryside many homes are very humble.

There are signs of hope and progress, however. We would soon visit one of these signs, Finca (Farm) Magdalena, an agricultural co-op at the base of Maderas, the southern volcano. We heard that they grow great organic coffee and that it would also be a good place to begin our climb of the volcano. But that was still a day or so away.

First, we planned on spending the afternoon at the beach. Between the two volcanoes is a connecting isthmus with a great beach at Santo Domingo. We got off the bus at Finca Santo Domingo and immediately wished we had planned to spend the night in one of the bright, cheerful rooms in the lovely setting by the lakeshore. Instead, we ordered beer and staked out a couple of hammocks with amazing views of the lake and volcano. After a short while of quietly swaying in our hammocks, we were visited by the blue-tailed jays called *urracas* that are found in abundance here. The distinctive plume on their heads stood up like a question mark as they checked us out.

The lake is so huge it is easy to forget that you are actually looking at a lake, and not at the sea, which is why it looks odd to see horses walking to the shore to drink. There are unusual houses along the beach, some vacation homes, and lots of open space. I had noticed during my Internet research that places around here were for sale, but I never saw a For Sale sign. It is a good walking beach, and the wind kept us cool as we explored. I kept looking down as I went along, scanning for seashells until I remembered again that it was, after all, a lake.

CLIMBING THE VOLCANO...OR NOT

We took off again the next day on the bus to the south side of the island, dominated by Volcán Maderas. The bus to Balgues, the closest town to Finca Magdalena, goes through lush tropical forests and past fields full of grazing cattle. We were let off in this very small town and asked a local for the way up to the farm. It takes a good 20–30 minutes to hike up there, depending on how much you are packing, but the destination is worth the effort. Don't be afraid to hitch a ride.

The finca is an old hacienda that the workers turned into a cooperative farm after the revolution in the 1970s. The cooperative has done well after years of struggle and is a great source of pride among its associates. They grow lots of crops, including coffee, much of which they sell to the Bainbridge Ometepe Sister Islands Association near Seattle. The association roasts the beans, bags them, and sells the coffee in Seattle and on the Internet. The profits have been used to fund schools, uniforms, scholarships, and lots of improvements for the lives of the people. The coffee is organic, and it is delicious. Visitors can buy cups of coffee and bags of the roasted beans to take home.

At the finca, we stayed in a small private room with a surprisingly comfortable double bed and a mosquito net for about $5. It wasn't that buggy, but I imagine it is a different story in the rainy season. The showers (no hot water) and toilet were down the hall. The finca can accommodate up to 80 people with cots and hammocks set up on the porch as needed. There are also a limited number of cabins for rent. It is possible to arrange work exchanges, especially during the coffee harvest, if you contact the finca in advance.

Since the finca is a mile or so up the slope of the volcano, the panoramic views are spectacular. From the massive porch, we could see the lake and Volcán Concepción to the north. There are some excellent petroglyphs on the finca grounds, just to remind you how ancient this place is. This farm is an international crossroads, attracting adventurers from all over the world. The meals for sale are quite good, the beer is cold, and the hammocks are the best. Watching a multihued sunset from the Magdalena porch can't be beat.

The people at the finca can also arrange for taxis, visits to other areas of the island, and guides to accompany hikers up the volcano to the cloud forest and lagoon at the top. It is foolish to attempt the climb without a guide; hikers have become lost on the way and died. It is not a technical climb, but you need to be prepared. We had thought we might climb the volcano, but as we sat on the porch the first day, we watched people returning from their climbs covered in mud. Every one of them wore boots. We had only sandals. "Can we make it to the top without boots?" we asked them. The answer was an emphatic and unanimous, "No way!"

We did climb some of the way up into the forest and saw the crops of beans, corn, and coffee growing under the shade and in dappled sun. You do not have to go far to see tropical birds, flocks of parrots, and howler monkeys in the trees. We spoke with one of the co-op members there, and he pointed out some of the local flora and fauna.

Even though I was disappointed that we could not climb the volcano, the many other wonders of the island more than made up for it. I would still like to try the ascent, but the conditions would have to be ideal as it is a hot and slippery trip. Now we have another reason to return to this special place, in addition to lounging on its uncrowded beaches, hiking through its lush forests, and visiting with its friendly people once again. There are many other things to do on the island, but I still hope to someday climb to the top of Volcán Maderas, soak in the view from the top, and make that dip into the cool water inside.

WHY GO: Isla de Ometepe is one of those special places where you can (and must) slow down to get into the local rhythm. Here is a place that seems to be a bit removed from the rest of the world by more than just a few miles of water. It feels like it exists in its own time zone, so the traveler does not find the usual consumer culture to define what there is to do. There are no fancy hotels and tourist shops to distract from the local culture and natural beauty of the island. Sit in the plaza and talk with the people who live here—this is a "real" place defined by the inhabitants and their history.

SPECIAL ISSUES AND CHALLENGES: Nicaragua can be *very* hot, making ambitious activities like volcano ascents extremely difficult if you are not in good shape and acclimated to the heat and humidity. The rainy season (May to October) can be especially humid, and the rain makes the trek up the volcano even more muddy and difficult. Fall provides a nice balance of weather. It is the end of the rainy season, so there are still a few showers, but it is not as hot as the dry season. We were there in late March and it was fine. In any case, the lake cools things down a bit on the island.

The buses run fairly often, but they are old schoolbuses, so they are not the most comfortable means of conveyance. They also break down a lot, probably because of the bad roads. If you are prone to motion sickness, this could be a difficult place to travel. Between the ferry and the bus, it can be a pretty stomach-jarring experience. Bring Dramamine.

There is not a lot of English spoken here, but a phrase book should see you through.

VARIATIONS AND OPTIONS: I am already planning my return to the island and will make sure to visit Merida on the west side of Volcán Madera. From Merida, you can access the beautiful Cascadia San Ramón, a magnificent waterfall. I will also try out the zipline at Santo Domingo and rent a kayak someplace, perhaps at Charco Verde, a lovely lagoon between Altagracia and Moyogalpa. There are nice places to stay in all of these areas.

If we had had the time, we would have gone to Granada via another ferry. Granada is the largest city on the lake. We went there recently (by road) and found it charming. This city, with its long and fascinating history, was established by the Spanish when they sailed up the Río San Juan from the Caribbean in 1524. To us, the city felt similar to Old Havana, probably because both cities were settled by the same people at almost the same time. The notable difference is that modern-day Granada is abuzz with construction and restoration work. This is a destination where a visitor can find history, including amazing colonial architecture, plus all the comforts of home. There are great international as well as Nicaraguan restaurants, horse-drawn carriages, nice hotels, and historic churches. It is a city in transition, but lovely still for visitors to enjoy and share some time with the local people in the Plaza Central as the sun sets and the birds fill the trees for the evening.

RESOURCES AND INFORMATION: For all kinds of information about the island, including general information, where to stay, ferry schedules and prices, where to eat, and more, go to *www.vianica.com/visit/ometepe*. A more complete listing of hotels and other accommodations can be found at *www .vianica.com/go/hotel/19.0.0.simple.0.0.html*.

Finca Magdalena has a very informative website at *www.fincamagdalena .com*. You can also follow a link to the Bainbridge Ometepe Sister Islands Association, where it is possible to order their excellent organic coffee and help support the collective.

For general background information about Nicaragua including maps, history, and tourist information, go to *www.nicatour.net*.

KAYAKING IN THE SEA OF CORTEZ (MEXICO)

DON MANKIN

I have idyllic memories of my first kayaking trip years ago in Mexico's Sea of Cortez—easy, warm-weather paddling through a unique environment of turquoise seas, long curving beaches, and stark desert cliffs. I also remember the lazy afternoons dozing on the beach, climbing the mesas, and snorkeling through schools of tropical fish. I figured that this could be the trip that finally turned my wife on to the joys of wilderness sea kayaking.

I didn't want to repeat the same trip, however, a partial circumnavigation of Espíritu Santos Island 20 miles off La Paz, a city about two-thirds of the way down the eastern coast of Baja California, Mexico. Besides, this trip has become so popular in recent years that it seems as if every kayaking company in the Western Hemisphere is now competing for campsites on the once secluded beaches of the island. So, I went looking for a more obscure trip in the region that would offer the same idyllic conditions as my earlier experience, but was different enough that I wouldn't feel like I was repeating myself.

I found it in a six-day trip exploring two islands a few miles off of Loreto, a small, sleepy town about 120 miles north of La Paz. I assured Katherine that it would offer her a true wilderness kayaking experience that would be, for the most part, well within her comfort zone. The parts that did not fall within her comfort zone almost did her in until a pod of dolphins transformed a potentially difficult few days into a great trip for both of us.

TRIP DESCRIPTION

The first few days were less than perfect. The good news was that the scenery was outstanding. From the kayaks, the Sea of Cortez seemed to go on forever, broken up only by the rugged profile of the imposing desert islands that would be our home for the next several days. Both of the islands, Isla Danzante and Isla Carmen, are rocky, barren, and dotted with cactuses. The russet peaks and headlands of the islands are interspersed with wide, white sand beaches and narrow coves. Carmen is about 19 miles long, Danzante only four.

The other good news was that our group was small, five clients and a guide paddling in three tandem (two-person) kayaks. They were very congenial companions—Rachel, a 27-year-old recent medical school graduate; Jan, a 50-something mother with her 16-year-old daughter, Hanna (the trip was Hanna's birthday present, of her own choosing); and Sergio, our easygoing Mexican guide who prepared great Mexican meals throughout the trip (and margaritas every evening). We got along well, hanging out together at the campsites or comfortable enough to go off on our own to read, nap, explore, or reflect whenever we wanted. It all made for a very cohesive group and an intimate experience.

The best news of all was that Katherine was able to manage the paddling despite the bursitis in her shoulder that had been nagging her for several weeks prior to the trip.

However, she did have some difficulty sleeping on the ground (with pad and sleeping bag, of course), going without fresh water to wash and, most of all, with "el baño." To the credit of the Mexican government, which has adopted some of the strictest policies I have seen to preserve their pristine wilderness, solid waste, including human waste, cannot be left behind on the islands or in the waters. We had to use a portable toilet—essentially a large black can fitted with a removable seat—and carry it and its contents from one campsite to another strapped with bungee cords onto the back of Sergio's kayak.

We all had some difficulty with this arrangement at first. Sergio helped by setting the toilet up in areas that were not only private but also afforded great views of the sea. Among all of us, Katherine had the most trouble. For the first few days of the trip, it was a toss-up for her whether the attractions of beautiful scenery, pleasant company, and invigorating exercise outweighed the restless nights and the dubious charms of el baño.

DOLPHINS IN THE DANCE OF LIFE

The turning point for Katherine came on the third day. It was the dolphins that did it. We had reached our first campsite on Isla Carmen the day before, after a long paddle of nine miles to make up for a first day that had been cut short by high winds and big swells. Since the plan was to stay here for two nights, we essentially had the day off. Instead of breaking down camp and packing up our kayaks to move to the next campsite, we would take a leisurely paddle up the coast for the day to a secluded beach with supposedly great snorkeling.

Unburdened by gear and supplies, our kayaks glided almost effortlessly on water that was smooth as glass. After about 45 minutes, we spotted a pod of dolphins a couple hundred yards away. We approached slowly, not making a sound. The dolphins alternated between swimming on the surface and diving for fish. We couldn't predict where or when they would surface, so we had to keep our eyes open and constantly scan the waters around us. This ballet played out in almost complete silence except for the gentle splash and exhale when they surfaced and the squawk of pelicans following in close pursuit, diving for the same fish.

We were now within a few yards of the dolphins. Katherine was transfixed. She had seen dolphins from boats and observed them surfing the waves off Venice Beach, but she had never seen them so close. There was no engine noise or crowds of gawking people intruding on the experience. We were able to view the whole scene from the perspective of a marine animal, which we essentially were, sitting in our kayaks waist deep in the sea.

In an instant, too fast for me to aim my camera, I saw a small fish leap out of the water. The fish was followed a split-second later by a dolphin in hot pursuit. Several pelicans were close on its "heels," ready to swoop in on the fish if the dolphin missed. For a moment, all three—fish, dolphin, and pelicans—were frozen in time in my mind's eye, only to disappear in splashes and ripples as the fish, then the dolphin, followed by the pelicans dove deep into the water. I gasped in astonishment and whispered to Katherine, "Did you see that?" She did and was as awed as I by what we had seen.

The rest of the day wasn't quite as dramatic, but it was still very special. We paddled into a large sea cave and peered out on the sea from the dark. We then pulled into a long, narrow, rocky cove for lunch. After lunch, we climbed to the top of the cliff that hung over our lunch spot and alternated between looking off in the distance at the stunning views from the top and looking down to peer at the hundreds of fossils—shells, bodies of other marine animals—embedded in the flat, primeval sediment, now rock, at our feet.

That evening as we acted out our own modern interpretations of hunting and gathering—Katherine creating complex mosaics from the varied shells she found on the beach as I scanned the horizon for game (whales?) and intruders (other kayakers)—we talked about the day. Clearly, seeing the dolphins that close, at their level and without distraction and noise, had had a profound impact on her. She was both excited and reflective at the same time.

I saw my chance for a breakthrough. I pointed out that the conditions that created the magical moments with the dolphins were the same conditions that required us to sleep on the ground, go several days without showers, and use a can for a toilet. "I don't do these trips for the discomfort and inconvenience," I explained, "I *put up* with the discomfort and inconvenience to have the kind of experience we had today."

Nothing profound happened at that point—no leaping to her feet shouting "Aha!"—but I could sense that that was the turning point of the trip for her. She slept better that night and the nights that followed, she made do with daily dunks in the sea with our container of biodegradable soap, and most important, she finally made peace with el baño.

OTHER HIGHLIGHTS

The dolphins weren't the only noteworthy animal sightings on the trip. The first day, we watched a couple of blue whales a half-mile or so out in the bay surface, spout, roll, and dive. As with the dolphins, I have an award-winning missed photo op memory of the late afternoon sun reflecting off the glistening back of one of these magnificent mammals as it prepared to dive. We also saw lots of birds—ospreys, pelicans, frigate birds, boobies, and a particularly regal-looking pink egret that posed on a rock against the backdrop of the sea for a good minute as I drew closer, squeezing off one picture after another. The pelicans were especially bold, dive-bombing one after the other into the sea just a few yards off the beaches where we camped.

For most of the trip, the water was too churned up by winds for good snorkeling. This was the only disappointment of the trip. The Sea of Cortez is known for great snorkeling, and this had been one of my fondest memories from my previous visit.

While the dolphins were the trip's highlight for Katherine, our last campsite was the highlight for me. I have seen stunning scenery in the dozens of wilderness trips I have taken over the years, but the rocky bay where we spent the last two nights has to be one of the most astonishingly beautiful places I have ever seen. The wide crescent of empty beach where we camped must have been over a mile from end to end. The beach was hemmed in from behind by very steep ridges and cliffs of red rock, and in front by an increasingly unruly sea.

At one end of the beach was a rocky headland with a large arch cut through the rock by erosion, providing a peekaboo view to the sea and the ragged stone ridges of the next bay. The arch is so squared off that it looks almost like a door cut by a stonemason of Bunyanesque proportions. In the other direction was a large sea stack shaped like a lotus bulb, and beyond that another rock shaped like a giant sail. By walking to one end of the beach, I could, in one view, take in the sea stack, the arch, three headlands layered into the distance, and the wild waters of the three bays lying between them. I was able to take this picture and have yet to grow tired of looking at it even though I see it every time I look at the desktop on my computer.

A low ledge of level rock wraps around each of the headlands making it relatively easy to walk around the points to the beaches on the other side. This gave us a fair amount of territory to explore as the mounting winds and waves kept us landbound for the day. We spent the day napping, reading, and taking leisurely walks around the ledges to check out the tidepools and watch small crabs scurry over the rocks, marvel at the view in all directions, and stand at the edge where the waves lapped. This latter "activity" felt weird and oddly satisfying, almost like walking on water a dozen or so yards from the shore. As much as I enjoyed the paddling and seeing the dolphins on the previous days, this was my favorite day of the trip.

But it wasn't over yet. After our outstanding final dinner of savory chicken *machacca* and margaritas, we returned to our tents for an early night in anticipation of a wake-up call at dawn to get on the water before the winds picked up. As usual, my bladder woke me up sometime in the early morning, and I stumbled out of the tent to the water's edge. Hanging over the horizon was a bright crescent moon, casting a cone of moonlight over the sea. I stood there for several minutes wanting to wring every last bit of moonlight and silence out of the experience. The need for more sleep finally won out, but the surprises were not yet over. I awoke again before dawn to make another trip to the water's edge, and caught the sun rising out of the sea in almost the same spot as the moon had only a few hours before.

THE END OF THE TRIP AND BEYOND

After our day of relaxation, we were ready for our last adventure, a short but adrenaline-pumping paddle across three miles of open water to our takeout point on the peninsula. The wind and surf that had kept us landlocked the day before were still whipping up, but Sergio figured that with an early start we could make it safely across before the conditions reached that fine line between excitement and folly. He was right, but it was still pretty hairy most of the way. As the white-capped waves broke over the sides of our kayaks and lifted and carried us along like surfboards—an unstable situation in a kayak—we hunkered down and paddled with singular purpose. It was hard but exhilarating work that made the idyllic days preceding it sweeter by comparison.

Over lunch of fish tacos and cold beer a couple of hours later, I popped the question (no, not that one—we were already married). I asked Katherine, "Would you do this again?" Specifically, did she want to bail out of the river-rafting trip we were scheduled to take in six weeks, or was she up for another week of sleeping on the ground, using a portable toilet, and gaping at spectacular scenery? She was. (To see how that trip worked out, see p. 65.) I had guessed right—this was just the trip to spark her interest in wilderness adventure. We'll see what happens with the next one.

WHY GO: The attractions of this trip should be apparent from the description. What may not be apparent is the thoughtful planning by the Mexican government to protect the area and make it a successful example of sustainable wilderness tourism. In a conversation after the trip with Grant Thompson, the founder and director of Tofino Expeditions, the company that conducted our trip, he described his contacts with the Mexican government, first to help them develop ecologically responsible policies, and then to qualify for a license to operate in the area.

I was very impressed with the careful, thoughtful, and open process he described. I was also impressed with the policies themselves: removal of all human waste; restrictions against taking shells, rocks, and other natural objects from the islands; restrictions against hiking off existing trails; and a system for allotting, reserving, and limiting the use of beaches for camping. Altogether, this demonstrates an impressive commitment to sustainable wilderness tourism that is worthy of the support of adventure travelers concerned about protecting the fragile areas they visit.

SPECIAL ISSUES AND CHALLENGES: This is an easier wilderness trip than most. Except for the constraints imposed by the policies on human waste and the occasional long paddles and windy days, this does not present any particular difficulties for reasonably fit travelers. Since the campsites are on sandy beaches, sleeping on the ground with a decent pad or air mattress should not be a problem for most people.

VARIATIONS AND OPTIONS: Tofino runs other trips in the area, including a longer one down the coast from Loreto to La Paz. In addition, Espíritu Santos

Island is another option that also offers warm-water kayaking, spectacular but slightly different scenery, and excellent snorkeling. That trip has become very popular in recent years, so the area is often crowded with kayakers.

RESOURCES AND INFORMATION: Tofino Expeditions *(www.tofino.com)* is one of the pioneering companies in the increasingly crowded wilderness sea kayaking field. Their motto says it all: "High Adventure and Great Food since 1988." In addition to conducting and outfitting the trip, Tofino provides airport transfers and accommodations in a local hotel before and after the trip and can provide information on flights from various cities in the U.S. Tofino also offers sea kayaking trips in the Queen Charlotte Islands, the Galapagos Islands, Vietnam, Norway, and Croatia. Contact them at 800-677-0877 or *info@tofino.com*. Other companies offering similar trips include Sea Kayak Adventures *(www.seakayakadventures .com)* and Paddling South *(www.tourbaja.com)*.

EXPLORING THE
HIDDEN GEMS OF BRAZIL

SHANNON STOWELL

Until my first visit to Brazil, I had the standard view that it was all beaches and jungle, Carnivale celebrations, and Amazon River cruises. I soon learned that it was much, much more. I've traveled to Brazil twice and have yet to hit any of the normal hotspots—Rio de Janeiro, the Pantanal, and the Amazon. Brazil is enormous (larger than the continental U.S.) and has a staggering range of geography, peoples, wildlife, and plant life, so there are many destinations for the adventurer who wants to get off the beaten path. So leave your thongs at home—the ones on your feet, as well as the other ones—and grab your hiking boots and Tevas and come with me to explore its hidden gems in the wild and lightly visited regions of Tocantins and Bahia.

TRIP DESCRIPTION

Although the states of Tocantins and Bahia share a common border in the center of the country, they have very distinct cultures, topographies, and economies. Bahia has a long coastline and a rich architectural and cultural history that reaches back to the earliest years of the country. The beaches and the historic capital of Salvador are among the most popular tourist destinations in Brazil. Tocantins, on the other hand, didn't exist as a separate state until it was carved out of the northern two-fifths of the state of Goias in 1989. It is a developing frontier area sandwiched between the Amazon jungle and the savannah. Cattle raising and agriculture are its main economic activities, and few tourists from outside Brazil visit its beautiful grasslands, forests, and river valleys. These two adjoining states offer a diverse geographical and cultural landscape. Between the two, the attractions are varied and abundant, but most have yet to appear on the tourist radar.

SAFARI CAMP AT KORUBO

I spent most of my time in Tocantins in Jalapão National Park. Jalapão is the perfect Brazilian remedy to the stresses of overcrowded cities like Rio and São Paulo. It is the least-populated place in all of Brazil, with fewer than one person per square kilometer. Wildlife still abounds in this humid subdesert region that marries two of Brazil's distinct ecosystems—the Amazon and the savannah. With its sandstone *chapadas* or plateaus more than 3,000 feet high, at times it's hard not to imagine that you are in a greener version of Utah or somewhere close by in the American Southwest, until the unique wildlife reminds you that this is the land of jaguars, toucans, macaws, anacondas, and capybaras, the world's largest rodent.

The first three days of my week in Tocantins were spent in the Korubo Safari Camp, located within Jalapão about a six-hour drive from the capital, Palmas, where my travel companions and I landed on our flight from São Paulo. We were all travel professionals who had come to Korubo to check out a new adventure destination. Having spent three chaotic days in São Paulo, it was wonderful to suddenly find myself in Korubo's quiet, sand-floored tent camp next to the Rio Novo, a tributary of the Amazon. That Korubo is named after the fierce Indian tribe in the northwestern end of the Amazonian jungle just added to its allure.

Korubo's safari camp is a low-tech, sustainability-oriented affair. Each tent has two cots and enough space for the typical traveler. The bathroom is a more attractive version of an outhouse, complete with camp toilets and a hand-washing station. The dining area overlooks the Rio Novo and is screened to keep out annoying insects, but there were not that many anyway. While the camp is not luxurious, it is clean, beautiful, and exotic. When we arrived at dusk, the camp was dimly lit by tiki torches. The night was soon transformed into brilliance by a full moon. Since the daytime temperatures in August are in the humid 80s and 90s Fahrenheit, we stowed our gear in the tents and went immediately to the river for a refreshing swim.

Before leaping in, we asked whether there were anacondas in the water. The owner and manager of the camp, Luciano, laughed and said he had never seen one right here. "Oh well, once," he added, "but it was a small one—only about 10 feet long and it was swimming across the river to move downstream." Considering all of the inglorious ways one can die in this life, like falling in the shower, getting hit at a crosswalk, or choking on a piece of steak, it seemed a pretty special opportunity to be known as the guy whose life ended while grappling an anaconda in the wilds of Brazil. So I ran the risk with the others, and we plunged into the cool water and had a glorious swim.

The next day, we headed out in Korubo's safari truck, a beast of a vehicle that allows you to ride up front in air-conditioned comfort on a cushy seat or on a butt-pummeling plank in the back, open to the elements, dust, and wind with an awesome view. Feeling tough and flush from our successful swim in the anaconda-choked river the night before, we of course chose the open back, scoffing at the thought of injury, litigious American attitudes, and seatbelts. It was an intoxicating ride toward the huge chapadas rising out of the dry plains with occasional patches of palms and jungle whisking by. Only once did we have to breathe the kicked-up dust of another vehicle passing by. We felt very much alone.

After a few hours of driving we arrived in the area known for its amazing chapadas, sand dunes, and waterfalls. The chapadas are the most salient landscape feature of the region, jutting up into the sky with red, white, and brown sandstone, providing for great hikes and views in all directions over the desert plains and nearby red sand dunes. The dunes were incredible! If you've ever been to Colorado and seen the Great Sand Dunes at the base of the Sangre de Cristo Mountains, you know what I mean. It has a very similar feel—huge red dune fields thousands of miles from any ocean. We ran down some of the steeper ones and watched the sun go down and the moon come up. Everything came together for several magical minutes—perfect temperature, few insects, silence broken occasionally by a call of an animal in the distance, and moon shadows playing on the dunes.

LIQUID LEVITATION

One morning we drove to a couple of *fervedouros* or fresh water springs for a swim. After a 90-minute drive from the safari camp, we hiked about five minutes through a banana forest to a roughly circular fervedouro about 25 feet in diameter with a small outflow at one end. The water was crystal clear, and the bottom was pure white sand. It was a beautiful sight.

Then it got weird. We could clearly see every feature on the bottom of the pool, and the constantly shifting sand on the bottom. Finally we could see that a hole on the bottom, a vent, was actually spitting white sand up into the pool and creating an illusion of a false bottom several inches above the actual bottom. Our guide, Luciano, encouraged us to step into the pool above the vent. We hesitated at first, then took the plunge and were immediately and forcefully spat out. There was incredibly strong water pressure pushing up out of the vent, and yet the sand was so heavy and dense that it didn't cloud the water. You could stir up the sand on the bottom and in seconds, the water was again crystal clear. And it was impossible to sink. Luciano told us that he actually had climbed up a banana tree once and plunged into the hole, only to be shot back up so strongly that he nearly cleared the water surface.

It was bizarre, like touching a power much stronger than it appeared. We experimented for the next hour and found that, with just the right stance, we could levitate right over the hole with our legs hidden by shifting sand up to our shins and yet nothing under the soles of our feet. We dove headfirst into the hole until our heads went into the silt layer and all went dark for a second until we were thrust up backwards out of the hole, feet first. We stood in the fervedouro, near the edge away and from the vent, and listened as the sand underneath our feet groaned and chirped while sucking our bodies down. I suppose this is where quicksand is born. It would have been disconcerting if we weren't also sticking out of the water at the level determined by our weight-to-volume ratio. Some of us were more buoyant than others.

All of us in the group were world travelers, and to a person we all agreed that this was the strangest natural phenomenon we had ever experienced. It appeared to defy some natural law—maybe of gravity or thermodynamics or at least normality. That night, one of our group members dreamed of levitation.

We got most of the sand out of our clothes, ears, and other strategic sand-capturing spots with a swim in the Cachoeira da Formiga, a waterfall-fed pool in a nearby river. The falls drop 10 or 15 feet into a shockingly blue pool—clear, cool, and clean. That perfect day was capped off with a dinner back at camp featuring pumpkin beef, beans—Brazilian style, of course— passionfruit pudding, and the local drink called caipirinhas made with cachaça, a sugarcane liquor.

RAFTING THE RIO NOVO

Following the three days in the safari camp, we were transferred to a put-in on the Rio Novo for a rafting trip. The guides gave us the usual safety instructions—what to do and not do when in the river, how to position yourself if tossed out of the raft, etc.—but skipped the part about how to successfully wrestle an anaconda. Perhaps they figured we already knew how to do that.

The standard trip is a three-day float, with the first day being the quietest, mostly a series of long quiet sections with occasional riffles and one or two Class II rapids. But it is a great five hours of scenery, calmness, and wildlife watching. We saw two capybaras run up to the river, squealing, then dive in and disappear. Apparently they walk their little, dense, pig-like rodent bodies along the bottom of the river for as long as five minutes before resurfacing.

The birds were stunning. Colorful macaws in pairs, ungainly toucans, and hunting vultures were almost a constant presence.

When it got too hot, we'd dive from the raft and just drift alongside and watch the world go by. I practiced a few back flips and tried to flop on my back—the loud slap designed to keep the anacondas away. At one point after swimming for about ten minutes alongside the raft, I decided to walk the shore. Deeply imprinted in the white sand on the beach were large cat tracks. It was an awe-inspiring moment realizing that jaguars were real and present.

We spent the first night on a picture-perfect white sand beach with a sand-bar just a few feet offshore. We made camp and then sat, sunned, and swam while the guides prepared a fantastic meal. Around the campfire that night, we swapped stories and enjoyed the beautiful night. We slept with sleeping bags in small tents nearby the river. The nights were cool and silent other than the sounds of the river (and perhaps the super-soft padding of jaguars).

Days 2 and 3 provided more exciting rafting, with Class III and IV rapids giving us a much-appreciated hit of adrenaline. The river water is incredibly clean and clear, and the guides drank directly from the river. To be on the safe side, though, I treated my drinking water with chlorine. I have friends back home who have gotten "beaver fever" or Giardia, and it's not pretty. I didn't want to think what capybara fever could be like. In the biggest rapids, quite a bit of untreated water did splash into my mouth, but I didn't get sick. I guess that the water is safe to drink, but I still think it was a good idea not to take the chance.

The very end of the rafting trip was punctuated with a fantastic exclamation point in the form of a huge waterfall. The guides lowered the rafts by ropes and we hiked down. Once beneath the falls, we all reboarded and paddled up to the crashing water, but the force was too powerful to get close to them, even with all six people on each boat paddling with all their might. We then circled behind the falls and edged into the cascade, feeling just some of the power of the crashing water but staying out of the pounding center, which could certainly pulverize the unlucky or careless.

CHAPADA DIAMANTINA PARK
IN THE STATE OF BAHIA

Whereas Tocantins is a wild state with few people, Bahia has many attractions usually associated with civilization. We started off by flying into Lençóis airport, which is very new, clean, nice—and utterly empty. Apparently it was overbuilt relative to the air traffic in the region, and was the least crowded airport anyone in our group had ever seen. The town of Lençóis has incredible charm, with narrow, cobblestone streets, a friendly populace, and big open squares. Restaurants seat their patrons in the square and people congregate there late into the evening. There is a small night market where vendors hawk handmade crafts and jewelry, and beautiful crystals and rocks sparkle in the shops, indicating the mineral wealth of the area.

In the past, this mineral wealth included diamonds, hence the name "Diamantina," but most have already been mined. There are still diamond hunters and miners, but they represent a mere shadow of the old days (the turn of the 20th century) when the area was the site of a rip-roaring diamond business. Even today on hikes, you can see creekbeds that have been dug 10–15 feet down, never fully recovering from the boom days of yore. You can still buy diamonds in Lençóis from local miners.

Today the gems are more architectural than mineral. We stayed in a fantastic hotel resort in Lençóis, Canto das Aguas, which is a beautifully landscaped wonder of nooks, porches, and crannies, each begging the visitor to sit for hours and sip a drink or enjoy a good book. From the beautiful, warm swimming pool and most of the rooms, you can see the Lençóis River cascade 400 feet down a sheer red rock face. It is a magical place to stay, surrounded by the never-ending whisper of falling water. We were there in late August, in the middle of the dry season (May through December); the whisper turns into a roar during the rainy season (October through April). There are many other comfortable, affordable resorts, hotels, and small pousadas in town. At the moment, there are no chain hotels or restaurants.

We took a number of day trips while staying in Lençóis. One involved a short drive through the brush to the wetlands known as Marimbus. We explored the clear, river-fed swamp in wooden dugout canoes. We piled in three to a boat and slowly launched into the clear water. At the same time, a few fishermen also hit the water, looking for dinner. As we paddled into the river through lily-pads, the land flattened out and we found ourselves in a huge marsh. The stream coursed in a serpentine pattern through the center of the marsh. Since we were headed gently downstream, the paddling was easy and we could enjoy the scenery, the birds, and the plants. Our guide, Roy Funch, is a fantastic naturalist, and he described the plant and animal life with great gusto and interest. Roy is an American who fell in love with the town of Lençóis and the surrounding area almost 30 years ago and decided to stay. He brought a unique flavor to the experience with a sensibility that is both American and Brazilian.

After pulling the canoes to the shore several miles downstream, we hiked up the Roncador River, which was colored like red wine from tannins—clean but dark and mysterious water. The plan was to hike up a massive red stone riverbed. If one was purposeful (which we weren't), one could get up the rock slope in about 20 minutes of good solid hiking. We took two hours.

The bed bends the river at varying angles and plunges it—sometimes gently, sometimes more forcefully—into inviting stone bowl pools or *caldeirões* (cauldrons). We couldn't resist these cool dark pools as the heat of the day intensified. Our group of ten adults played like a bunch of kids let loose for the first time in years. We repeatedly jumped in. Most of us just spent the day in our swimsuits, going in and out of the water like happy amphibians.

A local guide terrified and delighted us with his seemingly death-defying dives from the rocks into the small dark pools. At one point, he jumped into one pool and reappeared in a completely different pool several feet away. Apparently the two pools are joined by a tunnel running out of sight through the solid rock between them. Of course he knew about the tunnel and we didn't. For a moment, we thought it was Brazilian magic. In a way, I guess it was.

This pretty much summed up my trip to the center of Brazil—pure magic. It is a wonderfully unspoiled region of wildlife, geological beauty, and unusual features available only to the intrepid traveler willing to step off the mass tourism track. I am very happy that I took that step.

Saúde!

WHY GO: Brazil offers some of the most varied tourist attractions to be found within a single country—beautiful beaches, thick jungles, mighty rivers, diverse wildlife and plant life, sophisticated cities, great music and food, and a rich historical and cultural tradition. It has also become a dynamic economic and technological powerhouse in recent years. Brazil is a fascinating place that is changing rapidly. It is still reasonably inexpensive and relatively uncrowded once you get beyond the heavily populated coastal strip that is so popular with tourists.

SPECIAL ISSUES AND CHALLENGES: The trip described here is pretty active, but nothing that a healthy, reasonably fit traveler can't handle, except for maybe the backflips into the river to scare off the anacondas. The hikes up the chapadas and the river can be challenging, especially on a hot and humid day, so travelers should do some hiking back home to prepare for this trip. Also the long ride in the back of the safari truck could be a problem for someone with a bad back, but there is always the option of riding up front in cushy seats in air-conditioned comfort. Camp accommodations are rustic but comfortable. The shared bathroom facilities are clean and well maintained.

VARIATIONS AND OPTIONS: There are many other places to visit in the region. For example, from Lençóis you can also take day trips to:
• Pai Inácio Mountain, an impressive 3,800-foot-high chapada loaded with local legends and a fantastic view
• Fumaça Waterfall, which held the title of Brazil's tallest waterfall until a recent discovery in the Amazon region. Fumaça Falls is more than 1,000 feet high.
• Lapão Cave, the longest known quartzite cave in Brazil
• Numerous swimming holes in the local rivers, including the Serrano on the Lençóis River
• Modern archaeological sites, including the abandoned diamond miners' homes dating back to the 1840s

You'll want a local guide to get you to the best (and least known) spots since there is very little tourist infrastructure in the region. We traveled with Roy Funch, who also wrote *A Visitor's Guide to the Chapada Diamantina Mountains*. He can be found in the town of Lençóis with a little asking around or email him at *funchroy@yahoo.com*. For more information about the area, see *www.fcd.org.br.*

RESOURCES AND INFORMATION:
How to Do It: The only company that offers rafting on the Rio Novo is 4Elementos *(www.4elementos.tur.br)*. For other adventures in Korubo, see Korubo Adventures *(www.korubo.com/br)*. In addition to Roy Funch, I also recommend the following tour operators in Bahia: Andar por Ai *(www .andarporai.com.br)*; Bahia Adventure *(www.bahiaadventure.com)*; Venturas *(www.venturas.com.br)*; Brazil Ecotravel *(www.brazil-ecotravel.com)*; Ambiental Expeditions *(www.ambiental.tur.br)*; and Freeway Brazil *(www .freeway.tur.br)*.

Where to Stay: In Tocantins, we stayed in the Korubo Safari Camp *(www .korubo.com/br)*, operated by Korubo Adventures. In Bahia, we stayed

A cyclist rides through the heart of Italy's Chianti region during a six-day bicycle tour of the Tuscan countryside (see p. 141). Along with Tuscany's beautiful scenery, historic inns and villas, and rustic medieval villages, riders enjoy sumptuous meals and fine wines at many stops along the route. As a bonus, the active days of cycling allowed author Thomas Kramer and his wife to indulge themselves fully without gaining weight.

A panoramic view of the guest tents at Patriot Hills camp in interior Antarctica (see p. 263). The dining tent is on the left and the landing strip for the flight from Punta Arenas is at the base of the hills. Author Don Mankin lived for eight days in the tent behind the man pulling the sled. While not exactly balmy, air temperatures in the interior Antarctic summer are reasonable, hovering in the 15–25°F range.

ABOVE: Young girls from the minority Dong tribe in China show off their silver and hand-embroidered finery (see p. 227).

LEFT: Rafters on the Yampa River float past a stratified rock face in Utah's Dinosaur National Monument (see p. 65).

RIGHT: A Buddhist monk walks through the grounds of Wat Wisunarat, the oldest operating temple in Luang Prabang, in northern Laos (see p. 217).

ABOVE: A relaxed silverback mountain gorilla in Uganda's Bwindi Impenetrable Forest contemplates his midday snack while awestruck humans take his picture. Tracking mountain gorillas was the focus of an 11-day wildlife safari (see p. 179).

RIGHT TOP: A camel and its riders cast a shadow on the Sahara Desert near the Tunisian oasis town of Ksar Ghilane. The Sahara was only one of the attractions of a ten-day trip to Tunisia that also featured ancient Phoenician and Roman ruins and exotic medinas and souks (see p. 189).

RIGHT BOTTOM: A kayaker takes a break from paddling to celebrate the scenery in Gwaii Haanas National Park in the Queen Charlotte Islands, British Columbia. The seven-day sea kayaking trip also showcased eagles, bears, and the culture of the indigenous Haida people (see p. 75).

A colorfully decorated wigman prepares for a sing-sing at Ambua Lodge in the highlands of Papua New Guinea (see p. 247).

Kayakers glide by an iceberg in a fjord near Baffin Island during a 14-day sea kayak trip in the Canadian high Arctic (see p. 47).

at Canto das Aguas in Lençóis *(www.lencois.com.br)*. Another hotel in Lençóis is the Hotel de Lençóis *(www.hoteldelencois.com)*. And, for accommodations in Chapada Diamantina, check out Pousada Candombá *(www.infochapada.com)*.

EUROPE

—◦◦◦—

HIKING THE OUTER HEBRIDES (SCOTLAND)

DON MANKIN

I first visited Scotland for just a few days in August 1968 and enjoyed it so much that I returned the following summer for a longer visit. My idea was to hitchhike to the Hebrides, the legendary, remote, and notoriously moody islands off the west coast. However, my plans were thwarted one morning outside Inverness when every car passed me by, so I headed instead to the bus station to get on the first bus, wherever it went. I lucked out. Serendipity—and the bus, plus a ferry—took me to the Orkney Islands off the north coast and introduced me to their incredible Stone Age and Viking history.

I promised myself that I would return soon and visit the Hebrides, but other priorities and places intervened. Almost 40 years later, I finally made it back, this time with my wife, Katherine, and enough wherewithal to rent a car. Our plan was to hike the hills, moors, and beaches of the contiguous Isles of Harris and Lewis. As I researched the trip, I discovered another series of islands that were even more wild and remote—St. Kilda, 50 miles farther out into the North Atlantic and the site of an old, isolated, abandoned community with a unique history. I was more than intrigued and added these islands to our must-see list. What I didn't plan on was some of the worst summer weather in the memory of most everyone we met, making this trip more of an adventure than we had planned.

TRIP DESCRIPTION

My knuckles are white as I grip the steering wheel and try to keep the rental car from drifting into the stone wall on the left or the approaching cars on the right. It is pouring rain, and I am sitting on the "wrong" side of the car and driving on the "wrong" side of the road on a narrow, winding "highway" just an hour or so outside of Glasgow. This was not supposed to be part of the adventure, but it is, whether we like it or not.

Over the next several hours, it got worse—the fog settled in and it rained even harder. Water cascaded down the banks along the side of the road and I could barely make out the outlines of the breathtaking valleys, lochs, and mountains that surrounded us.

I had never driven with such unwavering focus for so long—almost seven hours to our B&B in the town of Uig on the western edge of the Isle of Skye, where the next morning the ferry would take us to Tarbert on the Isle of Harris. Our plan was to spend the next eight days on Harris and Lewis in the Outer Hebrides.

Harris and Lewis are actually two parts of a single island, Lewis to the north and Harris to the south, off the northwestern coast of Scotland. The two are separated by a rugged range of mountains, thereby creating two virtual, if not actual, islands. Harris and Lewis are the largest members of the Western Isles, as the Outer Hebrides are known in Scotland. They are isolated, wind-swept, almost treeless, ruggedly beautiful, and culturally distinct from the rest of Scotland. Sixty percent of the population speak Scottish Gaelic, a heritage that is widely displayed and honored in signs on the roads and on buildings throughout the almost 100 miles from the Butt of Lewis at the north end of Lewis to the settlement of Rodel at the south end of Harris.

I was especially looking forward to the one-day boat trip to St. Kilda. This group of rugged islands 50 miles off Harris in the North Atlantic are all that remains of an ancient volcano. They contain some of the tallest cliffs and sea stacks in Europe and the largest colony of seabirds in northwestern Europe. The main island, Hirta, was continuously inhabited for thousands of years by a hardy, self-sufficient community that lived primarily off the birds—they ate them and their eggs and traded the feathers and oil for other staples and supplies. They were able to preserve their unique society until 1930, when a number of factors and influences—missionaries, increased contact with the outside world, and World War I—changed their culture, lifestyle, and work in ways that could not support their hardscrabble existence.

The last remaining inhabitants, 36 in all, left Hirta that year and resettled in Scotland and elsewhere throughout the English-speaking world. Since then, the remnants of the village and other archaeological sites have been managed by the National Trust for Scotland. In recognition of its unique archaeological, ecological, and cultural heritage, Hirta is one of only two dozen global locations to be awarded World Heritage status for both natural and cultural significance.

Our rain-swept, white-knuckled welcome to the Outer Hebrides did not bode well for the rest of the trip. This was just the latest example of one of the coldest, windiest, rainiest summers on record. It was bad enough that it could have impacted our plans for hiking and exploring, but the implications for the St. Kilda trip were especially disturbing. The boat captain would not chance the almost three-hour trip—a difficult crossing under the best of circumstances—in high winds and seas. All we could do was get out our raingear, waterproof our boots, and hope for the best.

THE ISLE OF HARRIS:
BEACHES, MOORS, AND LOCHS

The next morning, the sun was shining brightly but the winds were blowing at just about gale force, making for an exciting two-hour ferry ride to Tarbert. The drive from Tarbert to our accommodations for the next four nights introduced us to another dimension to adventure driving in Scotland—the single-track road. Wide enough for only one car, driving on these winding roads requires vigilance, patience, courtesy, and a quick foot on the brakes. Fortunately, there are designated passing places every 50 yards or so that drivers can duck into to avoid head-on collisions. Traffic was light as the road ran across open moors and along the vast beaches on the ocean side of the island, so I didn't have to jam on the brakes too often. But the driving kept me from lingering too long on the spectacular views of wide beaches of golden sand, the craggy green hills, and the wild ocean with wind-whipped waves that would make a Malibu surfer salivate.

Over the next four days, we explored these hills and beaches and sat for hours in the sun room of our B&B, the Beul na Mara ("Mouth of the Sea" in Gaelic), looking at what is advertised as the best view on Harris. I would have to agree. In fact, it was probably the best view I have ever seen while eating a meal with bone china and linen napkins. The B&B overlooks the beach at Luskentyre, which stretches as far as the eye can see in both directions and almost as far out at ebb tide. We could see breaking waves in the distance at the mouth of the bay and the Isle of Taransay across the way. The view changed as the tide came in, filling the very shallow tidal flats of the bay in front of us. As the sun set, the color of the sand changed, from blazing white to gold to silver, and the sky from silver to orange to red to gray. Most evenings we sat and watched the changes for at least two hours after dinner until the sky and the beach grew dark.

For our explorations, we relied heavily on the recommendations, maps, and route notes supplied by Wilderness Scotland, a leading adventure tour operator in Scotland. On our first full day on the island, we took advantage of a break in the weather to hike across flower-filled coastal meadows called *machair*, along the white beaches and cliffs a few feet above the beach, to the ruins of a 16th-century chapel. The ruins are perched on a rocky rise above the sea with a large hill known as Ceapabhal looming behind it. We hiked past the ruins farther along the coast, the southern edge of a peninsula jutting out into the ocean. The views were magnificent the entire way—wide-open sea, islands, distant dark hills covered in clouds, and green fields. It was a stunning walk, and we inhaled deeply of the sweet-smelling breezes that filled the air. We saw only a handful of people all day.

As we headed back to the B&B, our good luck changed and it started to pour. Our trip to Kilda was scheduled for the following day, and the weather didn't look promising. With some trepidation, I called Angus Campbell, the owner of Kilda Cruises, the company that runs the boat trip. As I feared, the trip had been canceled. Maybe the day after.

The next day, the weather was even worse. It began with a drizzle, but as we drove to our next hike at Husinish at the western tip of Harris, it started to rain much harder. The road snaked between the rugged mountains of North Harris and a long sea loch to the south. It passed by rushing streams and the Western Isles version of an infinity pool—inland lochs ending at a dropoff, framed against the sea in the background, creating the impression of a continuous body of water. The road even took us through the grounds of a castle, now a private residence. By the time we got to the end of the road, at the neck of a very narrow peninsula, it was pouring.

We changed into our "full waterproofs" in the car and ventured out into the rain. The wind almost knocked us over as we stepped out of the car. For the next two hours we had a blast—literally. We hiked across a meadow and up a hill with views of the sea on both sides of the peninsula. Surrounding us were rocky rises, green boggy depressions, fields covered in heather and wild purple, yellow, and white flowers, and dramatic cliffs plunging down to rocky inlets and crashing waves below. There were no discernible trails and no people.

We wandered around until the wind-driven rain started to sting and threatened our balance as we approached the crest of the highest hill on the peninsula. It was all very exciting but also a little scary, the very essence of the Hebrides—incredibly beautiful and wild. We returned to the car, wet but exhilarated.

That evening I called Angus, and he told me that the next day's trip was also canceled. I was not surprised. He did hold out some hope for the day after, though, since the forecast was more favorable. The problem was that the boat was fully booked, but he told us not to give up hope. "Maybe there will be a cancellation," he said. "Call me again tomorrow."

The next day things looked more promising. At least it had stopped raining. We headed down the "Golden Road" (named for how much it cost to build) to the east side of the island. It is very different from the west side. Rather than wide-open views, beaches, and big islands off shore, the east is indented with narrow, rocky coves and features small islands, often little more than oversized rocks, off the coast. The road was very twisty and narrow, with steep dropoffs at the side. It was a challenging drive since the temptation was to gawk at the incredible scenery around every curve. We stopped to take a short hike on a portion of the Harris Walkway, a series of old paths that cut across the island. The lunar-like landscape is broken up by lochs, moss, and machair, with views to the ocean in one direction and the Minch (the body of water between Harris and Skye) in the other.

We called Angus three times that evening to find out if there had been any cancellations. On the last, desperate call at 10 p.m., he gave me the bad news—no cancellations. I sighed and slumped in disappointment. But he continued, mentioning almost in passing, "If there was only one of you, I could take you as an extra member of the crew. You wouldn't have a seat, you would have to stand on the outside deck." Katherine, who had been standing next to me, listening in, quickly says, "Do it, Mankin." She knew how much I wanted to take this trip.

The boat would return to Harris by 7:30 p.m., just enough time to make the two-hour drive to our next destination at the northern end of Lewis before the sun set (I didn't want to drive the single-track roads in the dark). The plan was for Katherine to drop me off at the boat dock in the morning, hang out for the day, and then meet me back at the dock when the boat returned. It would be tight, but it should work.

ST. KILDA

The boat, all 42 custom-built feet of her, bounced across the North Atlantic, its 700-horsepower engines pounding us through the oncoming swells at 18 knots, trailing a big, graceful wake. I was the only Yank among the group of passengers from England and Scotland, most of whom were in their 50s or older. The trip across was part of the adventure—the engines roared and the boat tossed and pitched the whole time. It was all very exciting.

During the two-and-three-quarter-hour crossing, I stood on the rear deck with legs wide to absorb the tosses and pitches and keep my balance. We all held on for dear life. Several people got sick, and one fell on the pitching deck. The mate told me that it is a rare trip when someone doesn't get sick going to St. Kilda. He also said that these conditions were "as good as it gets in the North Atlantic." Despite the name of the company, Kilda Cruises, this was no cruise! And then it started to rain.

But the sight of the islands nearing in the distance lifted our spirits, and the sun started to peek out. We pulled into Village Bay in streaming sunshine. Village Bay, on the main island of Hirta, is the site of the historic settlement, the only place in the islands continuously inhabited by humans.

The bay plus the slopes and hills that almost encircle it—the remnants of the ancient volcanic ridge—form a huge bowl. On the lower reaches of the slope, just up from the shore, is the abandoned village. Old stone houses line the path running from one end of the village to the other, and long, narrow fields extend up and down the slope in front of and behind each house. These communally owned fields were used to grow potatoes and other hardy crops for the villagers. A stone wall to keep sheep out of the fields runs behind the entire length of the village. The village, the fields, and the slopes are dotted with a number of Stone Age and medieval archaeological sites and many *cleits*, small stone structures used to store eggs, seabird carcasses, hay, and peat. Several of the buildings have been restored and house staff and volunteers from the National Trust for Scotland. There is also a small Ministry of Defence presence on the island housed in a collection of nondescript buildings near the shore. We were free to wander, except in the area occupied by the Ministry.

I slowly walked through the village, looking at the houses and trying to imagine what life was like for the hardy people who lived here. Then, I headed up to the "Gap," a saddle between the two highest hills on the island. The climb was steep and boggy, but the views back down to the village and the bay were spectacular. I approached what looked like a ridge at the top, but as I got closer I saw that it was the top edge of the bowl. The outside of the bowl is actually sheer cliffs that plunge 500 feet straight down to the sea. The cliffs ran as far as I could see in either direction, up to the crest of the two hills (1,300 feet at the highest point). It's as if half of the island dropped away into the ocean. Birds were everywhere. It's easy to picture, but hard to believe, that the residents used to hang by ropes off these cliffs to catch the birds and pick their eggs off the tiny ledges hundreds of feet above the sea. Off nearly four miles away I saw Boreray, the other major island in the Kilda archipelago, and the sea stacks Stac Lee and Stac an Armin.

It wasn't easy getting to this spot, but it was well worth it. For the next hour, everything fell into place—the sights, sounds, feel of the air, and solitude. I wandered along the edge of the cliff, mindful that a gust of wind could sweep me over the edge if I was not careful. I even crawled on all fours to peer over to look at the crashing sea below and the birds swooping along the face of the cliff. I took dozens of pictures.

After a while it was time to work my way down and return to the boat. But the show wasn't quite over. Before heading back to Harris, Angus took us over to Boreray and the stacks for an up-close look at some of the highest cliffs and the largest concentration of birds I have ever seen—puffins, kittiwakes, gannets, guillemots, and fulmars, among others. They hovered directly overhead, giving me a human's-eye view of the biomechanics of flight.

The trip back seemed calmer. At least no one got sick. We were back on the dock at 7:15 p.m. and Katherine and I were on the road by 7:30, headed to our next destination, the Galson Farm Guest House in northern Lewis.

TIME TRAVELING ON THE ISLE OF LEWIS

After our four-plus days on Harris and St. Kilda, I didn't expect that much from Lewis. My initial impression was in line with my expectations—from the road, Lewis looked flat and featureless. But that was okay. Despite the weather, the trip so far had been great. The historic Galson Farm was quaint and filled with antiques, but it mattered little to us at that point, since we just wanted to get in bed and go to sleep.

In the morning, we discovered why the views from the road were so uninspiring: Most all of the buildings, villages, towns, and main roads are set back at least a quarter-mile from the low cliffs overlooking the water, probably because the early crofters who lived on and worked the land feared losing their homes to coastal erosion. Therefore, while the views from the main roads were not that great, from the fields and local roads near the water they were spectacular. As far as the eye could see, there was nothing but uninterrupted views of bluffs, beaches, and surf, except for the occasional old farmhouse, crofter's cottage, or cemetery, all of which seemed to fit in with the natural scenery.

That day we headed to the northern tip of the island, the Butt of Lewis, which completed our tour of the combined island from end to end. Weatherwise, it was the best day we had had since we arrived in Scotland—bright, sunny, and what passed for warm in that part of the world (in the 60s). Near the beginning of our hike, a man walked toward us with a cane. I guessed that he was in his 50s, and the sag of his face on one side and his limp suggested a recent stroke. As we approached he greeted us with, "It's a good day for a walk, isn't it?"

In that moment, I finally got the Scottish attitude toward walks—not hikes, as we call them in the U.S., but something more casual, a part of everyday life, rather than a special activity to be noted with its own word implying something long and arduous. Everywhere, in the route notes from Wilderness Scotland, in the guide *Walks: Western Isles,* and in casual conversation, what I call a "hike," the Scottish call a "walk." It seems that there is nothing better in Scotland than "a good day for a walk," especially when the very act of walking can no longer be taken for granted.

And a good day it was. The walk around the Butt was one of the best of the trip: few people, and lots of gently rolling hills covered with bright green machair and dotted with sheep—as Katherine described it, a "golf course for sheep." Our route followed the bluffs above the coast, and waves crashed onto the rocky shore. It was sublime. I couldn't resist sitting down when we reached the Butt—in effect, the butt of Mankin on the Butt of Lewis—and stared at the rugged cliffs as we ate our lunch. It was one of the most serene moments of our trip.

The next day was quite different. This was a day devoted to history and culture. Driving 40 miles south from the guesthouse, we covered about 7,000 years of history—from the Stone Age, through the Dark Ages and the arrival of the Vikings, to the era of the crofters, both before and after the notorious "clearances" forced them off the land in the 18th century and initiated the Scottish Diaspora. We saw neolithic stone circles and obelisks, visited meticulously reconstructed "blackhouses" (early versions of the crofters' chimneyless cottage), and an imposing stone fortification from the Iron Age, called a *broch,* built to house families and defend against hostile neighbors and distant raiders.

Most impressive of all were the Callanish Standing Stones, a prehistoric stone monument second only to Stonehenge for mystery and grandeur, but surpassing Stonehenge in its setting, accessibility, and lack of crowds (just a handful of people). From different angles and framed against a changing sky, the stones offered varied looks. With little to distract me from the aura of the monoliths, it was easy to get in touch with my primeval self, my links to the distant past.

To cap off the day, we headed to the island of Bernera, which is connected to Lewis by a single-lane bridge. This was one of the most scenic drives of the trip. At the end of the road at Bosta Beach, we came upon a single, restored, thatched-roof, Iron-Age dwelling nestled in a grassy glen by a small stream between two ridges of rock. It overlooked the beach and a protected bay, with rocky islands and sea stacks in the distance. Maybe it was the sun, but the colors seemed to be the most vivid of the entire trip—white and yellow flowers, green moss and grass, gray rock, and deep blue water and sky.

The essence of this trip was captured in this one evocative scene—breathtaking beauty and history that reached back to our deepest cultural roots. And for a couple of hours at least, we were able to enjoy it while dry, warm, and dressed in T-shirts and shorts.

WHY GO: Why not? The Western Isles are reasonably accessible, they offer both adventure and amenities, and everyone speaks English, though the accents are so strong you may occasionally have your doubts.

SPECIAL ISSUES AND CHALLENGES: Since this is a self-guided trip, travelers can hike/walk as much or as little as they want and can pick and choose among many hikes/walks of different lengths and levels of difficulty. The only serious challenge we encountered, besides the weather, was a lousy exchange rate on the dollar.

VARIATIONS AND OPTIONS: The options are many—explore the other islands in the Outer Hebrides, the Western Highlands on the mainland, or the remote north, including the Orkneys. We chose to end our trip with several days in Edinburgh for the acclaimed International Festival.

RESOURCES AND INFORMATION:

How to Do It: Wilderness Scotland *(info@wildernessscotland.com; www.wildernessscotland.com)* helped us organize our trip by arranging accommodations at Beul na Mara and providing a very helpful trip dossier and route notes with numerous recommendations for things to see, places to visit, and, most importantly, hikes. It also provided detailed topo maps, gave us information on how to arrange the trip to St. Kilda, recommended a B&B on Lewis, and generally helped us plan our trip. The cost in 2007 was £395 (about $800) per person for four nights, based on two people sharing a double or twin room. This included accommodations, all meals, and ferry fares.

For the trip to St. Kilda, contact Angus Campbell *(www.kildacruises.co.uk)*. The cost in 2007 was £140 (about $280) per person.

Where to Stay: If you want to organize this trip on your own, you can contact the Beul na Mara directly at *morrison.catherine@virgin.net* (also see *www .beulnamara.co.uk*). The Galson Farm Guest House *(www.galsonfarm.co.uk)* charges £84 (about $170) for two people per night, including breakfast.

Where to Eat: Both the Beul na Mara and the Galson Farm Guest House serve excellent dinners. Galson also has a full liquor license and a good selection of single malt whiskies, including several that cannot easily be found in the U.S.

We also recommend the Rodel Hotel in southern Harris for lunch or dinner *(www.rodelhotel.co.uk)*. Their mussels are exceptional. For reservations, call 44 185 952 0210 or email *reservations@rodelhotel.co.uk*.

CYCLING—AND EATING AND DRINKING—THROUGH TUSCANY (ITALY)

THOMAS KRAMER

Tom, an academic administrator and psychologist in his early 60s, and his wife, Mary, have traveled throughout western Europe, the Caribbean, the U.S., New Zealand, and Australia. For the past 20 years, their vacations have included some mix of golf, cycling, and snorkeling while searching for good wine and food. When traveling outside the U.S. they always look to experience local customs and culture, especially in the local markets. While he likes his comfort, Tom is not hesitant to mix it in with a significant physical challenge, much like the one described in this chapter. —Don Mankin

TRIP DESCRIPTION

I have fond memories of my first trip to Tuscany with my family several years ago. We did the typical tourist trip then, driving here and there, visiting the region's charming medieval hilltop villages, standing on the Leaning Tower of Pisa, and tasting good wine and excellent food. Mary and I have also taken several bike trips over the years. So, when we ran across the description of a six-day, 150-mile biking trip through Tuscany with Backroads, an outdoor adventure company, how could we resist? The idea of coasting through the beautiful scenery, stopping for roadside picnics, eating grand meals in classic villas in the evening, and best of all, burning off all the calories consumed the night before with a vigorous bike ride the next day was too tempting to ignore.

The only question on my mind was, could I do it? While the description in the Backroads catalog noted that the trip included steep hills, we decided to ignore the warning and take the plunge. We focused instead on the knowledge that the trip would include tasting some of the wonderful Tuscan cuisine and wines. While it did occur to us that the physical demands of the trip (especially pedaling up steep hills) might be a bit more than we could handle, we did not let that discourage us from signing up.

THE DAILY RIDES

Tuscany is an area of small medieval towns perched on hilltops separated by rolling fields and valleys. It is one of the 20 regions of Italy and includes such well-known cities as Florence (the capital), Siena, Pisa, and San Gimignano. The area of Chianti lies in the center of the region with Florence to the north, Siena to the south, and stretches west from there. Chianti is justifiably famous for producing the wine that carries that name. Over the six days of our trip, we managed to cover some of the most scenic and interesting parts of this area and to sample many of the wines.

The routine for the trip was established early on. After a generous buffet-style European breakfast, our group of 20 cyclists would head out for a ride on our high-tech, 21-speed bikes. Most days, we rode for about two hours in the morning, stopped for lunch, then rode some more in the afternoon. For those who wanted to ride longer, there was always an option to take an additional trip, and those who had had more than enough could always ride in the van that followed us wherever we went. Three of the days we rode 35–40 miles, another day was 25, and the last was only 15.

The countryside was beautiful, but indeed there were many hills, sometimes even steep ones with many switchbacks. After grinding our way to the top of a hill, we would usually stop for a panoramic view (and a rest) before plunging back down. We meandered through forests, past Etruscan ruins and a Roman amphitheater, through the occasional small town, and past rolling fields of vineyards, flowers, or grain. The most memorable part of the rides, however, was when we rode past fields of red poppies intermixed with white wildflowers. At times, there were poppies as far as we could see, with an occasional barn, house, or stand of trees breaking up the view of the fields. A couple of times, we just stopped and walked into the fields to immerse ourselves in their beauty. We saw few cars. Our experience of Tuscany on a bicycle was very different than seeing it by car. It was all very peaceful.

While there was a routine to each day, each was also different. On three days, we returned to the same hotel, riding out and then back by a different route. On two days, we rode from one town to another while Backroads staff transported our luggage in the van.

Lunch, always a treat, was handled differently from one day to the next. Once we had lunch in a small park along the way, prepared by our two guides. It was delightful. The beautiful spread included Italian meats and cheeses, pasta salad, marinated red peppers, and some sweets for dessert. We all sat around in the shade and relaxed. After such a meal, it was hard to get up and head back out on the bike. I guess that is why so many Europeans take siestas.

On another day, my wife and I and two friends who were also on the trip found a little restaurant at the top of a hill. The meal, which more than made up for the long climb to get there, included salad, bowtie pasta in spinach sauce, *caprese,* and gnocchi in tomato sauce, as well as Prosecco, a light, refreshing, low-alcohol sparkling wine.

One of our most memorable lunches was on the day we stopped at a little grocery store that made panini to go for all four of us. Before we could find a good place to stop and eat, we had to climb our way up yet another long hill, a tough four-mile ride. We all hung in there, though at one point we did consider going back for the shuttle van. At the top we perched ourselves on a wall overlooking a long, verdant valley and had a relaxing lunch. It was a nice reward for sticking it out during our long, arduous ascent.

PUSHING IT

Throughout the trip, our two guides, Emily and Alexis, kept track of all of the riders. One would be on her bike while the other would track the group in the van. If we needed a ride, all we had to do was signal and the van would pick us up. As a result, we were never concerned that we would be unable to get back to the hotel or make it up a hill. The two guides watched over us without hovering and made sure that we all completed our daily rides safely. The group had some real "rabbits" who liked to speed ahead, as well as more leisurely bikers like the four of us who often brought up the rear. Emily and Alexis were able to track and assist everyone, not an easy task given the wide range of capabilities and riding styles within the group. Their unobtrusive but helpful attention made the rides enjoyable, safe, and comfortable.

All bets were off, however, when we went off on our own. On the last full day of the trip, we had a short ride in the morning and the afternoon was open. Some in our group chose to go shopping; others decided to lounge by the beautiful swimming pool overlooking a stream at the rear of the hotel. As the trip progressed, I had grown more adventuresome and, dare I say, cocky, so I decided to go on another ride, by myself. It was a 25-mile round trip over fairly flat roads to an Etruscan tomb. On the way, my competitive nature kicked in, and I ratcheted up the pace up a few notches to see how quickly I could get there. It was a great ride along a beautiful ridge to the tomb. Once

I got to the sign that said the tomb was just up the hill, I took a picture of the sign just to prove that I made the trip, drank some water, and headed back.

After a mile, however, my bike froze up! Here I was, 12 miles from our hotel, without any tools, no phone, little ability to speak Italian, and not much of an idea of where I was. Once I realized the depth of my predicament, I sat down for a moment to calm down. Then I quickly diagnosed the problem—my chain had come off and lodged itself in the frame and the gears. Fortunately, all the times I had thrown the chain on my bike as a youngster held me in good stead. I had never worked on a 21-speed before, but I was able to release the chain and rethread it onto the gears. I pedaled the rest of the way back with great care. I returned unscathed, aside from my greasy hands. I felt relieved and very lucky, vowing to never again go off into unknown territory without a backup plan.

This one instance of foolishness aside, I was very pleased with my overall performance on the trip. At age 54, I was the oldest person on the trip, but for the most part I was able to keep up with the younger members of the group. I might have been a bit slower than some, but I never fell far behind. Most important, I fulfilled my goal of riding the whole trip and never walking the bike or taking the van, despite some serious eating and drinking most every evening and often during the day.

I also didn't gain any weight. We often rewarded ourselves with a gelato or other treat for working hard and holding our own, telling ourselves that we had burned so many calories we could easily justify it. We used this rationalization throughout the trip as we ate and drank wine without worrying about gaining a few pounds. Much to our surprise, it worked!

WHERE WE STAYED

The towns and hotels in which we stayed were among the highlights of the trip. Our first stop was the walled medieval city of San Gimignano. The town itself rose from an Etruscan settlement around the third century B.C. Its first walls were built around A.D. 1000, followed by the construction of more than 70 towers that have earned it the unofficial name the "City of Beautiful Towers." Much of the wall and a few towers still stand today. It is an old city with narrow streets and a large piazza in the center of town that is the focus of daily activity.

We stayed two nights in the Hotel l'Antico Pozzo. The building that houses the hotel has been completely restored to its original style from the 15th century. Everything has been faithfully preserved or reproduced to keep the charm of this superb structure intact. The dining room where we had breakfast was large and beautiful. Our room was also huge and overlooked the piazza teeming with people. While we were concerned that it would be noisy, the town quiets down by about 10 p.m. We slept soundly.

We spent one night in Siena, one of the most beautiful cities of Tuscany, nestled in the heart of the wine and olive-growing country. The town sits on three hills, with the Piazza del Campo, famous for its shell shape, located in the heart of the city. Another interesting site is the *duomo* or cathedral of Siena. It is a beautiful building containing a mix of Gothic and Romanesque architecture with dark green and white marble in the façade. In the same piazza as the duomo is the hospital of Santa Maria della Scala, which now houses a museum complex, exhibiting frescoes, works of art, and treasures collected during its millennial history.

Our accommodations were in the Park Hotel Siena, which is in a 16th-century patrician villa. Like our previous hotel, it has been restored carefully and has large guest rooms, meeting rooms, and a beautiful restaurant where we had breakfast. The hotel contains salons with vaulted ceilings, antique furniture, and terra-cotta floors. It is located on the edge of the city with a beautiful view overlooking a refreshing pool and the valley below. The grounds contain spacious gardens for walking.

Our last hotel was the Albergo l'Ultimo Mulino between Gaiole and Radda in the Chianti region. This too was recently redone, but in a more contemporary style. The hotel was once a medieval mill and had recently been carefully restored to preserve much of its original character.

WHAT WE ATE AND DRANK

Eating local food and drinking wine in Tuscany is a true pleasure. Every meal, from simple lunches to elaborate dinners, was outstanding. We were never disappointed. On one of our first nights, we had a real feast at one of the many fine restaurants in San Gimignano. After a wine tasting, we settled down for a dinner served family-style with huge bowls of food: Bruschetta with tomatoes and eggplant, homemade ravioli with truffle sauce, *riboletta* (vegetable soup), spinach, French fries, rabbit, wild boar, fish, and a fantastic chocolate dessert. Along with the great food, we had generous quantities of wine. It was 11:00 when we finally left the restaurant. That meal motivated us to ride especially hard the next day to burn off the calories.

One of the highlights of the trip was what our guides called a "cooking school," where everyone on the trip participated in preparing our final dinner. Our host and hostess for the evening showed us around their 13th-century farmhouse, which had been lovingly restored and converted into a restaurant. After the tour, they went over the menu and invited us to help in the preparation of the meal. We each took turns preparing different parts of the menu at different work stations in the large kitchen. There was, of course, plenty of wine to enliven the conversation and add to the fun. People moved from station to station to try their hand at coring the peppers, slicing tomatoes, preparing eggplant, etc. It took us about two hours to prepare the meal, which included antipasti; bruschetta with tomatoes, cheese, and basil; rice-stuffed red peppers (the peppers were eight inches long); spaghetti with olives; and tiramisu for dessert. And, as always, there was plenty of Chianti. We left stuffed.

Another highlight was the olive oil tasting, at Badia a Coltibuono, the Abbey of Good Harvest. Before the tasting, we took a tour of the grounds and the olive oil–making equipment. The place was adorned with hanging plants, gardens, and ponds. We received quite an education about distilled and undistilled olive oil, the difference between cold press, first press, second press, and more. Not surprisingly, the best part was the tasting. What struck me was how many different kinds of olive oil there are. It wasn't so much a matter of which ones tasted better, but rather how different methods, presses, and quality of the olives affected the taste. While we previously might have thought that "olive oil is olive oil," we came away with the realization that there was much more to learn and appreciate.

Probably the most memorable culinary adventure was the formal wine tasting. Mary and I had been looking forward to this evening from the moment we signed up for the trip. We boarded a taxi at about 6 p.m. with our friends and took what Mary called a "kamikaze" ride to the Enoteca (wine bar) San Domenico in the middle of Siena. The cabbie met all of our stereotypes of a crazed Italian driver, darting in and out of traffic the entire way. Once at the bar, we tasted four reds—a Chianti Classico, a Vino Nobile di Montepulciano, a Brunello di Montalcino, and a Brancaia Vino da Tavola—accompanied by a very informative discussion of each by the owner of the enoteca. The wines were full, deep, and very different from each other, and they gave us an excellent opportunity to appreciate the style and quality of wines from the region. Besides tasting great, the wine also helped to calm our nerves in preparation for the equally chaotic taxi ride back to our hotel.

A TOTAL EXPERIENCE

After many group photographs and hugs after lunch on the last day, we loaded ourselves into the bus for our trip back to Florence. This was a time for reflection. We had seen a part of Italy in a way that one could never experience by car or bus. I cannot imagine a better way of sampling Tuscan cuisine. The cooking school was a unique opportunity to learn about Italian food preparation. Our experience in the countryside would be difficult to accomplish without a guide. And everywhere we went—restaurants, hotels, shops, and wine stores—we met the friendly people of Tuscany.

When we initially decided to take this tour, we focused on the biking and the scenery. What we really came to appreciate and value, though, were the cuisine, history, architecture, and people. And as the oldest members of the group, we learned that we could hold our own on a physically demanding trip, self-knowledge that has stood us in good stead in the cycling trips we have taken in the years since. It was an experience we will always treasure.

WHY GO: The main reason to go is, simply, Tuscany. It has history, fantastic food, excellent wine, interesting scenery, rustic towns and villages, and friendly people. Touring by bicycle gives you a whole different experience of the countryside, something we missed on our first visit there when we traveled by car. Doing the tour with a group adds an extra dimension of camaraderie. The exercise was also a plus.

SPECIAL ISSUES AND CHALLENGES: Except for a few of the hills, the cycling is not that difficult. Most, if not all, tour companies have a van to pick you up if you tire out or if a stretch is too demanding. Best of all, you can go at your own pace. Some people dart ahead and ride a lot farther than others. Our group of four tended to bring up the rear, but that was no problem. I would sometimes pedal ahead and then come back to ride with my wife and friends.

There is a small risk of injury. One woman on our tour fell and got scraped up, but that was the only such incident. Most everyone on the trip had some soreness from time to time, but it usually went away in a few days.

VARIATIONS AND OPTIONS: Backroads now offers a lodging choice of "casual inns" or "premier inns." The tour we took stayed at premier inns and costs $3,798 to $4,498 per person for six days/five nights for 2008, not including international airfare to and from Florence. This Tuscan tour turns out to be one of their most expensive trips on a per-day basis. Casual inns run about 30 percent less. Backroads also offers "Insider Trips," which focus more on culture than on activity.

RESOURCES AND INFORMATION: We have used Backroads *(www .backroads.com)* for four cycling tours. It offers biking, walking and hiking, multisport, and Insider tours in 42 countries and provinces. Almost everyone we have met on our four tours have done multiple trips with the company. For all the tours we have taken, Backroads arranged the hotels and most of the meals and provided transportation of luggage, maintenance and repair of the equipment, van support, and guides to follow behind to make sure everyone is doing okay. Backroads is not inexpensive, but we feel its tours have been very good. A similar trip is offered by Duvine Adventures *(www.tuscanybiking .com)* and Breakaway Adventures *(www.breakaway-adventures.com)*.

GREENLAND AND THE RELUCTANT WIFE

SUSAN MUNRO

I met Susan's husband, Bruce, a few years ago on a kayak trip in the Canadian High Arctic (see p. 47). Bruce obviously shared my love for adventure, as well as for places that are cold and remote. He was also articulate and thoughtful, so I immediately thought of him when Shannon and I started to ask our friends and colleagues to contribute trip chapters to our book. Bruce suggested that his wife, Susan, write the chapter instead, since she had a different take than his on adventure travel in polar climates. I figured that if she liked the trip, it must be a winner. Apparently, it was—a far more temperate and complex trip than either she, Bruce, or I had any reason to expect. —Don Mankin

TRIP DESCRIPTION

For several years, my husband, Bruce, has been fascinated by "the North." He's hiked and paddled in the Arctic for several summers. I am less intrepid than he, and our sole joint Arctic venture—to Svalbard in 2000—left me decidedly cold. I hadn't been back to the Far North since.

This trip to Greenland, he assured me, would be different—no sleeping on the ground, no carrying a pack, and possibly even toilets! And we wouldn't have to take turns staying up all night in case of polar bears. The description of the two-week hiking trip in southern Greenland, with accommodations in hostels and on sheep farms, won me over. In truth, when Americans hear "Greenland," they think "cold, glaciers, global warming." But Greenland has it all: history, culture, great hiking, and enough comfort for even this reluctant wife.

Until very recently, there have been no direct flights to Greenland from the U.S., so like most tourists, we fly via Copenhagen. Approaching tiny Narsarsuaq airport on a long fjord near the southern tip of this huge island, we pass over snow-covered mountains and ice fields before descending to the spectacularly bright green coast. We've arrived.

Here we meet our companions for the next two weeks. Our guides are Helle, an almost-50-year-old veteran guide from Greenland Travel, our tour operator, and Jamal, who is leading his first trip. They are both Danes, as are the other two couples in our group, both in their 60s. Three Norwegian friends in their late 30s round out our group.

At the airport, Bruce pulls Helle aside and says, "When we hike, I'm going to want to go faster and farther than anyone else. Is that going to be a problem?" It's not for her, but will it be for me? I love to hike, but I'm slow and steady. At five-foot-one, I have a short stride. It's already clear that this is going to be a primarily Danish-speaking trip, and if he's off ahead of the group, where does that leave me?

SCENERY, HIKES, AND HISTORY

Our trip starts as soon as we get off the plane. We walk to the end of the runway, where a boat arrives to take us to Qassiarsuk, a small farming village across the fjord. As we step out onto the lush, purple-tipped grasses, dotted with red, yellow, and blue wildflowers, my anxiety dissipates. Suddenly, I am transported back in time. This is thought to be the spot where Erik the Red first settled in 985, after he was banished from Iceland. Nearby there are Viking ruins, including that of Tjodhildes Kirke, the church Erik built for his wife after she converted to Christianity.

Before coming on this trip, I had read Jane Smiley's novel *The Greenlanders*, which depicts the last 75 years of the Norse habitation of Greenland, ending sometime in the mid-15th century. Smiley so wonderfully evokes the life and landscape of the Viking settlements that each time we visit one of the archaeological sites, I expect to meet her characters.

The Vikings died off, probably because their livestock could not survive as the climate grew colder. The Greenlandic natives (Inuit) and later the Danes tended to settle in these same areas, since they provide access to fresh water, good fields, and some protection from the sea. As a reminder of its past, a huge statue of Erik the Red's son, Leif the Lucky, overlooks the village. He is better known in the West as Leif Erikson, who was, as any Dane or Norwegian will eagerly tell you, the first European to discover America.

We settle into our accommodations in an old guesthouse on a working sheep farm. It is a snug fit for our group of 11, but at least we have it to ourselves. Everybody pitches in to help cook dinner and clean up. After dinner, with the sun still bright, we take a hike to the top of the hill that overlooks the village. It's an easy walk on dirt roads and sheep trails, and when we reach the top (Bruce in the lead, of course) we see a cruise ship anchoring in the fjord. The prospect of hordes of tourists jamming the Viking sites the next day makes us happy that we are scheduled to move on in the morning.

Early the next day, we hike through a valley to Tasiusuaq, a sheep farm on the other side of the peninsula. Except for our day packs, our luggage is transported by truck. For the hike, we split into two groups. Bruce, Jamal, two of the Norwegians, and I take the long route along a road that abruptly ends after a few miles and then turns into a trail leading through fields and spongy bog, all lush and green. The bay at Tasiusuaq is thick with bergy bits (small icebergs), brilliant in the bright sun. After five hours of hiking, we are sweaty and tired. We strip down to our T-shirts, and one of the Norwegians takes a dip in the bay. I am tempted to join him, but the comfortable air temperature (in the 60s most days) soon cools me down.

Our home for the next three nights is a small hostel, where we sleep on single and bunk beds and make do with a barrel of water on the porch, an "earthen" toilet (no plumbing), and no electricity. It's not luxurious, but is very cozy. The scenery is spectacular, and some of our group dip their fishing lines in the bay and catch cod and arctic char.

On our first full day in Tasiusuaq, we hike around the bay and up to a point where we can view the vast ice field in Sermelik Fjord. By lunchtime, Bruce has walked ahead, but the rest of us stop by a brook at the base of a waterfall, nestled in verdant and chartreuse vegetation, looking out at the bright blue water. As we listen to the icebergs crack, groan, and shift, I sense that we are being watched. And we are—by four beautiful Icelandic horses and two foals. One has a blonde mane that falls over one eye and hangs to the ground, Greenland's Paris Hilton without the questionable behavior.

We lose track of time, test different routes up a mountain that wasn't even on the agenda, and fight the wind all the way back to the house. Helle says we've hiked about 18 miles in ten hours. Even the folks who took a shorter route are sore and exhausted, and I can barely stand.

The next day is a recovery day. We need it! The wind is so strong that the idea of hiking a long distance is out of the question anyway. It's still howling when we go to bed, but when I wake up at 3 a.m., the sky is bright blue and the air is calm. I can't wait to get moving again. In fact, we are all up early to hike back to Qassiarsuk to catch the boat to our next destination, Qaqortoq.

When we get back to Qassiarsuk, we have plenty of time for a guided tour of the reconstructed Tjodhildes Kirke and a Viking longhouse. After visiting the structures, we see our guide, a young Icelandic woman, saunter back to the little café in her long, homespun Viking robe. A minute later, she emerges transformed into a 21st-century woman, wearing jeans and a black T-shirt, clutching a cigarette and a mug that says "BOSS," and furiously punching her cellphone.

While we wait for the boat, the wind comes up again and churns the sea into whitecaps. I take the Dramamine Jamal offers. That turns out to be a mistake, since by the time our boat comes a half-hour later, it is perfectly calm. Meanwhile, I'm drowsy all the way to Qaqortoq, barely able to participate in the conversation with our captain, Stefan Magnusson. He moved to Greenland from Iceland 18 years ago and now has a ferry business and a reindeer farm on the edge of the glacier. That has made him the local expert on global warming, sought out by film crews from Germany and Australia.

Captain Stefan is especially proud of the boat he has designed, noting that it could take us to Boston in only 60 hours. This reminds me that Greenland, as part of Denmark, is politically European, but that geographically it is in North America. Culturally it is also split—people with roots in Denmark identify themselves as Europeans, while the Inuit are more likely to identify with their cousins in northern Canada. Increasingly, though, many Inuit straddle the cultural divide.

IN THE "BIG CITY"

With 3,100 residents, Qaqortoq is South Greenland's biggest town, with well-stocked supermarkets, a hotel, a museum, a sealskin-processing plant, and a thriving port. Its beauty is marred by several Soviet-style apartment blocks built in the 1960s, when the well-meaning Danes encouraged the Greenlanders to move into towns. The idea was to provide access to jobs, education, health care, and social services, but this was at odds with traditional Inuit lifestyles and values, and the effort met with mixed results.

We walk by these rundown buildings on the way to our rooms in the high school dormitory at the top of a long winding hill. Climbing into bunk beds here reminds us that we are not teenagers, and the kitchen and dining area are cramped for our group of 11. Luckily the weather is perfect, and we spend little time at the dormitory.

By now we have fallen into patterns with regard to who cooks and cleans up and helps with the food shopping. Breakfasts and lunches are simple—cereal, fresh-baked bread, cheese, cold cuts, jam, etc. For dinner, we often have something Greenlandic, feasting on lamb, seal, reindeer, whale, or delicious fish.

Fresh green vegetables are in short supply, however. I become creative with cabbage, and we are all ecstatic when we find crates of apples and oranges on sale in the stores. The supermarket in Qaqortoq is truly "super," with everything from undershirts and toys to papayas. Bruce happens upon a bottle of 1968 Spanish wine, still quite drinkable! We even eat out one night at the town's fine restaurant, Nappansivik, for a traditional meal of fish soup and whale, which tastes to me like a fishy chunk of beef.

Despite these trappings of modernity and sophistication, the people of Qaqortoq are down-to-earth, free-spirited, and easygoing. Before coming to Greenland, we spent two weeks in Denmark, where pedestrians wait for "walk" signs whether or not cars are coming. In Qaqortoq, I am struck by how differently Greenlanders approach life's daily tasks. One day, at the bottom of the hill where we are staying, I see a pickup truck piled high with huge, shrink-wrapped packages of toilet paper rounding the corner to go up the hill. The load slides off and scatters on the road. Three men jump out of the truck, laughing as they pitch the packages, now loose from their wrapping, back onto the truck. Passersby also laugh and clap. Off they go, only to have the load fall off partway up the hill. And again they laugh as they reload.

But the real charms of Greenland are found outside the confines of the "big city." My favorite memories of Qaqortoq are of two trips outside town. One morning Helle, Bruce, and I hike around Tasersuaq, the lake next to the town. It is a glorious, warm, and sunny day, and when we reach the high point at the end of the lake we can see a huge amount of pack ice in the distance, blown in from the coast. As so often happens in Greenland's clear, dry air, distances are compressed. It seems as if we can reach out and touch the ice, though it is many miles away.

The next day we take a late-afternoon boat trip with Captain Stefan to Hvalsey, site of the last recorded events of the Viking era, a wedding in 1408 and the burning-at-the-stake of a man charged with witchcraft in 1409. These are pivotal events in Jane Smiley's novel, and the moment we step off the boat, I slip back into the mysterious last years of the Norse settlements in Greenland. Despite the importance of this archaeological site, we have the place entirely to ourselves. Sitting on a bluff looking down on Hvalsey, I'm back in "Smileyland." I know *The Greenlanders* is only a novel, but I feel that I have intimate knowledge of the people who lived here.

Basking in the sun, we delay leaving Hvalsey as long as possible. I drag my heels even as the rest of the group boards the boat. Captain Stefan wants to give us our money's worth, so on the return trip we stop at an agricultural station, where the Greenlanders are proving that they can grow flowers, turnips, potatoes, and lettuce. The fields of pansies and zinnias are gorgeous, although the project seems to make little sense economically.

MODERN GREENLAND:
PEOPLE, CULTURE, AND THE FUTURE

A ten-minute helicopter ride from Qaqortoq takes us to Narsaq, our next destination. Narsaq is a town of 1,700 people on a lush green plain on the coast. When we arrive, we discover that a wedding is in process. We slip into the back of the church near the end of the ceremony. The bride and many of the other women in the church wear the traditional Inuit costume of brightly colored, heavily beaded, and embroidered tops over sealskin pants and boots. By comparison, the men look very casual in their white anoraks. The church is exquisite, with a sky-blue vaulted ceiling and butterscotch trim. No one seems to mind our crashing the ceremony.

Narsaq's primary industries are farming and fishing. It's sleepy now, but up in the mountains changes are afoot. On our second day, we get a ride in a van to Kvaneveld mountain, where the sharp-eyed can find a pink semi-precious stone called tigupit laying on the ground. We all hike up to a closed uranium mine, and then Bruce, Jamal, and I climb a short but steep trail to the top of the mountain. As we take in the fabulous view, with water, icebergs, and mountains in all directions, a helicopter buzzes back and forth overhead, ferrying supplies from Narsaq to a nearby mining camp. Here Australian, Canadian, and Greenlandic mining engineers are searching for diamonds and maybe even oil under the ice cap. It makes me wonder. While we are all wringing our hands about global warming, are the Greenlanders thinking that having more land and less ice might be a good thing for them?

Suddenly it's very foggy. Coming down the steep trail is slow, and by the time we hike six miles back to Narsaq, I'm exhausted. It's been a strenuous but very satisfying day.

The next day, we travel by boat and then on foot through lush farms to the settlement of Igaliku, which is best known for the ruins of Gardar, once the religious heart of 12th-century Norse Greenland. Igaliku has only 36 permanent residents, all of whom are related to one another in some way. We arrive in fog, but it soon lifts, and we spend the afternoon exploring the ruins of Gardar and enjoying the sun.

The next morning is rainy but warm. We shake off our lethargy and take a short hike. Bruce has slowed his pace, and he and I are hiking together, around a lake, as the sky clears. We keep going up the trail, and at one point stop to look back toward the rest of our group. We notice one person striding toward us whom we don't recognize—the first time we've seen another hiker who was not a member of our group.

Soon we are joined by this mystery person, a young woman named Qupanuk or, as she says, "Q—that's what my friends call me." Q was born in Igaliku, grew up in Qaqortoq (attending the high school where we stayed), moved to Denmark to go to the University of Aarhus to study engineering, and then left the university to join the Danish marines. When I ask, "What was it like moving to Denmark?" she says, "At first, I missed nature so much. The trees got in the way of the view in Denmark. Now, when I visit Greenland, I am homesick for Denmark!"

Meeting Q turns out to be one of the highlights of the trip. She's an authentic Inuit, but she's also Danish—and cosmopolitan. As we walk, she chats about her family, her boyfriend in Denmark, and her plans to become an engineer and an entrepreneur. I'm a bit taken aback when she says that next week she and a friend are going seal hunting. She is great with a gun but has never shot a seal, a rite of passage for modern-day Inuit that keeps them connected with their cultural heritage. Clearly, Q keeps one foot firmly in the Inuit culture even as she identifies herself increasingly as Danish.

Q and I have fallen behind Bruce, and when we join him at the end of a long plateau at the top of the mountain, the view is startling. We look down on the glacier that is the source of all the icebergs in the fjord. Caught in the glacial moraine, the icebergs look like a city on a bay.

We have three more days of hiking, most of it in rain and fog, over wet rocks, through boggy high valleys, and up steep ledges. One afternoon, while drying out in the hostel, I flip through a glossy brochure that outlines a plan for Greenland's future. It includes an extensive transportation system, with major highways and massive bridges over fjords. While the Danes are known for their well-engineered and graceful bridges, this all looks improbable. It is hard to imagine a time when nature will not trump humans' plans in Greenland. Still, I'm glad that I've come now, when such plans are only a glimmer in someone's eye and the roads often disappear at the edge of town.

WHY GO:

- Go to disabuse yourself of typical conceptions of Greenland as being only snow and ice.
- Go for the hiking, as strenuous as you desire, and for unparalleled views of a virgin landscape.
- Go for the culture and history, with its layered and distinct Viking and Inuit influences.
- Go because, unlike everywhere else in the Far North, there are no mosquitoes. According to Helle, mosquitoes are repelled by sheep urine, and in southern Greenland you are never far from sheep.
- Go to escape any sense of ordinary time and space. Throw away your schedule and commit to "walking time." Wander thousand-year-old ruins with no fences, no fees, and sheep as your only companions.
- Go to remind yourself of what small creatures we humans are and how fragile our relationship is with nature.
- Go now, while you can look for miles and not see another tourist.

SPECIAL ISSUES AND CHALLENGES: It is important to be honest with yourself and the guides about any physical limitations. Hiking is strenuous but never dangerous, and there is always the option of turning back or taking a shorter route.

There may be psychological challenges for travelers who like more privacy than is possible on a group tour or more comfort than is offered on a hostel or sheep farm. For more comfort and privacy, you can stay in a hotel in the towns (Qaqortoq, Narsaq, and Narsarsuaq), but not in the more remote villages.

English-only speakers are a minority. Only 4,500 American tourists spend a night in Greenland each year. The majority of tourists are from Denmark, and most of the rest are from Norway, Sweden, and Germany. Everyone in our group spoke English as a second language, but everyday conversation tended to be in Danish.

The Greenlandic diet is based on meat and fish. Vegetarians will want to talk with the guides before setting out and should expect to eat lots of bread, cheese, and potatoes.

RESOURCES AND INFORMATION: This tour was organized by Greenland Travel *(www.greenland-travel.com)*, which also operates Greenland Air.

Another outfitter doing similar trips is Go2Greenland *(www.go2greenland .com)*. The trip cost about $3,100 per person, including airfare between Copenhagen and Narsarsuaq.

THE CAMINO DE SANTIAGO: AN ADVENTURE OF BODY AND SOUL (SPAIN)

DALE A. JOHNSTON AND ELSA P. PAULEY

D ale and his wife, Elsa, are frequent visitors to Europe. As a long-time academic, Dale has also been able to spend several sabbaticals in Europe, usually accompanied by Elsa. Like many travelers in Europe, they visit museums and sit in cafés, but unlike most, they also seek out more adventurous activities like windsurfing in the Greek Isles, kayaking the remote southern coast of Crete, and hiking in the Parque Nacional de los Picos de Europa in Spain. Since Dale is also a scholar of comparative religion, it seemed fitting to ask him and Elsa to write about their most recent adventure, a hike along the historic pilgrims' trail, the Camino de Santiago. —Don Mankin

TRIP DESCRIPTION

The giant *botafumeiro* swung from side to side in the tall transept, the cathedral packed with eager pilgrims. The Mass had been celebrated, and now the botafumeiro soared back and forth, higher and higher, spitting sparks from the burning incense inside until it seemed to touch the ceiling of the massive building. Everyone held their breath as the incense burner reached its apex. The feeling of jubilation was palpable.

It was Ascension Day 1999, and we had accidentally stumbled into the Pilgrims' Mass at the huge cathedral in Santiago de Compostela, Spain, to commemorate Jesus' return to Heaven. Thousands of strangely garbed, modern-day pilgrims from all over the world filled the Cathedral. They had walked the long and physically challenging Camino de Santiago (the Way of Saint James) across northern Spain, as millions have done since the Middle Ages.

We were spending a few weeks in northern Spain at the end of a year-long sabbatical. Now, in this beautifully preserved city filled with medieval and Renaissance architecture, we found ourselves pulled back in time to when people traveled hundreds and thousands of miles in pilgrimage, taking months, even years, to reach this destination, make penance, and be absolved of their sins.

By the Middle Ages, three great pilgrimage routes—to Jerusalem, Rome, and Santiago de Compostela—flourished within Christendom. Santiago was the most popular, because the travel was less dangerous than it was to Jerusalem and, for many, it was closer than Rome. But the path—more than 500 miles from the French side of the Pyrenees Mountains in the east to its final destination, Santiago, in the farthest northwestern reaches of wild Galicia—was not easy. Pirates and brigands harassed pilgrims. Storms disrupted travel over mountain ranges. Extreme cold in winter and heat in summer were typical on the plateau. Rivers needed to be forded and shelter found.

How did this remote city first emerge as a pilgrimage site? Ancient legend tells us that a ninth-century peasant, guided by a *stella* (star) to a spot in the *campos* (fields), found the remains of the apostle *Sant'Iago* (St. James), one of Jesus' first disciples. Thus is derived Santiago de Compostela, St. James of the field of stars. According to later legends, St. James miraculously led Christians to victories over the ruling Moors, and by the tenth century, he had become the patron saint of Spain. Since then, millions of pilgrims have flocked to Santiago to view his tomb.

After the Middle Ages, the popularity of this pilgrimage waxed and waned, but it rebounded after 1985 when Santiago was declared a UNESCO World Heritage site. In 1992 the Spanish government began restoring the trail, and in 2000 the city was selected as a European capital of culture by the European Union. In 2004, 179,000 pilgrims walked the camino.

Why are so many pilgrims willing to endure the physical and psychological hardships of the route? Not all of the pilgrims are even Catholic. But still they come, on foot primarily, trudging their way day after day—but some also by bicycle, horseback, and car. What was the lure? We asked a few of the pilgrims we met over the next few days. Their responses ranged from, "This is a marvelous trail to walk. It is beautiful, Spain is cheap, and the wine flows freely," to "It's the ultimate spiritual journey."

What would it be like to be a pilgrim, we wondered? What would we discover out there on the camino? Peace? God? Ourselves? We wanted to find out. Pilgrimages and quests have been an important part of life throughout the ages. We wanted to connect with that history as we walked on Roman roads and crossed medieval bridges, lodged in historic buildings, and imagined ourselves back in the 11th century. Walking the road would be physically challenging and give us the opportunity to reflect on our lives and refresh our souls. So in May 2007, we enthusiastically set out to experience the Camino de Santiago.

Traditional pilgrims walk the entire route carrying their belongings in backpacks and staying at *albergues* (pilgrims' hostels) each night. Others walk only a portion of the camino, or walk it while having their luggage transported from place to place. Since we had only three weeks, walking the entire 500-mile route was out of the question. Instead, we drove, stopping at several towns along the way for a few days to walk local sections of the route, explore the surrounding area, reflect on our experiences, and write. We walked only every other day to give our aching muscles ample time to recover. The book *A Pilgrim's Guide to the Camino de Santiago* by John Brierley was our constant companion, offering guidance about routes, water availability, restaurants, and lodging.

Our trip started with a climb through the Pyrenees, continued across the sun-baked plains of northern Spain, and ended with a descent into Santiago. Each segment was different, with distinct charms and challenges, but they flowed together and led us to one of the most interesting and fulfilling adventures of our lives.

THE PYRENEES

We followed the most popular of the several routes to Santiago, the Camino Francés (the French Way), which ascends the Pyrenees from Saint-Jean-Pied-de-Port, France, and makes its entry into Spain at Roncesvalles. Saint-Jean-Pied-de-Port has served as the main entry point to the camino for centuries. Here we first saw pilgrims wearing traditional garb—sandals, a heavy cape, and a broad-brimmed felt hat marked with scallop shells, and carrying a stout staff with an attached drinking gourd. Of course, we also saw pilgrims outfitted with more modern gear—wearing Gore-Tex and a soft hat, carrying retractable walking sticks, and protected by full-body raingear.

We started our hike early in the morning, heading up the steep trail out of Saint-Jean. We immediately felt the pain in our legs as we ascended from the village past the houses and tidy farms. The landscape was rustic and serene, and we slowly left civilization on this difficult trek over the Pyrenees. It was a miserable day. The clouds hung heavy, and the sky was dark as rain fell. We walked, struggling against the grade, as other pilgrims passed by. Clad in ponchos, they kept their heads down, using their walking sticks to push themselves along and calling encouragement back to us in English, German, or French. Rain made the ground muddy and slippery, and unseen rocks often tripped us. An older couple stopped for a rest ahead of us. "You need better shoes, if you're going to keep hiking," the woman said as we worked our way up to them. We looked at her sturdy hiking boots, and then down at our walking shoes designed for the concrete sidewalks of Los Angeles. She was right. These mountains are dangerous, especially in bad weather.

Later that day, we retraced our path, retrieved our car, and drove farther into the mountains where we again began to walk. Here we met only wet bikers pedaling slowly up the road nearby. Water dripped from overhead trees. It was green everywhere. Quiet surrounded us. The challenge was both physical and mental. Saying "Be careful not to slip," "Take it slow," and "Just put one foot in front of the other," we encouraged one another. Our breathing was slow and labored. The rain had made the trail even more slippery, and we lamented our poor choice of footwear. Some miles later, we had dirty shoes and clothes, nascent muscle cramps, and a deep appreciation of what it takes to mount the Pyrenees.

BETWEEN THE MOUNTAINS

We stayed in three different locations on the route between the Pyrenees and the mountains of Galicia. Our first stop, Santo Domingo de la Calzada, a pueblo of 5,000 people, offers quaint medieval streets, a few good restaurants, two albergues, a three-star hotel, and two paradors (part of the state-run hotel system). We stayed for a few days in the parador situated in a restored 16th-century convent where the camino crosses the plaza. Every morning, we watched as backpack-carrying pilgrims quietly left, having bathed and slept well for one night before resuming their long trek.

From Santo Domingo, the route leaves the state of La Rioja and enters Castilla y León, the land becoming flatter and more arid along the way. We made our base in the city of León, population 150,000, a former Roman military garrison straddling the banks of the River Barnesega. Here we walked the camino through the narrow and winding old streets to the 13th-century Gothic cathedral filled with 182 stained-glass windows and oculi. It was a Saturday in June, so of course, in Spain as in the U.S., there were weddings. The brides were lovely, and the organ added its powerful touch as the Mendelssohn "Wedding March" filled the cathedral. Later we saw one newlywed couple dance until late while flower girls played in the garden at the Convento de San Marcos, the grand parador where we were staying.

We stayed in Villafranca del Bierzo, a small 11th-century village nestled in a valley, for a couple of days before entering mountainous Galicia. It was filled with pilgrims resting up before the steepest and most difficult climb of the journey. We enjoyed the chance to talk with them and admire the beautiful scenery before we tackled the mountains again.

One morning we struck up a conversation with the owner of a small bar. She asked us to sign her registration book and then proudly brought out two more leather-bound volumes filled with inscriptions and drawings by hundreds of pilgrims who had visited her spotless establishment. In her words, "The camino is a meeting place for the world," a common ground that brings together people from different locations with different cultures and different languages around a single purpose. The Camino de Santiago is a model for the world, she suggested.

Rolling hills covered in grapevines filled our vista as we walked over dirt tracks on our up-and-back hike for the day. Tall eucalyptus trees provided shade. Puffy white clouds floated overhead. The feeling of history, tradition, and continuity was everywhere, and we imagined ourselves as pilgrims in the 11th century. We felt especially attuned to the outdoors, appreciating the smell of overturned earth and the sound of birds. Cherry trees grew along the way, and we stopped to sample their fruit. Oh, they were sweet. Sometimes around a curve we saw cars on a road, but they didn't seem real. The camino was timeless.

Our conversation shifted from moment to moment. "My calves hurt" followed "Do you feel more spiritual?" and segued into talk of when Dale would retire and whether we'd sell our house and downsize. Searching for the signs marking the trail interrupted a discussion of our future. We entered a small hamlet, Villatuilla Arriba, where we stopped at a bar for a Coke and the restroom. Politely, the server offered us a small tapa, which Elsa immediately popped into her mouth, then quickly spit into a napkin while thanking the server. It was *pulpo*—octopus—for we had unknowingly entered a *pulperia*, a bar specializing in this acquired taste that we hadn't yet acquired. Thus ended our talk on the meaning of life for that day.

Later, in a remote spot, we stopped at a pilgrims' refuge run by a young man sitting atop a table in the front yard, gently strumming his guitar and softly singing an enchanting Spanish lyric. The sounds perfectly matched the scene as we visited a world so different from the one we normally experience.

Toward the end of the day, we met a couple in their 70s from Wales— two of the many older adults we met along the route. We asked them why they were undertaking this journey, a two-month enterprise for them, and the feisty Welshman proudly asserted, "I know I'm still alive if I can walk this trail."

The walk that day challenged us. Our calves hurt from the ups and downs of the trail. We grew thirsty and tired. On our way back to Villafranca, the path sloped downhill, and we took care not to slip. Our guidebook had warned that the last downhill, when feet are sore and eyes dull, can be the most risky for falls, sprained ankles, and broken bones. Finally we spied church steeples, heard children's voices, and smelled freshly baked bread. We collapsed onto chairs at a café on the Plaza Major for a late lunch, tired but inspired by our journey that day.

THE END OF THE CAMINO— SANTIAGO DE COMPOSTELA

Monte de Gozo, the mountain of joy, is the last ascent before the long downhill into Santiago. We took our trip in late May and June, when Spanish weather is typically good—not yet too hot, nor too cool—but the weather ranged from cool to cold and very rainy, particularly in the mountains. This day was no different, and we wore our ponchos as we climbed to the peak. It felt good to be this close to our final destination, and we were on an emotional high that could not be dispelled, even by the noisy pilgrims crowding around us and the several miles of bleak industrial buildings and suburban streets stretched out in front of us. From here we first viewed the cathedral spires marking the culmination of our journey to Santiago. The old town's perfectly preserved buildings, grand squares, university students, and street scenes beckoned.

Like millions before us, we entered the old medieval city through the Porta do Camino (the Gate of the Way) and walked along the ancient stone street, the Rua da Azabacheria. We paused under the final shaded arch and looked back up the street, reflecting on the journey. For eight years we had thought about this pilgrimage, and now we didn't want it to end. We hugged and stood quietly. Rain dripped around us. The sense of timelessness that we had so often experienced on the trail came over us again, and hundreds of years ceased to exist. Eleventh-century pilgrims were all around us; we could imagine their journeys, and we realized that we were not so different from them.

We didn't walk the entire trail, nor did we endure the Spartan conditions of traditional pilgrims. But we had walked more in the prior three weeks than at any other point in recent years, and for us, it was a challenging hike. Maybe it was the many days of arduous walking, or maybe the uninterrupted time together immersed in the history and spiritual legacy, but we were affected very deeply by the experience. We felt a rush of joy, relief, and a sense of accomplishment.

That moment of reflection exploded as we entered the Plaza Obradoiro. Tourists, pilgrims, and students were everywhere! Street musicians played flutes and bagpipes, flags were flying, the mood was joyous. Did the sun really come out, or were we just exhilarated? We had done it! Proud, we cried tears of joy.

The cathedral dominates the plaza. We climbed its steps, marveled at its baroque façade and were awed by the Portico de la Gloria (Doorway of Glory). One stone pillar bears finger marks where millions of pilgrims traditionally place their hands to mark their safe arrival. Now our handprints are there as well. As it does every day, the Pilgrims' Mass began at noon, and the bells in the giant towers rang out marking the celebration. The botafumeiro soared higher and higher. We joined in, exhausted and content, our pilgrimage complete.

WHY GO: The Camino de Santiago takes the visitor to portions of Spain where Americans rarely go. Because of the physical nature of the adventure and the tranquility of the experience, you may return a bit sore but refreshed and restored in body and soul. Whether the goal of the adventure is a challenging hike, a respite from the hustle and bustle of modern life, a chance to connect with history, or a spiritual journey (whatever your religious persuasion), the Camino de Santiago does not disappoint.

SPECIAL ISSUES AND CHALLENGES: If done in its entirety, this is a 500-mile adventure through some very rugged terrain with many weather variations. You need to assess your physical preparedness and modify the experience accordingly by varying the length of the trip, what you carry in your backpack, and the exact portions of the journey you tackle.

You also need to invest in good hiking gear to make this a pleasurable experience, not an ordeal. We recommend comfortable hiking shoes or boots, hiking shorts and/or pants, a fleece jacket, a broad-brimmed hat, a rain poncho, a small day pack, and possibly a walking stick (or poles).

In addition, many Spaniards do not speak English, so you should have a simple Spanish dictionary and phrase book with you. Further, the Spanish schedule can be mysterious to Americans. Be ready to change some of your habits, particularly regarding shopping and eating. Many shops close during the afternoon, reopening later in the day. And Spaniards eat dinner very late.

VARIATIONS AND OPTIONS: Like us, travelers can adapt this trip to their particular schedules and interests. Many walk from beginning to end, but some cycle, others with limited time drive cars from one location to another to walk selected portions of the trail, and still others make repeated trips to piece together the different segments of the total route. You can also tailor this trip to accommodate individual needs for comfort and privacy by choosing among the many different lodging options available.

RESOURCES AND INFORMATION:

Getting There: Getting to Spain is relatively easy, with direct flights to Madrid from numerous East Coast cities via major U.S. international carriers. From the West Coast, generally a connection has to be made before arriving in Spain. Within Spain, Spanair and Iberia offer inexpensive connecting flights to most cities. It is possible to fly into Bilbao or San Sebastian near the eastern beginning point of the Camino, and then fly out of Santiago de Compostela after completing it. Train and bus transportation within Spain is reliable and affordable.

How to Do It: We made all our own travel arrangements, and it was not difficult to do so. Determine the length of time you can commit, the amount of the route you wish to walk, bike, or drive, the quality of the accommodations you desire, and the time of year you will set out on your adventure. Then consult *A Pilgrim's Guide to the Camino de Santiago* and other guidebooks and use the Internet to make reservations. If you require more guidance in planning your adventure, we encountered pilgrims who used Chemins de France *(www .chemins-de-france.com)* to make hotel arrangements and transport luggage.

Pilgrims' albergues are never more than 12 miles apart along the camino. Reservations are generally not accepted. Hostels are simple, beds may be dormitory style, and costs range from about $6 to $14 a day. Most accept only cash. The hostels can fill up fast; plan your day so that you do not arrive too late.

Also available in small towns and villages are rooms in private homes, pensions, and small hotels. There are signs posted along the camino advertising these lodgings, and guidebooks list specific pensions and hotels. Of course, in larger cities such as Léon, the full range of accommodations is available.

We did our own Internet searches for small hotels and found lodging in even very small towns such as Burguete on the Spanish side of the Pyrenees. We also stayed at paradors *(www.parador.es)*, both on the camino and while taking side trips. They are often situated in historic buildings and offer good value through either their five-night or Golden Days discount programs. If you want to treat yourself at the end of the journey, spend a night in the Hostal de los Reyes Catolicos, perhaps the most magnificent parador and reputedly the oldest hotel in the world. It is located on the Plaza Obradoiro in Santiago by the cathedral.

AFRICA

—⟶𝓋𝓋𝓋⟵—

A WALKING SAFARI
IN ZAMBIA

DENNIS HICKS AND STEPHANIE WAXMAN

My friendship with Dennis and Stephanie goes back many years. We have much in common, especially our shared love of adventure, and we frequently consult each other about where to go next. The trip described here is the result of one of these conversations, when we spent a couple of hours one afternoon flipping through my collection of adventure travel catalogs in search of the right combination of exotic destination, physical activity, and comfort. They found it in the Zambia walking safari. It was the quintessential Africa experience—personal, intimate, profound, and just a little bit scary. —Don Mankin

TRIP DESCRIPTION

"Smell that?" our guide exclaims enthusiastically, as we drive over rocky, sandy roads away from the tiny airfield at Mfuwe, where we have just landed, toward South Luangwa National Park. The air is dry, dusty, and smoky. "That is the smell of Africa!"

Jason Alfonsi was born and raised in Zambia, a land-locked country midway between the equator and the southern tip of the African continent. He has been guiding safaris in Africa for more than 20 years, and his love of this country will become contagious over the next nine days.

Suddenly he cuts the engine and points. A giraffe! We watch in awed silence as the giraffe nibbles on the leaves of an acacia tree. Jason explains that within 15 minutes the leaves will emit terrible tasting tannins that will cause the giraffe to stop eating. But like most everything else in Africa, the tree's survival may be short-lived as elephants tear its bark for nutrients and the tree eventually dies. This is the first of many lessons from Jason on life and death in the wilds of Africa, a lesson that will be illustrated in increasingly dramatic fashion as we venture deep into the heart of the continent.

A major reason for coming to Africa was to view wildlife in its natural habitat. Zambia surely offered that: "an untouched African wilderness," according to the literature from Wilderness Travel, our tour operator, with an amazing diversity of wildlife that has had little contact with humans. But the trip we chose offered something else: the opportunity to see them on their own terms—eye-to-eye, in effect—without the protective but distancing cocoon of a hulking four-wheel-drive vehicle. And it offered this in the context of a small group—a maximum of six clients (in our expedition only five signed on).

When our more skittish friends at home expressed alarm at the risks we might encounter—lions, pythons, cape buffalo, malaria—it gave us pause. But we were not deterred. This promised to be an unusual and special experience, and we were not disappointed. We may have come to Africa for the wildlife, but we found much, much more.

GAME DRIVES

The walking portion of the safari is scheduled for later in the trip, so our safari begins with a few days of traditional game drives. We start at Nkwali Camp, where we are greeted by our hostess, Susannah, offering cool, wet washcloths and cold drinks. This is our introduction to the many amenities of the trip, a cross between roughing it and a five-star hotel. Nkwali Camp is set on private land in the middle of an ebony grove overlooking the Luangwa River, the eastern border of the South Luangwa National Park. Our bamboo chalet is beautifully appointed with a private open-air shower, mosquito netting, bottles of water, and a view of the river with its large black boulders. Wait, that's no rock, it's a hippo! Actually, two or three hippos. And on the far bank, an elephant. We begin to see wildlife all around us.

In the late afternoon, we take our first game drive, ferrying across the river in a hand-cranked pontoon boat to gain entry to the park. The air has begun to cool, and by the time we step out of the 4WD to enjoy our first "sundowner" (a predinner cocktail in a scenic spot), we are wearing our jackets. As we sip gin and tonics, we watch elephants amble among the grasses. A warthog digs for his dinner. Birdcalls fill the air. The sun drops quickly over the savannah.

Riding back to camp, our spotter, John, holds a large spotlight so we can watch the giraffes, buffalo, and puku (a kind of antelope) enjoying the evening. The moon is barely a thumbnail in the sky. By the light of the searchlight, we spot a lion on the upper bank of the river about 200 yards away. Across the river, the men who operate the pontoon ferry have also spotted her and are none too keen on coming to get us. Nonetheless, they do, and we are carried back under the curious eyes of nearby hippos and crocs. The lion doesn't seem interested in us. The cable steadies our two-ton 4WD. We realize that faith plays a large part in our adventure.

Back at camp, Susannah explains that elephants and hippos like to wander into camp at night, so a night watchman has to accompany us back to our chalet after dinner. We know how dangerous these animals can be, especially if you get in their way. We don't have to be told twice not to leave our chalet until morning.

We awake at 5:45 a.m. to the sound of drumming, our wake-up call from the staff. Tea and porridge are delivered as the sun rises. By 6:30, hats and binoculars in place, we begin our morning game drive. On the far edge of the savannah, we see elephants, puku, and many guineafowl. Being in a wilderness with so many animals begins to feel normal, but spotting them is still a thrill. The oxbow lagoons, recreated annually in the bends of the river as the water level drops, are part of what makes the Luangwa Valley hospitable to so much varied wildlife.

The thickets and woods are perfect habitat for spectacular birdlife. We learn how to focus our binoculars on birds in flight and are amazed by the colors we see flitting through the sky. We spot a bateleur and a tawny eagle. On the shore, we see the great white egret and the lovely sacred ibis. We hear the hoot of a coucol owl and shrill cry of the "go-away bird." By 9:00 a.m. the day is heating up and our long-sleeved shirts come off. By 10, it seems as if all the color has bled out of the landscape and into the birds. The iridescent blue feathers of the long-tailed starling shimmer in the hot light.

We stop for tea and cake. Then, from a distance we hear a baboon's "alarm call." Like many other species, their warning call depends on visual clues, so we know they've seen a predator. Back in the vehicle, we come out of the tree line, down a steep embankment, and slowly drive across the hardpan of a drying lagoon. Then we see them: two lions feeding on the carcass of an enormous hippo! The head of the hippo is already gone and one lion is halfway inside the hippo's body gorging himself. The other is on the hippo's back, tearing off chunks of hide. It's like passing the scene of an accident: we want to look away, but we can't. One of the lions checks us out—we're only 40 feet away—but she is not interested; there's more feeding to be done. After a while, they leave the hippo for higher ground where they can relax in the shade while keeping an eye on their kill. Through the thicket, we make out four other lions, bellies bulging.

En route back to the camp, we encounter a herd of elephants. As we attempt to cross in front of one of the females, she threatens us with a mock charge, coming dangerously close to the vehicle, but stopping just short of contact. We could outrace her, but Jason does a surprising thing: he cuts the engine. Then he speaks to her in low, reassuring tones, "Now come on, girl. Don't be naughty." Suddenly she's like a big baby—docile and ashamed. She fake feeds herself, a face-saving move, before turning around and moving away. As we drive off, Jason explains that if we had run from her, we'd be reinforcing her bullying behavior. By standing our ground, we show the elephant that we are not intimidated.

After naps and tea, there is another game drive, and by the end of our first full day in the bush, we fall into bed exhausted. The rustle of nearby elephants (one taking a loud piss by our porch) and birdcalls are the soundtrack for the night.

ON FOOT

In the morning, we drive 70 miles north along a rocky bush road through remote parts of the park, arriving midday at our first mobile camp, situated on the Mupamadzi River, a major clear-water tributary of the Luangwa. We are shown to our tent-cabins, with washstands and a woven mat at the entry, and beds with fresh sheets inside. There is a shared latrine and a shower under a tree. Water will be heated and poured into buckets for four-minute showers. Our bread will be baked in an open pit. Our clothes will be washed in the river and ironed (hot coals heat the iron). A staff of 14 will be serving us—five clients and two guides—for the next four days. In two days, we will walk to the second mobile campsite which will have been moved—tents, latrine, and all—from the first site, set up, and made ready for us when we arrive at the end of our walk.

After lunch, served with linen and silver like all our meals, we take our first walk in the bush. We feel naked and unprotected outside the vehicle. There is nothing between us and "them"! While we were in the four-wheel-drive, the animals seemed indifferent to our presence (with the exception of the elephants). Humans in a vehicle are not perceived as a threat. To them, a vehicle is just a large benign beast. But once humans step out into the open, everything changes. On foot, we are something to be reckoned with. An unspoken fear permeates our group: What if a lion attacks us? Or a cape buffalo? Or an elephant? Even a giraffe could create havoc if it wanted to.

We are in the hands of Jason and Yonna, both experienced trackers. Jason teaches us three hand gestures he will use if necessary: (1) "Silence!" (2) "Don't move!" and (3) "Turn and quickly go back the way we came!" More importantly, he explains that this park isn't overrun with safaris, so the animals are shy and not used to humans. They are watchful and keep their distance. Animals pose no real threat, unless we surprise them or by chance come between a lioness and her cub. Hence Yonna will carry a rifle—but he assures us that, in his many years as a game scout on walking safaris, he has never had to use his weapon.

We form a line behind Yonna and Jason. The birds are calling. We feel a breeze. Jason points out paw and hoof prints in the dust: impala, elephant, and hyena. We spot a tiny bird's nest in a baobab tree. We stop to examine a purple blossom that has dropped from the sausage tree, a tropical tree native to Africa with hanging, sausagelike fruits. Puku run away at our approach but soon stop, keeping us in sight. We find the skull of an eland, its twisted horns untouched by decay. In the distance, we see our first zebras! They also keep their distance. A saddle-bill stork stands quietly with a gray heron by the river's edge. Hippos laze in the river.

Soon we understand the difference between a riding and a walking safari: It is the difference between watching a movie and being in one—the difference between being an observer and a participant. To walk is to slow down the experience, to taste every aspect of it. On foot, we are not just among the animals, we are animals, too.

We gather the next morning at sunrise for another walk. Before we start, Jason draws our attention to a low rumble, a "sawing" sound that lasts almost ten seconds. It is a leopard's territorial call, advertising its presence. We head in its direction, and in less than ten minutes we hear another call. We follow the sound, and when we hear a third call, we know we're getting close.

We come across fresh prints about four inches across, big ones. Jason "reads" the footprints, judging direction, depth, and gait. "Probably a male," he whispers. As we circle around a large termite mound, we see baboons and impala browsing quietly in the distance. Their silence is a big clue, telling us that they haven't seen the leopard, so it must be traveling away from them—in our direction. Silently, we wind our way through the trees and brush. It's getting hotter, and we're getting excited. We stop briefly to drink a few gulps from our water bottles, then continue. A short time later, we find the leopard's tracks again. Jason reads them and explains that the deep impression of his paws toward the front, plus the sand sprayed at the back, indicates rapid acceleration away from us. The leopard probably heard us when we stopped. We'd only been about a hundred yards away, invisible to the eye but not the ear. We didn't spot the leopard, but we've spent an hour with him, in his world, and we are elated.

LIFE AND DEATH IN THE BUSH

During the night, we hear lions calling. The following morning, we want to find them. We form our line behind Yonna and Jason and head toward a shady patch where lions tend to hang out, but there are none to be seen. We wander for a few hours in the woodland, enjoying the puku, giraffes, and various birds. We take a break under a large tamarind tree growing out of a termite mound. John offers us towelettes and a midmorning snack. Grateful for the rest and the shade, we sip our tea, eat our cake, and peer out into the hot sun.

After the break, we make our way toward the river. Suddenly, we startle a small group of buffalo, probably the bachelors of a larger herd. They run away, but one bellows and they change direction. We soon see why when we catch a glimpse of a female lion slipping around a big bush! We carefully creep up a small rise to get a better look. Now we can see the entire herd on the opposite bank, but no sign of the lion. Then, from the other side of the river, vervet monkeys create a ruckus. They see the lion. We figure she is below us, hidden by the reeds.

We watch the buffalo for a few moments, but then the wind changes and they catch our scent. Already on edge because of the lion, they panic. In their confusion, they stampede across the river in our direction, which is also where the lion lies in wait. They run along the bank, then disappear into the reeds directly below us. Jason estimates that there are 200 buffalo, but to us the thundering procession seems endless. They take our breath away.

Suddenly there's a loud bellowing! It sounds as if the lion has grabbed a buffalo. The herd continues to roar past and up the bank only 40 yards away. At the end of the line, we notice a straggling calf, limping. Its fate is clear. As it drops behind the reeds, the sounds of the lion with the first buffalo stop, then start again where the calf is.

We see the herd congregate on a slight rise to our left, seemingly in a help-less, mournful huddle. They stare at us, before shuffling away, as we listen to the lion throttle the calf. We move to get a better view, but the lion hears us, leaves her kill, and runs away across the river. We move off noisily so she can hear us leave, then we also cross the river at a spot too shallow for the hippos and crocodiles. From there, we can see the dead calf in the water. The lioness makes her way back across the river into the reeds, evidently content to watch her kill from the shade. Jason thinks she'll wait for the day to cool down before returning to finish her meal.

It was our presence that startled the buffalo and caused them to stampede. Had we not been there, the baby might have escaped its fate. To ignore that is to ignore our effect on any environment, at the peril of it and us. Once we put ourselves in the bush, we became part of the story. And suddenly, we realize that is what a walking safari is all about. We are part of the narrative of life and death in Africa, and it's an old, old story.

Occasionally, during our time with Jason, he picks up what appears to be rather unremarkable rocks. But they're not mere rocks, they are Stone Age tools! We can see that edges had been chipped on both sides so these small stones could be used to cut or scrape. Perhaps some of our earliest ancestors had altered these rocks. In the African bush, these artifacts are all over the place, reminders that to walk in Africa is to step into the past, a past when humans, too, had to forage and hunt each and every day to survive, just like all the other animals. That's what sometimes echoes through our minds in the middle of the night in Africa, the sound of our ancient past and the constant struggle for survival rummaging around just outside our conscious memory.

After another day, our walking safari is over. We return to the southern part of the park for our final three days at Nsefu Camp, a beautiful lodge set on a sweeping bend of the Luangwa River. Here we once again are offered morning and evening game drives, but we opt for walking instead. Accompanied by our guide and armed guard, we embrace the continuing drama of life and death up close—a drama that is writ large across the landscape of Africa.

WHY GO: During our walks, we did not encounter any other tourist groups. In addition, the Zambian government and the few tour companies that operate in the country are conscientious about preserving wildlife and practicing responsible, sustainable tourism. Trips such as this provide an economic incentive for wildlife and land-use conservation by the government and the local people. Also, despite our vague discomfort at the deferential service—especially at mealtime as several men would hover over us, pouring wine, offering more meat or dessert—this reminder of the colonial era did seem to serve everyone's needs, good employment for them and good times for us.

Another benefit of the trip was the more nuanced, in-depth perspective on the land and the wildlife we gained from being on the ground with experienced trackers, observing details and subtle signs up close. We would not have learned as much if we had spent all of our time observing the wildlife from the distant remove of a vehicle.

SPECIAL ISSUES AND CHALLENGES: The walking is not particularly arduous. The terrain is relatively flat and the straight line distance from beginning to end is not great, typically 5–6 miles. However, we rarely walked in a straight line. We meandered instead, to look for game tracks or something that Jason wanted to point out, so the actual distances may be greater than advertised. In the hot sun, the days and distances can seem longer than they are. Wilderness Travel strongly recommends that participants "be agile, in good health, and in good shape."

The biggest problem we encountered was Stephanie's motion sickness from the plane rides to and from Mfuwe and the long drives to get from one place to another. If you are susceptible to motion sickness, make sure that you bring appropriate medication.

The risks from wildlife are real but well managed, as long as clients pay attention to the guides and camp hosts and follow their instructions.

VARIATIONS AND OPTIONS: Wilderness Travel offers an optional three-day extension to the Zimbabwe side of Victoria Falls. Zimbabwe was in turmoil when we visited, and the famous old colonial Victoria Falls Hotel showed it. It had seen better days and the service was indifferent. Nonetheless, we didn't expect to get back to Africa any time soon, so we were glad we seized the opportunity while we were in the vicinity, because the falls are spectacular.

We also spent a few days in Chobe National Park, the legendary elephant refuge in Botswana, and made a brief visit to South Africa. Our most memorable day in South Africa was the tour of Cape Town offered by Selwyn Davidowitz, an opponent of apartheid since his student days in the 1960s. With a deep understanding of South Africa's unique history, Selwyn offers a personal experience of Cape Town, including a hands-on visit to the township of Kayamundi (for more information, see his website: *www .ilovecapetown.com*).

RESOURCES AND INFORMATION: The tour operator for this trip, Wilderness Travel *(www.wildernesstravel.com)*, made all the arrangements, including accommodations and transportation within Zambia. It can also book flights to and from Zambia, often at lower-than-advertised fares. The cost for the 2007 trip was about $5,000 per person, including everything but international airfare, tips, airport taxes, and meals not covered in the itinerary. Wilderness Travel limits the group size to six.

Other companies offering similar trips include Robin Pope Safaris *(www.robinpopesafaris.net)*, Vintage Africa Safaris *(www.vintageafricasafaris.com)*, and Go2Africa *(www.go2africa.com)*.

TRACKING MOUNTAIN GORILLAS IN THE BWINDI IMPENETRABLE FOREST (UGANDA)

KATHERINE BRAUN MANKIN

I 've dragged my wife along on numerous adventure trips over the years, so after the last trip, a river-rafting trip in Utah (see p. 65), I promised her that the next one would be her choice. Taking no chances, I suggested one I knew she would like and I would also enjoy. Since she loves animals, the bigger and more exotic the better, I was confident that she would jump at the chance to go to Africa to see mountain gorillas and other large, scary beasts up close. I knew pretty much what to expect since I had visited Kenya a number of years before, but even I was surprised by the sheer quantity and diversity of the wildlife we saw, as well as the beauty of the setting and the intimacy of the experience. —Don Mankin

TRIP DESCRIPTION

The sun begins to rise pink and gold and resolute over the lush green hillsides of Uganda. It is our second morning in Africa, our first in the countryside, and I know that behind the remnants of the dark night, the Rwenzori Mountains in the distance are thickly covered with tea plants, tropical trees, and flowers. The scenery is exotic and much more beautiful than I had imagined. But my reason for coming here is to see animals.

This morning, our Wilderness Travel tour group—three couples in their 60s and two single women in their 30s, plus two guides—is going on a guided walk around a swamp to see monkeys and birds. On the drive over, we pull off to the side of the dirt road to watch baboons. They are numerous and serious and not welcoming. One baboon in the upper branches of a tree starts throwing fruit and hits my husband, Mankin (I call him by his last name), in the head with an unripe fig. We will see baboons many more times during our trip but none with such accurate aim.

The walk takes us around the perimeter of the swamp. The trees, branches, and leaves are so dense that I can't imagine I'll see anything. But then I catch on and learn to watch for branches that shake from the weight of an animal. We see many colobus monkeys with their white faces and dark eyes, red-tailed monkeys, and vervet monkeys. At one point, we spot a mangabey monkey in a tree eating an ear of corn with another ear tucked under his arm. He chews with obvious pleasure and calls in a loud chatter to his mates, we assume to tell his friends about his good fortune. Another mangabey swings into view, but now the first appears to have decided that sharing is overrated and takes off through the branches with his ears of corn. The second pursues and their chatter is loud and manic. It is all very comical. I wonder why he announced his position in the first place. Maybe he was calling to a different mangabey (a girlfriend?), and this was not the one he was hoping for (the wife?).

We also see lots of birds on the swamp walk, as we will throughout the trip. Uganda is full of bird life, about 1,200 different species, but I am not a birder and will never be one. In my mind, you wait too long and must be much too patient for too little reward, and frankly, don't they mostly look like black dots anyway? That said, I gasp in amazement when a great blue turaco flies out of the foliage and swoops from tree to tree, its metallic blue wings and golden beak highlighted against the gray sky.

In the afternoon, we go to Kibale National Park to track chimpanzees in the equatorial rain forest. Much of the hiking is off-trail through dense underbrush. When the guide stops, puts his finger to his lips in the universal "quiet" gesture, and points up, my eyes follow and I see a dark spot moving in the tree limbs. Then I see that the dark spot is actually two chimpanzees. I'm entranced, but they are more than 50 feet away—I wish they were closer so I can get a better view. We spend the next three hours looking for more chimpanzees, but without much luck. Our first sighting was a tease. We return to the lodge in early evening, hot, sweaty, and somewhat frustrated.

The next day, we go back for more. Again, we start out on a trail, but we're soon off of it and stumbling through the underbrush. But we do find chimps, about eight of them, in the trees and much closer than the day before. I watch them in the treetops for so long that my neck begins to ache, so I lay back on the forest floor, prop my head on my day pack, and observe the chimps through my binoculars in comfort. They use their feet with the same ease as their hands, swinging through tree limbs, pulling branches to their mouths with their toes so they can eat the leaves.

Our guide leads us to another group of chimps just a few yards away. Suddenly, one of the apes descends to a lower branch within a few feet of us, then drops to the ground even closer, wanders about 20 feet away, and sits down. He is soon joined by another, and we watch the two sit and groom each other. It is quiet until suddenly there's a huge, ferocious noise, like a pack of dogs barking but at a higher pitch. It's coming from some of the other chimps in the group. Our pair joins in. Then they all quiet down, and the two go back to grooming. When we ask the guide what that was all about it, suspecting something sinister or dangerous, he says that's just how they communicate.

HIPPOS, ELEPHANTS, BUFFALO, LIONS, AND MUCH MORE

The next day we head to Queen Elizabeth National Park, our home for the next two nights. On the way, we see elephants, kob (antelope), waterbuck, warthogs, hippos, and guinea hens. We stay in the lodge inside the park and take early-morning and late-afternoon game drives on rutted dirt roads in the two four-wheel-drive vehicles we use for the entire trip. The vehicles have pop-off rooftops, so we are able to stand up and watch the animals from an unobstructed vantage point and in relative safety. Most of the time it seems as if we are the only vehicles out there. Of course, there are others, but they are well dispersed throughout this park of more than 750 square miles.

Within a few minutes of starting our first game drive, we spot a female lion with her cubs very close to the side of the road! The lioness moves about, slowly and gracefully. This animal has poise. I am surprised that even the cubs seem undisturbed by us. I mention this to Stephen, one of our guides, who tells me they are used to the vehicles. Besides, he tells me, they are never afraid. "Why should she be afraid? It is the lion."

Later, we watch a group of female waterbuck. They resemble deer with soft taupe-brown bodies and black noses surrounded by white fur, each a larger and more muscular version of Bambi's mom. We're about to pull away when I spy the male on the opposite side of the road. He has a large set of beautifully curved antlers and is running strong and fast like a thoroughbred across the road to guard his females. It is breathtaking.

On the drive back to the lodge for lunch, I see my first hippo up close. It is submerged in a mud hole by the side of the road and distinguishable only by the white of its eyes and the pink of its ears. When it lifts its head, which looks to be the size of a PT Cruiser, some cow dung decorates its long snout. When we get back to the lodge, we see two hippos on the lawn, chewing the grass next to the bar area, working away at it like lawnmowers. After lunch, these two hippos fall asleep in the shade of some trees on the property, oblivious to the sounds of 4WD vehicles passing by.

In the afternoon, we take a two-hour boat ride down the Kazinga Channel, which connects Lake George and Lake Edward. We drift along the shore and watch the animals at the edge of the water. We see tons of hippos (literally, of course), many cape buffalo (more ill-tempered and dangerous than their cousins, the water buffalo), elephants, crocodiles (ghastly!), a monitor lizard, and a great many birds, all up close. Mankin notes that this is easily the largest concentration of wildlife he has ever seen in just two hours. After the river trip, our guides drive us to an overlook above the lake for the most memorable cocktail hour of my life. On a distant spit of land, we spot our last wildlife of the day—except for the hippos and warthogs on the lawn of the lodge—a lone elephant, a couple of water buffalo, and through my binoculars, the unmistakable ears and eyes of hippos peeking above the water. A picture-perfect end to a fantastic day.

The next day is more of the same. The highlight of the day is our stare-down with a herd of elephants. We spot them eating tree branches just a few feet off the side of the road. They are huge and wrinkled, and they sway as they move. One large male walks close to our four-wheel-drive to check us out. My husband is standing with his head through the pop-out roof as the elephant fans his ears back and forth and extends his trunk out repeatedly toward him, coming closer and closer. Mankin thinks he is going to charge and starts to shrink into the interior of the van. Andy, our lead guide, hisses, "Don't move." Mankin stops, but the elephant doesn't, fanning his ears and stretching his trunk. Then he sways away from the side of the vehicle and crosses the road right in front of us. We watch the other elephants, mostly females with young ones, gather, hesitate, trumpet, hesitate some more, make a few false starts, and then cross the road behind their leader. Mankin looks very relieved.

MOUNTAIN GORILLAS

After three days at Queen Elizabeth National Park, we drive seven hours through forest, savannah, hills, and towns to the Bwindi Impenetrable Forest, home for almost half of the surviving 800 or so wild mountain gorillas in the entire world. The others live just over the border in Rwanda and the Democratic Republic of the Congo (DRC). Small as this number is, it is double what it was eight years ago, after poachers almost wiped them out. The Uganda Wildlife Authority (UWA) has worked very closely with researchers, environmentalists, and others to protect the remaining gorillas, the largest living primates in the world at about 600 pounds, while at the same time allowing visitors to see the few that have been habituated to humans.

There's a permit application process to limit the number of visitors, and those with colds or other infectious diseases are not allowed to participate to reduce the risk of infecting the gorillas with human viruses and bacteria. Once contact is made, visitors must keep a distance of several feet and are limited to one hour of viewing.

"Once contact is made" is the operative phrase here. The pretrip literature from Wilderness Travel made it very clear that there is no guarantee that the trackers will be able to locate them. The hike—usually in hot, humid weather, along rough trails—is tough and may take several hours. It is also fast paced, because once the trackers spot the gorillas, you have to get to them fast before they move on, deeper into the forest. I was apprehensive. I go to the gym regularly, but I am the world's slowest hiker when going uphill. A month before the trip, prompted by my insecurities and at Mankin's urging, I started working with a personal trainer—on the Stairmaster carrying a backpack with telephone books, and weight training to build lower body strength. I wanted to see gorillas.

Now I am here. After an orientation, during which we are told that anyone who can't keep up will be escorted back, we travel in a 4WD for 20 or 30 minutes to the trailhead. At first the trail leads through a small village of mud-brick huts and cultivated fields before heading straight up into the hills. After 30 or 40 minutes of this, we veer off the trail, first straight up, then straight down. We are moving fast through thick vines and over slippery grass and mud. "Impenetrable" forest, indeed! I am right behind the tracker, trying to follow in his footsteps, literally. I manage to keep up. I don't think about anything other than that I must keep moving. When I fall, because it's slippery and twisty and steep and we are going so fast, I get up in an instant.

Suddenly the tracker stops and points to my right. A silverback mountain gorilla is seated in the low branches of a tree about 20 feet away. I gasp. I can't help it. The silverback rolls out of his tree and moves deeper into the forest. We keep walking. Another gorilla, a blackback (a younger male), drops to the ground near us and disappears into the thick trees and underbrush. We follow him. We soon emerge from the dense forest into a field of high grass where the family of gorillas is eating, playing, sleeping, or just hanging out. This group is made up of two silverbacks—the larger one is the dominant male and the second one is the guy I saw on the way—three females, and three young-sters that our tracker estimates are six months to a few years old.

The silverback pulls a branch toward his mouth, strips the leaves with his teeth, and chews. The gorillas move with deliberation, except for one of the juveniles who climbs a tree to an outer limb and hangs and swings by one arm as he beats his chest, playing at being the dominant silverback. Seeing them so close—as close as eight feet at times—and in their own environment is so unusual and intimate that by the end of the hour when our guide leads us away, I am relieved, exhilarated, and very, very happy.

MORE GORILLAS

We return the next day for more gorilla tracking. Our group is lighter in spirit because the pressure is now off. If we don't find any today, it's okay—yesterday was so incredible.

The trekking this morning is even steeper and more difficult. The floor of the forest is thick with growth. But, there are also holes covered by grass and vines, and I often fall through. I hear the sounds of others in my group behind me, also falling, but I am still right behind the tracker and concentrating so hard on keeping up that I think of little else.

When the tracker stops, I see a silverback, even larger than the ones we saw yesterday, a few feet down the hillside to my left. I have a clear view of him. Then I hear a noise to my right. It's a blackback, about 10 or 12 feet down slope from us, and he's moving toward me. I watch him, he watches me. "Sit down," my guide whispers to me, and my butt drops to the ground like a magnet. "Slowly," he whispers. But it doesn't matter now what he says. Nothing matters, because the gorilla is studying me carefully. I forget to drop my eyes as we were instructed. I freeze under the gorilla's gaze. I want to back up but cannot as some of the group is behind me. The grass is slippery. I'm afraid if I move at all, I will slide forward in front of him. I just stay in my crouched position. Finally, I remember to drop my eyes.

The gorilla moves forward. There's no path, just jungle, but he is walking toward me, moving very slowly. I have never been so still. I feel as if my heart has ceased beating, and I no longer breathe. As he crosses in front of me, only two feet away, I can see the ridges in his ears and individual tufts of hair, he is that close. If I had stuck my foot out, I would have tripped him. And then he has passed. I watch him climb uphill and disappear in the thick leaves. The tracker reaches out and touches my shoulder. "Are you all right?" I nod.

I sit for a few minutes watching the silverback and two females with their offspring. Once again, I hear sounds off to my right. Another large gorilla approaches us, moving just as slowly, just as deliberately toward me. I grab the tracker's arm. My legs ache from this crouched position, and I am really afraid of slipping and sliding into the gorilla. He also passes just a couple of feet away. This time I remember to avert my eyes. Afterward, when I'm breathing again, I hear a noise behind me and turn to see the first blackback push through the bushes and sit down a few feet uphill from me and begin to eat leaves. Slowly I twist around and watch him eat. His belly is enormous—a Buddha belly blackback. When our hour is up, we move on. I don't try to keep up with the tracker.

The mountain gorillas were the raison d'être for the trip, and the ultimate highlight, but there is much, much more yet to come—the visit to the Bwindi Community Health center started by American missionary and physician Dr. Scott Kellerman (for more information, see *www.bchc.ug*), and the lunch by the river bordering the DRC where we watch two huge hippos play and then fight each other with open jaws. There are also the rustic but very attractive and comfortable lodges where we stay most every night—Ndali Lodge overlooking two crater lakes, the wonderful Gorilla Forest Camp on the edge of the Impenetrable Forest, and especially Mihingo Lodge at Lake Mburo National Park, where we watched zebras from the comfort of our private deck overlooking the savannah. But all of this was just icing on the cake, a bonus on top of the gorillas on what is surely the most amazing trip of my life.

WHY GO: Most people associate Uganda with the bloody reign of Idi Amin, an association recently reinforced by the award-winning movie *The Last King of Scotland.* In fact, many of our friends thought we were crazy to go to Uganda on vacation. But Uganda has come a long way since that era. It is a beautiful country that has one of the most stable and least corrupt governments on the continent, and, as yet, the parks are not crowded with tourists.

We were very impressed by how well managed the national parks were, especially how the UWA handled the chimpanzee and gorilla tracking. The guides and trackers were knowledgeable and very ecologically responsible and aware. It was an expensive trip, but much of the money helps to support the local communities and to protect the animals, so it's money well spent.

SPECIAL ISSUES AND CHALLENGES: Aside from making sure that you are physically fit for tramping through the "impenetrable" forest and taking the recommended medical precautions (e.g., malaria medication, pretrip inoculations, etc.), this trip does not present any particular special challenges. Wilderness Travel provides very clear instructions and information before you depart, and the guides give more detailed instructions after you arrive in Uganda. Following all these instructions carefully will minimize your risk and discomfort.

However, "this is Africa," as Andy reminded us one day when Mankin asked about exploring an area downriver from our lunch site. "Anything can happen." Andy also always checked behind bushes whenever we stopped for pee breaks to make sure that there wasn't a cape buffalo or lion lurking out of sight. Being careful and paying attention is important.

The borders with Rwanda and the DRC are much quieter than in 1999 when eight tourists were abducted from Bwindi and murdered, but armed guards are present in the camps and accompany all gorilla-tracking groups. Despite these cautions, I felt safe and was more concerned about the thorns and the biting ants than I was about terrorists or charging hippos.

VARIATIONS AND OPTIONS: It is possible to do this trip on your own for much less money, but Africa can be a difficult place to travel on your own. Unless you have lots of time and an especially adventuresome spirit, I would recommend the group trip.

Wilderness Travel also offers a three-day extension to the famous Masai Mara Reserve in Kenya. The airfare to Africa is quite expensive, so if you have the time and can afford the additional expense, it makes sense to get as much out of your trip to Africa as you can.

RESOURCES AND INFORMATION:

How to Do It: Wilderness Travel (*www.wildernesstravel.com*; 800-368-2794) offers four trips a year. The cost in 2007 was around $5,000 per person, depending on the size of the group, plus about $800 for tracking permits. This includes everything except tips for guides and porters (about $200 per guest). The company can also arrange air travel.

Mountain Travel Sobek (*www.mtsobek.com*; 888-687-6235) offers a slightly longer version that includes a visit to Parc National des Volcans in Rwanda for about $8,000, plus $1,500 in permits.

Volcanoes Safaris *(www.volcanoessafaris.com)* offers a shorter trip (seven days) for about $3,400.

Where to Stay: Wilderness Travel arranges all accommodations, but if you want to do it on your own, the lodges where we stayed are: Ndali Lodge near Kibale *(www.ndalilodge.com);* Mweya Safari Lodge in Queen Elizabeth National Park *(www.mweyalodge.com);* Gorilla Forest Camp in Bwindi *(gfcamp@africaonline.co.ug);* and Mihingo Lodge near Lake Mburo *(www .mihingolodge.com).*

EXPLORING TUNISIA'S HISTORY, CULTURE, AND DESERT SCENERY

DON MANKIN

T unisia has beckoned me since I first heard the name in my early teens in the title of one of my favorite jazz tunes, "A Night in Tunisia" by Dizzy Gillespie. In my overheated adolescent imagination, it represented someplace exotic, even slightly dangerous that I had to visit someday. It took almost 50 years before I finally had the opportunity to satisfy my curiosity. In November 2006, my wife and I traveled to Tunisia for a short but eye-opening visit.

TRIP DESCRIPTION

"What the hell are we getting ourselves into?" I thought to myself, as my wife and I followed our newfound "best friend," Mustapha, into the dingy bar on a dimly lit side street in downtown Tunis. We were the only Westerners in the place, maybe the only ones to have ever crossed its threshold. Katherine was the only woman, probably another first in this smoky, downscale, Arab workingman's bar. My worst fears about this trip to Tunisia were rapidly turning into reality.

The months leading up to this trip had been marked by increasing violence in Iraq, the Israeli–Hezbollah war in Lebanon, and further deterioration in the perception of the U.S. in the eyes of the average citizen on the Arab street. Our friends, colleagues, and family all asked "why?" when informed of our plans, usually followed with, "Are you crazy?"

We would tell them about the spectacular Roman-era ruins, the friendly people who were among the most modern and liberal in the Muslim world, and the beautiful beaches—which we had no intention of visiting since we live two blocks from the beach in Los Angeles. They would remind us— as if we needed reminding—of the Al Qaeda terror attack in 2002 on the ancient synagogue on the island of Jerba (or Djerba) that killed 21 people, mostly German tourists but a number of Tunisians as well. As an American Jew whose heritage is prominently written across his face, it was perhaps not surprising that my apprehension mounted as the date of our departure approached and tension continued to escalate in the Middle East.

So, there we were in this funky bar on a Saturday night in mid-November only a few hours after our arrival in Tunis. We had fallen for one of the oldest scams in North Africa. Mustapha spotted us on the street looking at our map and in halting English (Arabic and French are the primary languages) offered to take us to a Berber festival in the medina, where we were heading. We knew it was a scam, but he was persistent and we were overly concerned about appearing rude, so we followed him for a few blocks through an uninviting neighborhood before deciding to pull the plug on the scam and return to our hotel. "At least have a beer with me, my friend," he implored. It didn't seem like a bad idea—that is, until we entered the bar and looked around and realized that this was no tourist spot and we were way out of our element.

Everyone looked at us as we made our way to a table against the wall. Mustapha asked for 30 Tunisian dinar (about $23) to pay for the three beers he ordered—enough to buy at least one beer for everyone in the bar. I was not going to quibble. We settled into our chairs and looked around. Instead of the scowls I expected—at the infidel Americans forcing themselves once again into places they were not welcome—I saw broad smiles and heard laughter, at our expense no doubt.

Who cared? The vibe was anything but hostile. For the next half-hour, we had halting conversations with those who spoke some English and laughed loudly along with those who spoke none. My apprehension began to melt away. Who would have expected that going along with Mustapha would lead to a unique, eye-opening experience that was well worth the cost? What happened in that bar—or to be more accurate, what didn't happen—set the tone for our entire trip.

After half an hour, we decided that it was time to leave. We said our goodbyes and stepped out into the dimly lit street. We had no idea where we were. After getting directions from a helpful shopowner, we finally found our way to Avenue Habib Bourguiba, the main drag of the *ville nouvelle,* the "new city" built by the colonizing French in the 19th century and the heart of the entertainment and tourist district. The wide, brightly lit boulevard was packed with sidewalk cafés, families out for an evening stroll, and teenagers with cell phones wearing clothes with designer labels. It could have been Saturday night in Santa Monica, except there were fewer blondes. There were even street entertainers—Berbers on horseback and African drummers. It was glorious—an odd mix of the familiar and the novel, of comfort and excitement.

A DAY IN THE SUBURBS

Over the next two days, we explored Tunis and its suburbs. While the suburbs of other cities are rarely tourist destinations, other cities do not have the spectacular ruins of the ancient Phoenician city of Carthage, a World Heritage site, just outside the city limits. The setting is even more spectacular than the ruins. The city was strategically located; most of the sites overlooked the Gulf of Tunis and the emerald waters of the Mediterranean.

The history of Carthage has all the makings for an HBO series—sex, intrigue, wealth, and violence. Founded in 814 B.C., Carthage was one of the most important cities of the ancient world. It was the focus of epic battles with Rome, known as the Punic Wars, involving legendary figures like Hannibal, among others. This is the most important historical site in a country that is filled with them. Even though the ruins are primarily that—ruins, not intact or restored sites—they are evocative. It doesn't take much to imagine what it must have been like to be a soldier standing on the edge of Bysra Hill, the heart of the ancient city, scanning the sea for enemy sailors.

Since Carthage comprises several separate sites spread over several miles—all located within the larger, modern community of Carthage, one of the most exclusive suburbs of Tunis—we needed to hire a taxi at the hotel for the day to drive us around. At the conclusion of our sightseeing, our driver took us to the village of Sidi Bou Said, only a few miles from Carthage, for a late lunch. Situated on a cliff overlooking the Gulf of Tunis, Sidi Bou Said is upscale, artsy, charming, and just a bit touristy (but in a good way). The narrow cobblestone streets, little more than well-maintained alleys, wind upward past equally well-maintained, chockablock houses, all brilliantly whitewashed with blue trim and ornate blue doors.

After our lunch of lamb and couscous on a restaurant terrace overlooking the village, we made our way up the main street of the souk, past the immaculate shops into the residential district. On our walk, we frequently came across peekaboo views of courtyards and lush gardens aflame with bougainvillea, overlooking the blue-green sea. At the top of the street was a small cemetery and a park that offered 180-degree views of the Mediterranean and the hills of Cape Bon across the bay. Next time in Tunis, we promised ourselves, we will stay in Sidi Bou Said.

WANDERING THROUGH THE MEDINA

Carthage and Sidi Bou Said offer a dramatic contrast to the medina in central Tunis, which was the focus of our explorations the next day. The medina, also a World Heritage site, dates back to the seventh century and was the main district of the city until the French came and built the ville nouvelle. Habib Bourguiba, the wide tree-lined boulevard in the ville nouvelle that is, in essence, the Tunisian version of the Champs Elysées, leads to the "French Gate," a tall stone arch that is the symbolic gateway to the medina. Passing through the gateway is like entering a different world. Instead of the graceful, open sidewalks and leisurely pace of the boulevard, the medina—a maze of covered souks and narrow streets, passages, and alleyways—is confined, packed with people, and claustrophobic. The sides of the streets are lined with stalls, one after the other. It is all very disorienting, but once I gave in to the chaos and crowds, it turned into one of the most interesting places I had ever visited.

We wandered for hours. We ignored the merchants imploring us to "just look" at their wares—rugs, souvenirs, and cheap jewelry—and kept our eyes on the people bustling by and the close details of the architecture: the abstract decorative tiles, the domes on the mosques, the weathered doors, and the many archways and passageways leading to who knows where? Our route loosely followed the walking tour recommended in the Lonely Planet guide. As we wandered, we grew more confident that we would not get lost and that most people—except for the incessant shopkeepers and touts offering bargains and access to special places—either ignored or tolerated our presence as we brazenly poked our noses into their daily lives. We deviated often from the recommended walking tour, letting our curiosity lead us through gateways and down passageways.

In one such passageway, a number of teenagers, both boys and girls, walked in and out or sat and read on the benches along the walls. They were dressed like schoolkids in Los Angeles, except that their pants were less baggy and securely belted above their hips. We walked through the short passageway until we reached a courtyard, still not sure where we were. A slight man approached us and spoke softly in French: *"Interdit"* (forbidden). We finally figured out that we were in a medersa (or as it is more commonly known in the Western press, madrassa, a school for the study of the Quran) and were about to violate a religious taboo. We muttered an apology, turned around, and quickly left. What struck me was how gentle he was in barring our further entrance and how indifferent the students were to our presence. This was a far cry from the rabid reaction we might have expected from images of these schools in the Western press.

In fact, the entire day was like this. We often wandered into sections that were absent of tourists and Westerners. This, plus the crowds, close quarters, lack of direct sunlight, and general strangeness of the place could have easily seemed sinister. But it wasn't. In the U.S., we wouldn't think of wandering into neighborhoods like this, and if we mistakenly did, we would be justifiably terrified. But in Tunis, while I wouldn't exactly describe the experience as mellow, it was essentially nonthreatening. Most important, it was also one of the high points of our trip.

THE SAHARA DESERT: CAMELS, SAND DUNES, AND ATVS

After two and half days in Tunis, it was time for our desert adventure. After a short flight to the island of Jerba, our driver met us in a four-wheel-drive Land Cruiser for a three- to four-hour drive to the oasis town of Ksar Ghilane at the edge of the Grand Erg Oriental, where the rolling sand dunes of the Sahara Desert begin. After a short ferry ride to the mainland, we drove for two hours on paved blacktop through flat open country, past small villages and towns, and up a long winding road to the top of a plateau that reached all the way to the horizon. After a brief stop at an abandoned Berber settlement of mud huts, the road turned from blacktop to rutted gravel, then to packed sand. There were no longer any towns or villages or any other signs of civilization, save for the occasional hut or lean-to and, of course, the road, or at least what passed for a road in the desert.

After a bone-jarring hour and a half, we thankfully arrived at Ksar Ghilane, the southernmost Tunisian oasis. Our lodgings for the next two nights were at the Pansea Resort at the edge of the oasis. The only thing separating the resort from the sand dunes is a line of palm trees. Despite the cost of a night's accommodations ($195, including breakfast and dinner for two), the resort is far from luxurious, but it is comfortable, attractive, and appropriate to its setting. Instead of rooms, there are large tents with private bathrooms and a combination heating and air-conditioning unit. The grounds are spacious and beautifully landscaped, with a big pool and a tall viewing tower where guests can watch the sun rise and set over the desert.

The best thing about the resort, of course, is its location. From our tent, it was less than a hundred yards to the sand dunes, which stretched as far as the eye could see and much farther. It took only minutes to walk far enough into the desert to get a sense of its immensity, solitude, and beauty. Unfortunately we couldn't walk far enough in the little time we had that first evening to entirely escape the noise of the oasis—all-terrain vehicles and dirt bikes buzzing up and down the dunes and the sound of the resort's generator pumping out the electricity for our lights and heaters.

During the day, most of the ATVers either napped in their tents or took off in the desert on far-ranging, gasoline-powered excursions, so our desert walk the next day was much more serene. We were also able to escape the late-afternoon buzz of internal combustion engines by hiring a guide and his two camels for a sunset ride deeper into the desert. Sitting on that camel was probably the most uncomfortable ride I have ever had, but the setting was magical! In the silence and the soft light of the setting sun, the color of the dunes ran the spectrum from reddish yellow to burnt orange and finally to deep red before growing dark in the deepening dusk.

HISTORY, CULTURE, AND THE MODERN WORLD IN THE LAND OF THE LOTUS EATERS

We rode back the next day to the island of Jerba for the last stop of our whirlwind trip. As urbane, sophisticated, and secular as Tunis is, Jerba is small-town, down-home, and sectarian. The religious and ethnic mix is unique, reflecting its long history as a refuge and waystation for Berbers, Karijites (an Islamic sect of the eighth century), Jews, and pirates who swept through on their way to somewhere else and decided to stay. This is where, legend has it, Ulysses stopped for a rest during his mythical odyssey and lost most of his crew to the allure of the "land of the lotus eaters."

We stayed in Houmt Souq, the largest town on the island, in an old *funduq*, a lodging place for traveling merchants and their camels that had been converted into a spartan but atmospheric tourist hotel. The hotel was in the middle of the old souk, a miniature version of the medina in Tunis—narrow, winding streets interspersed with public courtyards and squares surrounded by cafés.

Like Tunis, the juxtaposition of cultures was compelling, maybe even more so given the compressed scale of this much smaller town. The calls to prayer, which started at 5 a.m., contrasted with the sounds of American blues filtering through the courtyard restaurant where we ate dinner our first night. The old fort, where the Turkish fleet defeated the Spanish in 1560 and erected a tower of skulls to ward off potential aggressors, looks toward the new luxury marina in one direction and the fancy resorts and hotels of the Zone Touristique in the other. Young women wearing headscarves and snug Levis walked along the beachfront promenade to meet their boyfriends. A bearded man wearing a yarmulke rode by on a motorbike.

This last image was especially compelling and unexpected for me. The Tunisians talk with pride about their history of diversity and inclusion and especially about the Jewish community that has lived for centuries in relative peace alongside Muslims, but to actually see this tolerance in evidence was a surprise. We saw schoolkids wearing Stars of David around their necks, and Hebrew was prominently displayed on several stores in Houmt Souq to advertise the silver jewelry produced by the renowned Jewish silversmiths of Jerba.

On the outskirts of Erriadh, just a few miles away, is the oldest synagogue in North Africa, La Griba, which supposedly contains one of the oldest Torahs in the world. The original synagogue was built in 586 B.C. The current structure is less than 100 years old, but it just reeks of history and tradition. It's not like any synagogue I have ever seen—all blue tiles, Moorish arches, and dark wood. The overall effect is strikingly beautiful, colorful, and hauntingly evocative.

I asked one of the men who handed out yarmulkes and shawls to visitors to the synagogue about the local Jewish community. I was surprised to learn that it was thriving. There are more than 1,300 Jews currently living on Jerba, he said, and there are Sabbath services every Saturday at La Griba and on Friday night at another synagogue nearby in Erriadh. Every spring, local and expatriate Jews from Europe make a pilgrimage to the synagogue to honor Rabbi Simeon bar Yohai, a revered Talmudic sage.

While the synagogue and the community around it suggest harmony and peace, recent history demonstrates that all is not rosy. After all, this was the site of the infamous Al Qaeda attack in April 2002. In addition, many Tunisian Jews have felt insecure enough over the years to leave the country for Israel, France, the U.S., and elsewhere. In early January 2007, just weeks after our return to the U.S., the Tunisian police fought a deadly gun battle with two dozen Islamic extremists.

With all of that, I would not hesitate to return to Tunisia. Like any remote or exotic destination, there are risks. But that is the point of adventure travel: to take calculated risks to visit places that may not be as comfortable and safe as home in the hope of learning and experiencing something new, satisfying our curiosity, and maybe even having a helluva good time.

WHY GO: There are many reasons for visiting Tunisia—the ancient history, ruins, and artifacts; the scenery on the coast and in the desert; a culture that is very different than any in the Western world; the luxurious beach resorts; and the window the country offers on what may well be the defining geopolitical/cultural conflict of the 21st century. Many argue that Tunisia is a shining example of the best of the Arab world—modern, prosperous, secular, and peaceful. For any curious, informed, educated Westerner with at least a modest sense of adventure, the attractions are irresistible.

SPECIAL ISSUES AND CHALLENGES: Aside from the incessant attention of con men, scam artists, and overly aggressive shopkeepers, most travelers should not encounter any significant problems or challenges. Some may be bothered, however, by the average Tunisian's late-night habits and schedule. Tunisians eat late—most restaurants don't open until 8 p.m.—and party even later. Our hotel in Tunis had a bar that stayed open very late on Saturday nights, usually for incredibly loud private parties. The throb of techno/Middle Eastern/disco music kept us awake until 3 a.m. or later on the two Saturday nights we stayed there, despite the fact that our room was separated from the bar by several floors.

Travelers should also be aware that summers can be very hot, especially in the desert. In November, when we were there, the weather was perfect—never too hot or too cold. The evenings in the desert were surprisingly cool, however. If you go there at that time of the year, make sure you bring a light jacket or even a sweater and something warm to wear to bed.

VARIATIONS AND OPTIONS: Depending on how much time you have and how much you are willing to spend, there are lots of other places to see and things to do. Our trip, nine days, was too short. If we had had more time, we would have visited the ancient Roman city of Dougga, the desert oasis of Touzeur, the Roman arena in El-Jem, and the holy Islamic city of Kairouan. We also would have done a trip into the Sahara at least overnight, possibly even longer, and capped it all off with a few days at a beach resort on Cap Serrat. Next time, we will hire a private guide and driver with a four-wheel-drive vehicle to take us around to these destinations.

RESOURCES AND INFORMATION:

Getting There: Air France and Lufthansa have connecting flights to Tunis from most major American cities. TunisAir has frequent nonstop flights from Tunis to Jerba.

Where to Stay: We stayed in the Hotel La Maison Blanche in Tunis (45 Av Mustapha V; 216 71 842 842, fax 216 71 793 842; *maison.blanche@planet.tn*). The rooms are huge and attractively appointed, with four-poster beds and marble-floored bathrooms, and rates are very reasonable (we booked online and paid about $79 a night, double, including breakfast), but there are those extremely loud parties most every Saturday night in the bar that never seem to end.

In Houmt Souq, we stayed at the Hotel Djerba Erriadh (216 75 652 691, fax 216 75 653 089; *hotel.erriadh@topnet.tn*), an old funduq that had been converted into a somewhat modern hotel. It was very inexpensive (about $24 a night with breakfast) and conveniently located in the souk. The hotel does not accept credit cards.

The Pansea Resort in Ksar Ghilane has a website at *www.pansea.com*. The resort does not accept credit cards.

CUSTOM SAFARI IN THE OKAVANGO DELTA (BOTSWANA)

HAZEL CAPER FURST

Hazel and her husband, Charlie, are my frequent partners in urban adventure. While most Los Angelenos let their fear of traffic confine them to their immediate neighborhoods, I can usually count on Hazel and Charlie to explore the exotic cultures of Los Angeles County with me, usually in the form of cheap ethnic restaurants. They have also explored well beyond the boundaries of Los Angeles, especially Hazel (Charlie prefers his sailboat). When she wanted to go on safari in Africa, she asked three women friends (none of whom knew each other), hoping that one would say yes. All three jumped at the chance, so they all went on a 15-day custom-tailored safari in the heart of southern Africa. This chapter reports on the highlight of the trip, the several days they spent in and around the Okavango Delta in central Botswana. —Don Mankin

TRIP DESCRIPTION

First there was the sound. That's what woke me. I had been told that a big male hippo, called Jeffrey by the guides (Jeffrey? Geoffrey? How would an African hippo spell his name?), frequented the area where we slept to graze at night. Under no circumstances were we to leave our little shelter. An armed guard had escorted us there earlier that evening and in case of emergency we were to shout out for him. Hippos are the most dangerous animals in Africa, accounting for more human deaths per year than any other animal. They feel vulnerable on land and will seek the safety of the water if at all disturbed. Anything between them and the water will be trampled. At three tons or more, this is a threat to be taken seriously.

Two of us were sleeping in a thatched-roofed, open-fronted, terra-cotta cottage right next to the lake. Built on a platform about a foot high, it had two sides with waist-high walls and was completely exposed in front. We were told that hippos will not go up a step and that we would be perfectly safe as long as we stayed on our platform.

All of this ran through my mind as I heard Jeffrey chomping. Then I saw him, within arm's length of our cottage. I whispered over to my friend Carol sleeping a few feet away. No response. I whispered louder and louder still, but she continued to sleep. I knew that she would be disappointed if she missed this close encounter. I wanted the comfort of another sentient being, but she didn't wake up. I was too afraid to hop out of bed and shake her awake. For 20 minutes I just lay there in bed, watching Jeffrey's bulk through the gauzy haze of my mosquito net, marveling and hoping, really hoping, that he knew that hippos don't do steps.

UP CLOSE AND PERSONAL

I wanted an intimate experience with Africa and not be confined to a fixed schedule and a van full of tourists following specified routes. I also wanted comfort and security, to be in the bush without sacrificing amenities. Most of all, I wanted to see a lot of wildlife, as up close and personal as was prudently possible. By arranging a custom tour of Botswana, I was able to have it all—flexibility, comfort, and being about as close to the animals as one could safely be.

The Okavango Delta region is one of the most biologically diverse ecosystems on the planet. The Okavango is the only permanent river in the region and is widely described as "the river that never reaches the sea." Instead it spreads through 6,000 square miles of the great Kalahari Desert, creating the largest inland delta in the world, made up of countless waterways and channels, lakes and waterholes, marshes, lagoons, and islands. It supports a huge variety of animals and plant life. No other part of Africa has a higher concentration of game.

Our custom tour provided us with a variety of adventures and experiences in the delta and the surrounding areas. It also enabled us to go at pretty much our own pace and to places of our own choosing. I could walk through the bush in the morning, touch warm elephant dung, and track lion paw prints. When I had had enough, I could go back to a beautiful lodge tastefully furnished with native fabrics, crafts, and furniture to be served fine food and drink in gracious style.

Despite the luxury and the careful attention of the guides, rangers, and the staff at the lodges where we stayed throughout our trip, being this close to wild animals in their natural habitat had its risks. We had to be cognizant of these risks at all times. There were a few instances when this was all too apparent.

Once we were on foot tracking a particular lion by his paw prints and our guide noticed that the lion had doubled back and crossed our path. He thought it wise to immediately vacate the area. Another time, we were stealthily crouched behind some trees in a heavily wooded area closely observing a small group of elephants. The wind shifted and they became aware of our presence. We hastily backed away. Perhaps the most harrowing time was when I was paddling a canoe and was carried by the current into a small cove filled with hippos. The only thing more dangerous than a hippo on land is a hippo in the water. They are very territorial and will attack anything that breaches their boundaries. I could hear the guide shouting from his canoe, "Get out of there. Paddle, paddle." Trust me, I paddled.

GETTING AROUND, HANGING OUT, AND EXPLORING

We flew from camp to camp in private, four-passenger planes with seasoned African bush pilots at the controls. What a great way to go! It allowed us to cover a lot of territory in a very short period, maximizing our time in the bush and offering us great diversity in ecosystems and wildlife. And the views from the planes were extraordinary. Imagine bird's-eye views as you fly at treetop level over savannah, veldt, desert, delta, river, lake, forest, swamp, saltpan, and floodplain. We could see to the horizon in three directions.

It was also very romantic and exciting to pack up my little duffle in the morning, walk from our camp down a narrow footpath through the bush to a primitive packed-earth landing strip, help shoo away any grazing animals nearby, and watch our plane come in just at the appointed time. Landing, we could see our new hosts performing the same get-the-animals-off-the-runway maneuver. Once there, we would either walk or, if the camp was far away, drive through the bush to be greeted with cold drinks and a totally different environment to explore.

As my nocturnal encounter with the peripatetic Jeffrey illustrates, the accommodations are an intrinsic part of the safari experience. Most lodges are built up high to take advantage of the incredible views and open-sided to catch the cooling breezes. Sleeping quarters are in either individual chalets or luxurious platformed tents with attached private bathrooms. The furnishings are reminiscent of Hemingway or Maugham: proper beds with soft linen and mosquito netting, dressing tables, comfy chairs, carefully chosen native pottery or baskets, and often a private veranda.

Camps usually accommodate between 12 and 22 people, thus ensuring personalized service. Because there are no large groups, it is easy to interact with fellow lodgers from all over the world, and equally easy to find quiet, private space to be alone to commune with the natural world uninterrupted by the chatter and commotion of other people.

The meals were simple but of high quality and served beautifully, often with native-themed tableware, sometimes accompanied by candelabra and silver. The food was fresh and locally grown, raised, or hunted. All of the camps served three substantial meals a day, plus snacks throughout the day and hors d'oeuvres and drinks every evening.

Each camp has its own naturalists/rangers/guides. This is their home. They know the habits of the resident wildlife and which animals have recently given birth or are new to the area. They share their vast knowledge in an unobtrusive way. When our ranger Harris pointed out a bird, it wasn't just a shrike, or a ground shrike, or even the long-tailed ground shrike. It was the white-lipped, long-tailed ground shrike. I had been a bit apprehensive about the almost constant presence of a guide, but their easy manner and expertise was welcome and significantly enhanced the experience.

Our usual wake-up call came with a cup of hot tea or coffee brought directly to our "room" early in the morning. One of the best viewing times is just after sunrise, so after a quick consult with the ranger about where to go and what to do, I was typically out in the bush at prime time. This was my favorite part of the day. The air is crisp, the animals are active, the vegetation vibrant. After a couple of hours in the bush, I would return to the lodge for a big, hot breakfast. I had had my wildlife "fix" and could then relax without feeling like I was missing out.

We were actively out in the bush all day, evening, and sometimes at night, and close to the animals at all times. One afternoon, I watched a leopard wake up from its nap, come down from its tree and gracefully move off. We followed him until his natural camouflage hid him from view. Another afternoon was spent watching lions mate, and another day we drifted for a few hours down a river in a canoe following a small group of bachelor elephants walking along the bank just a few yards away. They were perfectly comfortable with us being there because we were in the water. They would not have allowed us to get that close if we had been on land.

After such excursions, we would come home to freshly laundered clothes and cocktails. Even then, the wildlife viewing didn't stop. Often, I would be sitting at the table in the dining room eating my meal while watching kudu, or impala, or elephant or zebra or lechwe (a kind of antelope found in marshy areas like the Okavango), eating theirs.

INTO THE HEART OF THE DELTA

The only access into the heart of the delta is by light aircraft. We flew from Kasane, our starting point in Botswana, to Camp Moremi across "the whole of bloody Africa," as our pilot put it. Botswana is flat, and for an hour we flew at 300 feet over an area where there are no indigenous people, no water, no discernable animals, and precious little plant life. It was stark, forbidding, and mesmerizing. It so clearly illustrated why money is called *pula* in Botswana, which also means "rain."

Moremi is set on the Xakanaxa Lagoon, surrounded by huge ebony trees and more than 3,000 square miles of protected diverse habitat in the far eastern section of the delta. There were 19 guests total when we were there. Within hours of our arrival, we saw leopard, lion, ostrich, jackal, sable, lechwe, and other antelope of many varieties.

The four of us and our guide, Allen, tracked lions in our small open vehicle. We found a family—one male, two females, and four cubs. The females led the cubs away, but the big male made no attempt to move at all; in fact, he did not acknowledge us in any way. He was perfectly content going about the business of being a lion, unfazed by the five humans sitting in a metal box on four tires just a few feet away. Allen told us it would be very different if we were on foot. The lion would then pay careful attention to us—as prey. About 15 minutes later, we saw one of the females again. The cubs were out of sight with the other lioness, so she too now tolerated our presence, but she was warier than the male.

Later we found two young males and their sister lying together under a tree. They had just recently stuffed themselves, and their muzzles and paws were sticky with blood. Buzzing flies swarmed around to share in the feast. We watched quietly for at least 15 minutes. They were in a post-prandial stupor, content with full bellies, cooling shade, and each other's company. Although we could literally have reached out and touched them, we were again cautioned that, as relaxed as they looked, they had a very clear idea of boundaries and threat. Any quick move or startling noise or limb reaching out of the vehicle would cause trouble. We certainly didn't want to cause trouble.

That night as I walked down the narrow pathway to our bathroom, an elephant walked just a few inches away, on the other side of the reed wall that lined the pathway. We walked in parallel, side by side, for a few steps. I could see him through the reeds right there next to me. He apparently spent many nights around camp, so this was just an ordinary stroll for him. I, however, was astounded. According to our guides, the only time an elephant had damaged a tent was when one guide pulled a practical joke on another guide by burying a watermelon under the front of his tent, knowing that an elephant would come and push over the tent in order to dig up the melon.

The next morning, the four of us left by small speedboat for a three-hour journey through the delta past the heron colonies on Gadikwe Lagoon to Camp Okavango on remote Nxaragha Island. It was a thrilling ride. We sped through a maze of narrow gem-like, blue-green channels surrounded by reeds and rushes—papyrus, tsunga, devil weed—in spectacular colors. We passed by a red lechwe and hippos and a myriad of birds. Halfway there, we pulled over to a small island. It was perhaps four times as wide as my living room. There we found tea and snacks laid out on a picnic cloth, prepared by the guides from Camp Okavango who had come in their small boat to meet us and bring us the rest of the way to the camp.

One of my fondest memories is the last leg of our trip to the camp. We made the trip in a hand-made dugout canoe known as a *mekoro*. There were just two of us plus the guide in each of the two canoes. The guide stood in the back of the canoe, poling us along with a long stick. We glided silently for two hours, with a cocktail in our hands, through pristine, untouched wetlands. The smells were especially pungent here. I would find myself inhaling deeply, the better to savor the rich, layered, and complex aromas. The setting sun made everything iridescent—the water, the reeds and grasses that lined the narrow channel, and the faces of my friends and our guides. Golds and reds were displayed in every shade and hue. It was completely quiet save for birdcalls, the rustle of the wind in the reeds, and the water dripping off the poles pushing us silently along. The overwhelming sense was of peace and tranquility. For just a moment, despite the strangeness of the setting, I sensed an almost primordial connection and somehow felt like I belonged.

WHY GO: In addition to the diversity of the wildlife and the opportunity to experience it up close, tourism to Africa helps ease the economic pressures that are growing throughout the continent. Ecotourism provides much-needed monies and opportunities to the resident population. It is heartening to know that you will help preserve and protect this magnificent land by doing something that you treasure and love.

I need adventure and the natural world to get the cobwebs out of my head. To paraphrase Wordsworth, when the world is too much with me and there is mostly getting and spending, it is time to take a break from the modern, urban world. The contrast is refreshing, renewing, and spiritually necessary. To be immersed in Africa is to reawaken senses dulled by our usual daily routines.

SPECIAL ISSUES AND CHALLENGES: Remember, you will be in the wilderness, in the bush, not at the mall. Everything you *might* need has to be brought with you. In addition to the usual (medications, extra eyeglasses, personal toiletries) you should have a first-aid kit that emphasizes wound and insect bite care and protection from infection. Be sure to check with your physician or the Centers for Disease Control and Prevention for any immunizations or prophylactic medications recommended prior to travel. Also have mosquito repellent for your person and insect repellent coils or candles for your lodging.

Bring a good flashlight with a broad beam and plenty of power. It will be bulky and heavy, but it is important. One does not want to be surprised by (or worse yet, to surprise) an animal when walking around camp at night.

Clothes are greatly needed in many parts of Africa. Consider donating your "bush" clothes (T-shirts, shorts, shoes, sweaters, pants, or hats) when you leave.

VARIATIONS AND OPTIONS: We ended the trip in Chobe National Park, which is famous for its large herds of elephant, buffalo, zebra, and wildebeest. I strongly recommend adding this to your itinerary. It's relatively close to the Okavango Delta and is very different. Besides, Botswana is a long way to travel from the U.S.—you might not get this way again, so take as much advantage as you can of all that the country has to offer.

RESOURCES AND INFORMATION: The person we used to put all of the pieces of this trip together for us, including internal transportation and accommodations, is no longer in business. However, there are a number of tour operators that can design customized safaris much like the one described here for around $5,000 per person for a trip of several days, including accommodations. For example, see Africa Exclusive (*www.safariinstyle .com/about.html*; 800-958-1509), Safari Nzuri (*www.safarinzuri.com/index .html*; 888-723-2746), and Desert & Delta Safaris *(www.desertdelta.co.za)*.

ASIA

———

TEMPLES AND TREKS IN THE
UNREAL REALITY OF BHUTAN

CHRISTINA HEYNIGER

Christina is one of the few lucky ones who decided well before the age of 40 that life should not be lived sitting in traffic or a cubicle and left the corporate world to pursue adventure travel as a career and way of life. We traveled in a group together in Xinjiang, China, a couple of years ago, and I have come to appreciate her keen eye for detail and unabashed awe for the beauty of the natural world and diverse cultures. In the past few years, Christina has literally been all over the globe consulting, working, observing, and learning wherever she goes, which tends to be adventure destinations like India, Nepal, Ecuador, and Cambodia...so when she said that she experienced a trip that was "stunning," I sat up and listened. Here is her tale of Bhutan. —Shannon Stowell

TRIP DESCRIPTION

The center beam of the barn's roof was missing, and when I looked up all I could see were winking stars floating in the black, soupy night. I heard the wind as it whirled up the hill from the valley below, and the murmur of the two men discreetly tending the low burning fire outside the barn. I stretched my arms out, letting them dangle limply on the edges of the wooden tub where I sat up to my neck in steaming hot water. A single candle, lit just for me, flickered nearby. I watched as my toes floated up to the surface of the water at the far end of the bath. Tipping my head to rest it on the back of the tub, I alternately contemplated the stars, the barn, the candle, and the steam in a sort of rolling meditation.

A voice called from outside, "Madam, more rocks?"

With sweat trickling down my forehead, I called back, "No, thank you, it's still quite hot!"

I was enjoying my first Bhutanese hot stone bath, soaking alone in this barn at the top of a hill nestled in Bhutan's Paro Valley. Stones cooked for hours over an open fire had been carefully placed in a compartment at the end of my wooden tub. The principle is simple: stones heat the water, the water sizzles, and the soaker (me, in this instance) turns to putty. The effect is even greater if the bath is enjoyed on a freezing January night after a full week of walking, senses dazzled and exhausted by snowcapped Himalayan mountain views, black-haired yaks knee-deep in wild thistle, sightings of graceful soaring black-necked cranes, and hours driving over twisting roads.

After seven days in Bhutan, I felt quiet, calm, and imperturbable. I also felt like I had stepped into a Dr. Seuss story. Bhutan has a reputation for bringing out childlike wonder in its visitors, and like most everyone else who comes here, I was not immune to its magic.

AN UNFORGETTABLE ENTRY
INTO AN UNFORGETTABLE WORLD

The Kingdom of Bhutan—Druk Yul, "Land of the Thunder Dragon," in Dzongkha (the national language of Bhutan)—takes its name from the violent storms that frequently lash the Himalayan mountains surrounding it. The country inflamed my imagination from the minute my trip planning began, and the guidebooks I purchased only fueled this fire with descriptions of Bhutan as a "land replete with myths and legends" where "tales abound of ghosts who destroyed temples, and angels who rebuilt them."* I learned that Bhutan had been closed to the world for centuries until a few tourists began to trickle in during the mid-1970s. With an estimated population in 2001 of 690,000, most of whom are rural farmers who live at least an hour's walk from a road, it was easy to imagine that a rare and unusual journey awaited me.

The planning wasn't all fantasy, though. With government tourism policies oriented toward cultural and environmental preservation, travel to Bhutan requires more planning than other destinations in the region. The only way to obtain a visa is to be invited by the government, and for anyone who is not a foreign dignitary, this generally means joining a group tour or trek. In addition, the government has standardized and regulated all tour costs, charging about a 35 percent royalty on all payments in an effort to keep tourist traffic to levels that won't deplete the country's natural resources.

---

* Stan Armington, *Bhutan*, *2nd ed.*, Lonely Planet, Melbourne, 2002.

I signed up for a group tour and decided to enter the country via Druk Air, the national carrier of Bhutan (the only other entry point is by road, from India, through the town of Phuentsholing). On a searingly sunny morning flying from Kathmandu, I watched with the other lucky passengers seated in window seats on the right side of the plane in rapt disbelief at the sight of Mt. Everest hulking out of the earth. No matter that I'd seen probably hundreds of pictures of Everest in my life, the *feeling* I got from seeing the actual mountain, snowy whorls whipped to froth, its massive form higher than the airplane—was completely overwhelming. I found myself whacking the man next to me on the arm—"Do you see this?!" "Can you *believe* it?!"

After all that mountain madness in the air, the plane landed on the runway at the bucolic and gracefully designed Paro Airport, where the scene was one of almost preternatural calm and order, a perfect counterpoint to my airborne histrionics. In sharp contrast to other Asian airports, navigating Bhutan's airport is almost a soothing experience. Dorji Tshering, Himalayan High Treks' ground operator from Kuenphen Tours and Treks, quickly singled me out from the small throng of travelers. As a native of the country, he was dressed in the traditional *gho*—a long piece of fabric worn like a robe hiked up to the knees and held in place with a belt. I quickly discovered that I was the only person in the group and a custom itinerary had been created just for me. Bhutan was already working its magic.

AN UNEXPECTED INVITATION

My itinerary called for some easy day treks and cultural touring in western Bhutan—including Paro, Thimphu, Punakha, and the Phobjikha Valley—with relaxed days and a loose schedule.

That first day is a hard one to forget. I had been in this pristine mountain country less than two hours and just finished downing a plate of *em datse* or "chili cheese"—cooked strips of hot chilis slathered in melted cheese—before I found myself hiking up the moderately steep and rocky trail to Dorji's village. I'd been invited to join his household's annual "winter ceremony," a seasonal celebration presided over by Buddhist monks to bring good luck and prosperity for the coming spring.

I was very pleased at the invitation to participate in the ceremony—a treat Dorji says he offers to many of his groups if the timing of their visit coincides with the ceremony. Bhutanese people practice Mahayana Buddhism, the most open and accepting of all of the forms of Buddhism. When it developed, the aim of Mahayana Buddhism—translated as the "Greater Vehicle," or actually "Greater *Ox-Cart*"—was to accommodate believers from all walks of life. Dorji's openness in allowing visitors to participate in his family's observance of this ritual, an openness I found repeatedly in Bhutan, touched me deeply.

As we hiked up the trail to his village, I stopped often to look over my shoulder at the quiet fields in the afternoon sun or to stand aside so villagers carrying their baskets from the fields up the trail could pass me. After about an hour we reached Dorji's house, a traditional Bhutanese farmhouse, tall and square, with ornate painting and wood-carved details around the windows. After ascending a wooden ladder to the second floor, I found myself immediately included in a circle of monks seated on the wood plank floor, listening as their steady chanting reverberated throughout the room. The murmured prayers were occasionally punctuated by the deep-throated sound of the three-foot-long horns played by two of the red-robed men and the gentle tapping of the standing gongs manned by two others.

Nearly hypnotized by the sounds, the sights, and the overall atmosphere, I was surprised when I realized an hour had passed. One monk began walking from person to person with a small brass pot. I watched as each man held out a cupped hand to receive a small pour of the water. When the pot was finally held above my hand, Dorji next to me said, "Yes, yes, you too!" and so I raised my hand to receive a small pour. He told me, "Now drink a small bit of it, and then do like this." Sipping his water he quickly smoothed the last sprinkles of it in his hair, on his forehead, and over his eyes, then turned to me and said, "Rub it in your head."

Following his instructions, I tasted a faint ashy residue in the water as I swallowed, and then tried to gracefully rub the last bit through my hair and over my forehead.

"There," he observed happily, "now you have received some good blessing from this!"

Participating in this ceremony turned out to be one of the highlights of my trip. Entirely devoid of the artifice or showmanship often found in the cultural performances put on for foreign visitors in other countries, it was a true peek into the lives of the Bhutanese people.

RIDING THE "TIGER"
The next day brought even more "good blessings," when we hiked the steep path to visit the famed Taktsang Monastery, popularly known as the "Tiger's

Nest." Perched improbably on a rocky ledge high above Paro, at first glance the monastery seems ridiculously situated, and its lines and colors are so articulate and brilliant that it appears painted onto the gray rock that surrounds it. A central monument to the establishment of Buddhism in Bhutan, this revered place is said to have been established by Guru Rinpoche in A.D. 747. One legend tells of the guru riding a wild tigress through the air, vanquishing mythical demons across Bhutan before finally coming to rest and meditating in the spot where Taktsang Monastery is now located.

For mere mortals who do not get the chance to ride a tigress up the mountain, reaching the monastery requires a long walk up a moderately steep dirt and rooted path beginning in a wooded forest far below the monastery cliffs. We paused frequently to rest and saw other groups doing the same; there's never any hurry in Bhutan. At every stop, I peered through towering trees to look up, refusing to be discouraged even though our objective seemed to hover so high above us, small and far away. Prayer flags draping the trees flapped and floated in the breeze as we ascended, and looking through their clutter down into the heavily forested valleys gave me a sense of airy height. Even though it was January and I had been freezing while taking my tea in the guesthouse dining room that morning, by noon I was sweating madly. I stripped off my micro-fleece layers—those colorful staples of every good adventure traveler's wardrobe—and tied them on, one atop the other, around my waist.

The final climb to the monastery is a zigzag series of stony steps—steeply down, then steeply up, traversing the face of this rocky mountain and at one point bridging over a rushing clear stream totally invisible until one is upon it. To me, the quality of the light—filtered, golden, hazy, and warm as we made our way up these last steps—was a visual representation of quiet, a halo radiating out from the monastery to enfold and welcome us.

From the outside, the monastery is deceptively small. Inside the main gate, however, I saw that it was large, with separate buildings for monks and staff separated by wide stone courtyards. Built around a cave where Guru Rinpoche meditated for three months in the eighth century, the most holy room is ornately painted and populated by gold statues of the Buddha and Guru Rinpoche. I removed my shoes and prostrated three times in respect as Dorji had taught me. The slim monk guarding the room allowed us to pull aside a curtain sheltering one wall and peer into the darkness of a cool stone cave. Trays for money lay on the floor at the foot of a case containing a statue of the guru. A familiar image to me by this time, Rinpoche's expression had frequently seemed agitated and even a little scary, but in this chilled and shadowy lair even he appeared becalmed. Despite the cool breeze, the smell of incense was heavy and thick in the air.

FLOATING ROOFS AND FLOATING BIRDS

"More chilis?" Dorji asked me with a gentle chuckle as he watched the tears well up in my eyes in reaction to a particularly spicy round of chili cheese I'd been in Bhutan now for a few days and was feeling confident enough with the chilis to have boldly forked some from Dorji's serving dish this lunchtime. We'd spent the morning driving the twisty road from Punakha to Phobjikha Valley in the hopes of catching a glimpse of the famous Chinese black-necked cranes, which migrate to this valley in Bhutan during Tibet's harsh winters.

In Punakha, Bhutan's old "winter capital," we had visited the sprawling and beautiful Punakha Dzong at the confluence of the Pho Chu and Mo Chu Rivers (a *dzong* is the fortress-like administrative, military, and social center found in each district of the country). In the hold-your-breath stillness of January, the flapping of birds' wings in the courtyard sounded loud in my ears, and the elaborate paintings on every wall of the dzong seemed to scream out for attention. Incongruously, bright red roosters strutted in the corners of the formal courtyard, pecking at the ground and occasionally each other. The architect of this unusual dzong is said to have conceived the structure in a dream in which Guru Rinpoche led him to Zangto Pelri, the guru's heavenly abode. With never a sketch or drawing to guide the construction, the dzong is certainly something of a miracle, having weathered six fires, two glacial lake bursts, and one earthquake.

The dzong also provides an excellent example of the "floating" roof style found not only in the elaborate formal dzongs but also in simple farmhouses throughout Bhutan. The floating roof, well suited to Bhutan's wetter monsoon climate, is an adaptation of Tibetan pueblo-style flat roofs. The Bhutanese added four timber columns to the house at roof level to create a "hipped" roof that rests like an umbrella on the columns. The space between the Tibetan flat roof and the timber umbrella is used to store fodder in winter (which also adds insulation) and to provide shade and cooling in the summer. Because the umbrella roof creates a shaded dark space above the Tibetan flat pueblo roof, it creates the illusion of a floating roof.

The trip up to Phobjikha Valley from Punakha only deepened the hypnotic, fairyland spell that had been working on me for days in this country where roofs float above houses and ethereal, snowy mountains look over lush subtropical valleys. On the narrow twisting road, we ascended from Punakha's subtropical terrain through a dense forest where Chir pines, willow trees, and thick vines chaotically intertwined and sheltered wild orchids lying at their base alongside crystal waterfalls. It was imagination turned inside out, exploring these steep hillsides littered with boulders, waterfalls, and moss-festooned trees.

Bhutan's natural wonders are unusual enough that the country has been included in Conservation International's list of 19 "Global Hotspots" for biodiversity conservation. These hotspots around the world occupy less than 2 percent of the Earth's surface but include 75 percent of the world's most endangered plants and animals. Bhutan is home to more than 600 varieties of orchid alone.

Although we had made this drive for the express purpose of seeing the cranes on their winter holiday from Tibet, I had low expectations of actually sighting any—bird-watching has never been particularly rewarding for me. But, my God! They seemed to carpet the valley and fill the sky. These beautiful birds breed on the Tibetan Plateau and have six wintering areas, mainly at lower altitudes in China, but also in Bhutan. With a wingspan of nearly eight feet and a distinctive black head with red crown and whitish-gray body, they're easy for even pedestrian birdwatchers like me to appreciate. The cranes I saw seemed to be flying in slow motion, and I marveled at the gentle muscling of their cloudy wings, the smooth flapping carrying them in pairs over the treeless valley where we found them.

A TREK NOT TAKEN

I am a dedicated trekker, but with only a short amount of time in Bhutan, I was not able to do any of the multi-day walks through the pure wilderness and Himalayan views that have made this country so famous. I asked my friend Victor Saunders, a world-class mountaineer with extensive experience in Bhutan, to recommend a trek for my next visit. Victor's immediate recommendation for the amateur adventurer was the Druk Path, probably the finest short trek in the country.

This beautiful hike takes five days and leads from Paro to Thimphu, Bhutan's capital city and one-time home of the country's only traffic light (removed within days after residents complained it was "impersonal" and "ugly"). It follows the old trading route once routinely traversed by traders traveling from west to east but now rendered obsolete with the construction of the trans-Bhutan highway. It is interesting to note that what trekkers now enjoy in five days of trekking bliss was once a punishment for Bhutanese soldiers forced to complete the journey in a grueling one-day march.

The path is described as "moderately strenuous." It reaches 13,812 feet at its highest point and takes the trekker through remote wilderness and past monasteries unlike those found in the towns. Traveling through yak-herding country on the first two days, trekkers enjoy fine views of the famous Jhomolhari, a snowy peak with a silhouette that looms powerfully over Paro. Spellbinding to me from the road, I can only imagine its impact when viewed from the silence of a wooded trail.

The third day's walk meanders through rhododendron forests over the Jeli La pass to the delightful Jimilangsto (Sand Ox Lake), famous for its giant trout. The Himalayan views never stop—trekkers see Jangchu La (13,714 feet) before descending to the lake, where it's possible to see the south face of Jitchu Drake (22,930 feet), whose name means "Angry Bird."

On the fourth day, the route leads past dwarf rhododendron and, later, high alpine moorland to the high point of the trail at Phume La. The view at this point includes tangles of colorful prayer flags and of Bhutan's highest peak, Gankar Puensum (24,836 feet), on the Bhutan-Tibet border. On the long descent, trekkers pass close to the Thujidrag Gompa, a curious meditation center apparently stranded in the middle of a cliff.

The last day takes trekkers through gorgeous blue pine forests back into the bustle of Thimphu, no doubt leaving them with the overwhelming sense that they have walked into and out of another century in just five short days.

WHY GO: Bhutan is in the midst of major change. Several years ago, the people's beloved former king, Jigme Singye Wangchuck, set in motion his plans to hold real elections in 2008 and end absolute royal rule in Bhutan. After that, the monarchy will assume a more ceremonial role. Throughout the country, people are being trained in everything from the basics of voting to understanding a free press. Bhutan offers a rare opportunity to observe firsthand a country going through a profound and peaceful transformation.

SPECIAL ISSUES AND CHALLENGES: Although lavish accommodations are available, Bhutan is not a luxury destination. If one is very sensitive to cold, avoid traveling in winter months, and of course if one chooses to trek, it's best to be moderately fit and accustomed to walks of multiple hours and camping at high altitude. Check with your doctor about any health concerns that may limit your ability to tolerate extended stays at high altitude.

I traveled alone during this trip and did not encounter any problems. There is little crime in Bhutan and the people are very respectful of visitors and treat women well. That said, I am an experienced travel professional who has roamed widely throughout the world on my own. Others, especially women, might want to go with a companion, if for no other reason than for the company and support another person can provide. Besides, most trips to Bhutan are with groups, and few people will have the opportunity to travel as a "group of one" like I did.

VARIATIONS AND OPTIONS: The options are endless: Guides can tailor itineraries to suit any special interest—from difficult and technical climbing to soft adventure trekking or trips oriented around culture, Buddhism, or wildlife.

RESOURCES AND INFORMATION: I booked my trip through Himalayan High Treks *(www.hightreks.com)* because I was booking on short notice and wanted a person in the U.S. I could easily talk with about my plans. Contact Himalayan High Treks' founder Effie Fletcher in California at 415-551-1005 or email *effie@hightreks.com.*

For more experienced travelers who would prefer to deal directly with a foreign operator, two local Bhutanese operators who have good reputations and experience in working with Western tourists are Dorji Tshering from Kuenphen Tours and Treks *(dorjitshering1@yahoo.com)* and Etho Metho ("Rhododendron" in Dzongkha) through *www.bhutanethometho.com.*

Other operators offering cultural and trekking tours of Bhutan include Journeys International *(www.journeys.travel/destinations/asia/bhutan)* and KE Adventure Travel *(www.keadventure.com).*

SCENERY, SERENITY, HISTORY, AND CULTURE IN LAOS

DON MANKIN

I n the late 1990s and early 2000s, I had the good fortune to travel often to Thailand on business. The several times that my wife was able to accompany me, we added on a week or two of vacation in the historic north of the country or to other countries in the region. After a number of such trips, we were ready for something even more exotic. Over the years, we had heard glowing, though occasionally cautionary reports about Laos, and once even managed to squeeze in a day-trip across the border. We were intrigued by what we saw and heard, so when a recent business trip gave us another opportunity to spend some time in the region, we decided to head for Laos once again for a longer trip.

TRIP DESCRIPTION

"And the beat goes on...." The vintage sounds of Sonny and Cher wafted through the lounge of this rustic mountain lodge in the most unlikely of places: Phonsavan, in northern Laos near the border with Vietnam. The sounds, the smells, and the sights were disorienting—Sonny and Cher on the stereo, views through the pines overlooking the smoke of the cookfires below, an ice-cold bottle of Lao beer, and fragments of exploded U.S. ordnance from the Vietnam War arrayed along the bar. This is just a piece of modern Laos— a land of contrasts and irony, of beauty balanced with sadness, and of rustic poverty with urban sophistication.

A former French colony that has been under communist control since 1975, Laos has been largely overlooked by the wave of Western tourists that has swept through Southeast Asia for the last 20 years. There are no beach resorts, and until recently the government has not encouraged tourism. Because of its relative isolation, it is still an underdeveloped country that is only now awakening to its tourist potential. As a result, there are few crowds, aggressive street vendors, or the kind of development that has transformed the face of Southeast Asia. It is still a sleepy, charming country of very human scale that offers an excellent opportunity to experience life in Southeast Asia as it once was.

THE ANCIENT CAPITAL OF LUANG PRABANG

We began our trip by flying directly from Bangkok to Luang Prabang, a UNESCO World Heritage site of classic Buddhist temples; quiet, shady streets; and world-class dining and shopping. Established in the 14th century, Luang Prabang remains one of Asia's best-preserved ancient capitals. It is nestled at the confluence of two rivers, the Mekong and Nam Khan, and is surrounded by soft green hills. The city is a living museum of life, culture, and architecture in a beautiful setting, the jewel in the crown of this unique country.

Our guide and driver for the next few days met us at the airport. Wan, the guide, gave us an introductory tour of the city, then dropped us off at our hotel, the Grand Luang Prabang, a resort built on the grounds of the former villa of the Prince Regent before the communist takeover in 1975. Since the resort is small, only 78 rooms, and about 2.5 miles outside of town, it is very quiet and peaceful.

The resort's French-Laotian architecture, spacious grounds on the banks of the Mekong, and many reflecting pools and lotus ponds enhance the sense of peace. From early evening to late morning, a heavy mist hangs over the river. It all feels very mysterious and tranquil. Throughout our six-day stay in Luang Prabang, we spent many hours sitting on the chairs on the patio outside our room, watching the mist descend and rise, and listening to the gentle sounds drifting from the village across the river.

Most of the next day was spent on the Mekong. This legendary river begins in Tibet and runs through southern China, along the borders of Myanmar and Thailand, and through the heart of Laos, Cambodia, and Vietnam on its journey to the South China Sea. One could easily argue that the lifeblood of Southeast Asia flows between its banks. It is both the symbol of the region and the backbone of its economy and culture. Its name evokes a different kind of history for Westerners like us, linked as it is in our memories with the Vietnam War. This river would soon become the touchstone for our ten-day visit to Laos.

On this day, we were heading to the sacred Pak Ou caves several miles upstream. As our boat slipped through the current, the river teemed with life. Women washed the family laundry, men tended crops on the gently sloping banks, children splashed in the shallows, and junks from China ferried staples, furniture, and machine parts to cities and towns downriver.

After about an hour and a half, we reached the caves, about halfway up a towering limestone cliff overlooking the river. The local people, almost all of them observant Buddhists, have visited the caves for four centuries to place statues to honor Buddha and gain merit and good luck. There are now thousands of Buddha statues of all sizes, materials, and styles stuck in niches in the rock, on ledges, or anywhere space can be found in the dusky caves. The overall effect is both reverent and spooky.

Over the next several days, we wandered through the streets, temples, and markets of Luang Prabang and explored the surrounding countryside. One day we visited the Khuongsi waterfalls several miles outside of town, climbing up a steep trail past inviting pools of turquoise-colored water. Another day we crossed the river to walk down country lanes from one rustic temple to another. We stopped often along the way to interact with children who were only too happy to teach us how to count in Lao. Once we stood in the middle of a rural lane to stare for long minutes at the picturesque view of a farmer working his fields with his water buffalo.

But we most enjoyed our in-town explorations. On our first evening, we climbed the steps that lead up to the temple at the top of Phu Si Hill to watch the setting sun as it reflected in the waters of the Mekong. From the top of this hill, the highest point in Luang Prabang at over 300 feet, we could see the entire town, both rivers, the surrounding hills, and the *stupas* (spires) of several temples off in the distance.

We woke up early the next morning to participate in a daily ritual for the residents of the town, giving alms (handfuls of sticky rice) to the Buddhist monks walking in procession down the misty streets. A drum marks the start of the procession, then hundreds of mostly young monks with shaved heads, wrapped in bright orange robes, walk silently down the street past a line of kneeling locals and a smattering of early-rising tourists. Most place small handfuls of sticky rice in the black lacquered rice bowls carried by each monk. These donations, which make up a significant portion of the monks' daily diet, are said to ensure a good life for the donors.

This was followed by a visit to the morning farmer's market on the street running alongside the river. The variety, color, and abundance of the produce were stunning. For the rest of the day, we wandered on our own, poking down narrow shaded lanes hidden from sight off the main streets by overgrown plants and trees, leading to temples tucked away in quaint neighborhoods. We did this almost every day. The temples were never crowded or noisy—perfect places for reflection and meditation.

The serenity of the back streets and temples was a stark contrast to the bustling main drag which runs through the center of the town and the heart

of the tourist district. Lining the street on both sides are inexpensive restaurants and guesthouses, Internet cafés, and numerous shops selling the
high-quality handicrafts and art for which Luang Prabang is known—handwoven silk, products made of *saa* paper (from mulberry bark), silver jewelry, and artwork of various kinds. These handicraft shops attract high-end,
cosmopolitan shoppers. One of the stores we visited, which sold some of
the most beautiful and expensive products we saw on the entire trip, even
had a photo of Mick Jagger with the owner of the store pinned to the wall—
taken just the week before!

Dining can be as sophisticated as the shopping; it can also be very basic
and simple. In the best restaurants, you can find influences from Thai,
Chinese, and French cuisine. Luang Prabang even has a cuisine all its own,
featuring fish from the river, local greens grown on its banks, water buffalo
stew, purple sticky rice, and a fiery condiment called *jaew bawng,* a paste
made from pounded dried buffalo skin, garlic, and chilis. We had dinner one
night at a restaurant that displayed a blown-up copy of a recent review of it
from the *New York Times.* There are also several excellent bakeries around
town, a legacy from the many years that Laos was a French colony.

Most evenings after dinner we wandered through the night market along
the main drag. Local artisans ran extension cords from shops and restaurants on the street to power bare light bulbs so that shoppers could see the
colors and quality of their silk scarves, hand carved wooden boxes, and
other handiworks.

PINE TREES, JARS, AND BOMBS

After six idyllic days in Luang Prabang, a full day's drive along a winding
mountain highway transported us to another world. The distance from
Luang Prabang to Phonsavan and the Plain of Jars is only about 130 miles,
but it could easily have been much more, considering how long it took us
to get there and how different the landscape, climate, culture, and history of
the two regions are.

The drive itself was initially a source of some concern. Several guidebooks and websites had warned of bandits and a local Hmong rebel group
along a portion of the road. But when we asked our guide Wan about this,
she laughed and assured us that government forces had secured the highway and that there had been no incidents in more than a year. The scenery
was beautiful as we made our way slowly through the green mountains and

the simple but orderly hill tribe villages, past open fields and rice paddies, and across picturesque river gorges.

As we approached Phonsavan, the landscape and climate changed markedly. The area is on a plateau almost 4,000 feet high, so the air is cool and dry. Instead of jungles, there are pine trees and open, arid fields. The town of Phonsovan was not the reason for our visit, though. Except for the lodge, the town itself is unremarkable—few tourists, forgettable restaurants and shopping, and the slowest Internet connection I have experienced in years.

The few tourists in the area come for two very different reasons. One is to see the enigmatic Plain of Jars. This is actually several dispersed sites made up of meadows and wooded areas dotted with hundreds of large stone jars estimated to be around 2,000 years old. The jars are about five feet high and three to four feet wide. Many have fallen over and others are damaged, but a surprising number are upright and relatively intact. The purpose of the jars is still subject to debate, but most archaeologists believe that they are above-ground stone coffins. The jars themselves are quite impressive. One can only marvel at the skill and effort required by the early inhabitants who, using only rudimentary tools, transformed rocks into these symmetrical, well-shaped jars.

The setting is equally impressive—long views of rolling hills, meadows, fields, and woods. I was enthralled at the view, so different from Luang Prabang, until I realized that the pockmarks in the distance were actually bomb craters from the many years of carpet bombing by American forces during the Vietnam War. In fact, the path through the archaeological sites is marked by prominent warnings to stay on the path because of the danger from unexploded ordnance (UXO) still buried in the ground. Farmers accidentally digging them up while plowing their fields and children playing with found ordnance result in about 60 casualties per year.

This sad history is the second reason why the area is so noteworthy. Most of the UXO is left over from the Vietnam War. Bomb casings and fragments from exploded or decommissioned ordnance are displayed all over town, including the lounge of the mountain resort where we stayed. Despite this sad legacy of the American misadventure, people were unfailing friendly, polite, and gracious to us throughout our visit.

Instead of visiting the Tham Piew cave where hundreds of local people were killed by an American bomb during the war, we opted for a more uplifting alternative. Our resourceful guide was able to arrange a last-minute visit to a silk co-op, the Lao Sericulture Company. This co-op was founded in 1976 to create jobs for local women by teaching them how to tend mulberry trees, raise silkworms, make natural dyes, and weave scarves, cloth, clothing, and other products in traditional Lao patterns. Their handmade products, which are of exceptional quality, are marketed throughout Laos and in stores in the U.S. and Europe under the brand name Mulberries. The founder, Kommaly Chanthavong, was nominated for a Nobel Peace Prize in 2005 for her work in founding and managing the co-op.

For more than two hours, we observed the women at work and talked to Ms. Chanthavong and her staff. We also played with their young children who, until they are old enough to go to school, accompany their mothers to work. The playful children, the vivid colors of the dyes, the smiles of the women, and their spirited chatter made this seem like more than just another place to work. The co-op is also a community where people laugh, play, and look out for each other and for each other's children. It was a fascinating morning. This bit of serendipity was memorable—an uplifting end to our visit to a place marked by so much sorrow.

AN ALL-TOO-BRIEF VISIT TO VIENTIANE

When we visited Laos's capital city of Vientiane several years earlier on a day-trip from northern Thailand, we were not all that impressed. Our one-day tour was rushed, our guide was glum and rigid, and our transportation was a creaky taxi with a cramped backseat. As a result, we planned to spend only one night in Vientiane this time and only because it was our departure point from Laos.

Everything was different on this trip. Our guide was congenial and flexible, the vehicle was a new van with efficient air-conditioning, and we had some time to explore the city on our own. Furthermore, the hotel for our one-night stay was outstanding. The Settha Palace is an excellent example of French Colonial architecture, which meant that it exuded understated class and style. Every direction you looked offered a picture for a postcard or sales brochure—wood floors, marble bathrooms, classic furniture, and lush landscaped gardens. The hotel restaurant is also outstanding, and a bargain to boot, considering the quality of the food and service.

The city itself is a rarity among Asian capitals. The 360-degree view from the top of the Patuxai monument—a smaller version of the Arc de Triomphe, and a good starting point for a tour of the city—confirms that Vientiane is a relaxed, low-rise city. There are few buildings taller than three stories and the tallest has 12 floors. Of course, all of this will no doubt change as investment from Thailand and China continue to pour into the city and the country. The impression of the city from the top of the monument is confirmed by walking around the streets. This is easy to do since many of the boulevards are lined with canopies of trees and are relatively uncrowded.

Although Vientiane can't match Luang Prabang's spiritual grandeur, it does have its share of impressive temples, most notably Pha That Luang, which our Lonely Planet guide described as looking almost like a "gilded missile cluster." Also like Luang Prabang, Vientiane is on the Mekong, though it looks quite different here. It is much wider, and there is a broad beach separating the promenade from the river. In the fading light of the setting sun, the promenade was a magnet for all kinds of people. Teenage boys leaned on their motorbikes, flew model airplanes, and flirted with their girlfriends. Street food vendors set up tables, colored lights, and grills for their evening customers. Families and tourists strolled along the banks. This was an appropriate way to end our short trip to Laos—sipping a cold beer at an outdoor restaurant and watching the street scene and the sun setting across the river. I just wish we had had more time.

WHY GO: Besides the obvious attractions of scenery, serenity, history and exotic culture, Laos is also very inexpensive. It is one of the few places in the world where travelers of modest means can afford to stay in the best hotels and hire private drivers and guides to ease their way around what might otherwise be a difficult country. Our trip was about as upmarket as you can go, but even with the high-end accommodations and custom tour, it cost us only about $100 per person per day, including accommodations, excursions and day trips, entry fees to sites, drivers, guides, internal flights, transfers to and from airports, and breakfast every day.

SPECIAL ISSUES AND CHALLENGES: While Laos does not present any unusual difficulties for most travelers, those with health problems should be aware of potential risks. Probably the biggest ones are digestive and intestinal. This is true throughout Southeast Asia, or in any country or region with a warm climate, unfamiliar food, and old plumbing. Laos is no different and probably not that much worse than other countries of this sort. My advice is to bring lots of hand sanitizer and use it often. When that doesn't work, use over-the-counter medications, rest, and be patient. Also bring along appropriate antibiotics for more serious problems.

Another potential problem, for those with respiratory problems, is the pall of smoke from the open cookfires and burning agricultural waste that builds up in late afternoon. The pollution from other sources is minimal, but the smoke was a bit of a problem for me on some days. We were there in January, when skies are relatively clear, so the smoke was not that bad—but it can get pretty thick in March and April. The inhaler I use to deal with the occasional recurrences of my childhood asthma was enough to keep this potential problem at bay.

Heat, humidity, and sun can be another problem. There is no magic solution, but wearing a hat, using sunblock, drinking plenty of bottled water, and laying low during the hottest part of the day will help. In addition, I always wear travel pants with zip-off legs whenever I visit hot climates. I take the bottoms off when I am just walking around at midday and put them back on to visit temples and other places where short pants would be disrespectful. I also wear the bottoms to protect my legs in the excessively air-conditioned restaurants that are as ubiquitous in Asia as motorbikes and rice.

The government seems to have dealt successfully with the rebels and bandits that have made road travel unsafe in some parts of the countryside. However, it is always a good idea to check the Consular Information Sheets and travel warnings available on the U.S. State Department website *(http:// travel.state.gov/travel)* before you go, and to ask locally about current conditions when you are in-country.

VARIATIONS AND OPTIONS: Travelers with more time might wish to see the dramatic karst (limestone) formations and caves in central Laos and the hundreds of islands and wild rapids at the southern end of the Mekong, or add on visits to Cambodia, Vietnam, or the less traveled Isan region in Northeast Thailand just over the border from Laos. There is also a two-day cruise down the Mekong River from the northern Lao border town of Houeisay to Luang Prabang on a large, comfortable river barge. Overnight stays are at the Luang Say Lodge, an attractive ecolodge on the river *(www.asian-oasis.com/luang.html)*.

The best time to visit is during the "dry" season (there are three basic seasons in Southeast Asia—"hot," "dry," and "wet") from November through February. We had great weather on our trip—no rain and pleasant days. I even had to buy a lightweight jacket at a market in Luang Prabang because the evenings were cooler than I expected.

For those on tighter budgets, there are plenty of less expensive alternatives. For example, you can do this trip on your own and stay in budget hotels, guesthouses, or hostels. However, if you are a first-time visitor and have only a limited amount of time, a private, custom-guided trip is the most efficient way to travel and provides all of the flexibility you could want. In addition, as laid back as Laos is, things can get pretty hectic and noisy. Mature travelers may prefer to stay in places that provide a quiet retreat from the hustle and bustle of the street, especially from the high-pitched, barely muffled roar of the motorbikes.

RESOURCES AND INFORMATION:

Getting There: Bangkok Airways flies directly to and from Luang Prabang every day. Thai International Airlines has daily flights to and from Vientiane. It also has several flights a day to Chiang Rai, which is the closest airport in Thailand to the starting point for the Mekong cruise.

How to Do It: We booked our trip through Asianventure Tours Company, headquartered in Hanoi *(www.asianventure.com)*. They did a great job. The guides were excellent, the accommodations outstanding, and the itinerary was just what we wanted. Other companies that also can arrange tours in the region include Boundless Journeys *(www.boundlessjourneys.com)* and KE Adventure Travel *(www.keadventure.com)*.

Where to Stay: For information on the Grand Luang Prabang in Luang Prabang, see *http://grandluangprabang.com;* for the Settha Palace in Vientiane, go to *www.setthapalace.com.* The rustic mountain lodge in Phonsavan is the Auberge de la Plaine de Jarres (also known as the Phuphadaeng Hotel). For more information, see *www.viengchampatour.com/ho_plainof_jars.php.*

Other: For more information on the Lao Sericulture Company, the silk co-op in Phonsavan, and its products, go to *www.mulberries.org.*

ETHNIC TRIBES AND OUTDOOR ADVENTURE IN GUIZHOU (CHINA)

SHANNON STOWELL

I first heard of Guizhou from a Chinese friend in the travel business who, when he found out that I was an adventurous type, exclaimed that I had to visit Guizhou if I wanted adventure. Having traveled to some of China's best-known regions and having spent some time in the very adventure-filled far west province of Xinjiang, it was an intriguing prospect. Over the next several months, my wife, Shelly, and I read and learned more about Guizhou's stunning scenery, friendly people, and mix of unique cultures that remains largely untouched by the modern world. Clearly we needed to go. When we were invited by the Guizhou Tourism Administration to make an exploratory visit to the province as part of its efforts to promote tourism, we jumped at the chance. In March 2007 we spent eight days touring the southwest portion of Guizhou for a peek into the future of adventure tourism in China.

TRIP DESCRIPTION

"Twenty years ago," our guide says, "I came here for the first time in a four-wheel-drive on a buffalo path. An old woman came out of a ramshackle dwelling and, wishing to be hospitable, cut swaths of grass to feed my auto. She'd never seen one before." While it's hard to imagine an area in China that has not been overrun by industrialization and Westerners, these places still do exist. Guizhou is one of them—a land where mountainous geography makes it less interesting for builders of factories than other regions of China, a land where more than 40 percent of the population are not ethnic Chinese but a variety of minority hill tribes: Yao, Miao, Dong, Shui, Yao, Buo-Yei, and others.

Located in the south-central part of the country, Guizhou is bounded by the better-known provinces of Hunan to the east, Sichuan to the north, and Yunnan to the west. Peasant farmers make up 85 percent of the population. The landscape is all multihued green, terraced, cultivated hills dotted by laborers and water buffalo; sharp, unfarmable mountains rising from misty rice fields; and crystal clear rivers and unexplored caves. Guizhou, a little-known corner of the world's most populous nation, contains magical pockets of culture and geographic beauty and is inhabited by some of the warmest and kindest people in this vast and rapidly changing land.

STARTING IN THE BIG CITY

We started out with a night in the provincial capital of Guiyang, which contains three million people and, like most Chinese cities, is loud, bustling, and seemingly unable to slow down. There are few Western hotels or restaurants here. Clearly it won't stay this way for long, as Wal-Mart China just dropped a warehouse store into the heart of the city. In an interview I did with a reporter from Xinhua News Agency, she was visibly shocked that as a Westerner I did *not* want to see McDonalds, Wendy's, or even Starbucks in Guizhou. "I came to China to see China," I told her, "not New Jersey or Oshkosh." I'm not sure she knew exactly where Oshkosh was (nor do I), but I think she got the point.

We spent most of our day in Guiyang exploring a park at one end of town with a fairly good network of walking trails that go up the mountainside. We walked to the end of one of the trails and took a gondola the rest of the way. At the top, there were great views, but most important, for a few minutes at least, we were above the noise and mayhem of the city.

Guiyang, like most mid-size cities in China, is not a place to spend too much time, so we quickly moved to the countryside. We spent our first night in the southwestern city of Kaili, a small, quiet place where the sounds of chickens and dogs at dusk compete with motorbikes and street vendors. Our overall plan was to spend the next five days in a car with a driver and interpreter to do a loop through the southwestern part of the province, visiting different villages, viewing the stunning karst mountain scenery and rural farmland, going through a few caves, and wrapping up our visit back in Guiyang with a night at the opera.

THE MIAO VILLAGE

Our first real cultural experience with local tribes was a Miao village, which was preparing itself for an expected influx of tourists in the future. Some villages are further along in their preparations than others, ranging from communities that came off as overprepared and a little wooden with their cultural shows to those where the kids stare in wonder at us odd foreigners.

Over the next week, we experienced the whole range and appreciated all of them, but absolutely loved being in the villages that had not yet fully given themselves over to tourism.

The Miao village was somewhere between these two extremes. When we stepped out of the car, we realized that much of the village had gathered at the entrance to greet us. Immediately, two old women began a loud, mournful, long harmonized wail as an intro to a welcome song. Everyone wore long, dress-like clothing, brightly decorated in blue, purple, and red. As part of their traditional welcome to visitors, they offered us bowls of rice wine. It is polite to drink it, and we like to be polite, so we drank. After a while, my wife had to pretend to drink out of the water buffalo horn-bowl that was now being passed around, as the welcomes and especially the drinking were a little more enthusiastic than she could keep up with.

The interpreter who accompanied us on our trip was very helpful. She explained a dance that the villagers performed, details of their daily life, what crops they raised (mostly rapeseed and rice), even a little about the Mao Zedong–era propaganda that could still be seen on a few buildings, painted by the Red Army as it passed through decades before. We spent a couple of hours in the village and then got back into the car to move on to our next destination, LiBo County, a few hours' drive to the south.

A local guide took us on a beautiful hike along a river for a mile or so to a waterfall. The water was crystal clear. Our guide, who presumably knew where he was taking us, was dressed in a suit, which meant he had to take his loafers and socks off and roll up his pants whenever the trail crossed the river. We, on the other hand, were dressed for vacation in zip-off pants and water-proof sandals. He did just as well as we did, reminding us that adventure is not just about the gear and the clothing. While the zip-offs and sandals were certainly handy, our guide ably demonstrated that you can have adventures no matter what you wear.

One of the best things about traveling with an interpreter was that it provided an incredible window into life in Guizhou. On the drives between locations, we talked endlessly about what it was like to be a young person in China, music tastes, Brad Pitt, the Internet and its impact on Chinese culture, history, language, Jesus, spicy food, dreams, Britney Spears (pre-head shaving), eating water buffalo, the war in Iraq, children, who the most annoying tourists are for the Chinese guides (sorry, Germans, it's you), and much, much more.

THE DONG VILLAGE

The highlight of our trip was staying in a minority Dong village. Word had spread that a couple of Westerners would be spending the evening, and when we rolled into the cobblestone town square, we could tell preparations were taking place, as kids scurried around moving benches and adults fixed and fiddled with the children's beautiful silver headdresses.

The name of the village was Xiaohuang, and it had about 2,000 inhabitants. Most of the homes have two stories so that livestock can live downstairs. The houses are made of single-plank wood that is milled on-site from locally felled trees. Each home has limited access to electricity—most only sport a bare bulb in each room and possibly an outlet or two for a radio or TV. There were no bars, no bowling alleys, no restaurants, and no dance clubs—thank goodness. It was a functioning community that we were fortunate enough to peek into, even for just a short while.

We were housed with local families. Our rooms were spare but clean, and the mattresses were thin and somewhat hard, like most in China. The room rate of $3 a night included a noodle soup breakfast served in the family's main room in the morning. The bathroom was primitive, Chinese-style, and shared by several guests, but no one really minded.

The evening kicked off with a dinner in a communal house served to us by some of the young people of the village. The meal included a medley of vegetable dishes, chicken, fish, bee larvae, mushrooms, rice, noodles, and several roaring-hot chili oil dishes. Teacups were kept constantly filled, and the rice wine and *pi jio* (beer) also flowed. After dinner, about a dozen of the teenagers who ate with us, both boys and girls, got up and sang a few traditional songs. The effect was haunting in the dim light of the dark wood room with the smell of good food and woodsmoke filtering through the air. It was easy to lean back and realize that we had truly left our normal lives behind for a bit and were now living in someone else's world.

But we weren't done yet. We were then taken to the town square, where more than a hundred youngsters (aged about 6 to 11) waited, dressed in ceremonial costume garb, to sing traditional songs for us. The girls wore incredibly complex silver headdresses and everyone wore beautiful, painstakingly detailed clothing made up primarily of rich shades of blue and red. The children and young adults divided into four groups—teenage boys and girls, and young boys and girls. They began to sing. In one of the most memorable numbers, called "Forest Music," the ensemble interpreted and imitated in song the voices of the cicadas, birds, frogs, and other night creatures in a melodic but haunting chorus, lightly accompanied by a few string instruments.

All this unfolded under the drum tower, a 90-foot-high structure of wood that houses a huge drum, which is pounded loudly to bring the village together for community meetings, to fight fires, and in times past, to go to battle. In the center of the square under the tower was a huge roaring fire, probably eight feet across. There was no other light in the square. The event had an almost medieval feel, as all the performances were done with the most rudimentary of lighting and props. A short play followed the singing, and then, as was custom, it was the visitors' turn to sing to them. We croaked out a song by Creedence Clearwater Revival and followed that with "Amazing Grace." They either loved our singing or convincingly pretended that they did, although I'm sure that it had more to do with our enthusiasm than our virtuosity.

The final performance was a kind of line dance where everyone placed their hands on the shoulders of the person in front of them and followed. They of course expected us to participate, and after our rousing success with our singing, we were more than game. Other villagers jumped in, and soon there were perhaps 200 people in a huge line. We didn't realize that a trap was being sprung on us as the leader of the line began to circle in ever and ever tighter. All of a sudden, on a hidden cue, ten or so strong young men grabbed each of us in turn and flung us into the air as high as they could. I am a six-foot, 200-pounder, so my brain went into red alert as I rose into the sky, fearing the worst. Everything went quiet and into slow-motion for a few moments as I imagined the well-intentioned lads dropping me as I landed, not aware of how heavy Americans can be.

As I plummeted toward the stone pavers, I began to try to right myself and tensed for the inevitable crash when I felt 20 strong hands (these guys are farmers, after all) abruptly stop my fall and throw me into the air again. This time, I saw Shelly also airborne over the heads and outstretched hands and could not stop laughing as we were gently caught and set down on the ground. Everyone laughed along with us (at us?).

We then gathered with several of the adults and retired back to the communal house for a couple of hours of singing, drinking rice wine and tea, talking, asking questions (with the aid of our interpreter), and just enjoying each others' company. Since they had all grown up together, my wife observed that at times they were like one organism. The men or the women would all of a sudden break into the same song, and though we didn't understand any of the language, their deep understanding of and reaction to each other was something neither of us had ever experienced. The genuineness of the villagers and the overall experience of spending the night in a Dong village was one of the best cultural experiences I have ever had. We were sorry to move on the next day. I still have dreams of returning and spending a couple of weeks there and discovering more about them, learning some of their songs, and watching their lives go by in a completely different way from my own.

THE NATURAL BEAUTY OF GUIZHOU

The next day we visited a forest park and went hiking. The path was completely paved with stone. Our guide explained that when Chinese tourists hike, they don't want to walk on dirt. Stone is the preferred surface, and it was a little disappointing for us Westerners who prefer the feel of nature over a groomed path. Still the track wound through beautiful forests with Jurassic-era fern trees and other flora I had never before seen.

We ran into a similar scenario when it came to caving. I grew up wallowing through caves in Colorado with a few buddies, carrying packs filled with little more than backup lights, food, and a few safety items. In Guizhou, the only caves that people actually enter are those that have been developed with paths, handrails, lights, and guides. Guizhou's rock substrate is largely limestone and there are an estimated 600 known caves in the province and probably hundreds more on farmer's plots that no one has explored. I confirmed this hunch later on with some of the tourism professionals in LiBo County, who acknowledged that the locals don't go into the caves and that many have probably never been entered beyond the natural light emanating from the entrance. A caver's dream come true!

We visited three caves. In the Xiao Qikong Scenic Area, we went to the stunning Tianzhong Cave, which has an enormous entrance and a turquoise clear river that winds lazily out of the entrance. Also in the Xiao Qikong Scenic Area is Long Gong, which is filled with water, so we had to go through on a boat.

The most impressive was the enormous Zhijin cave, about a three-hour drive west of Guiyang. Zhijin rivaled any cave I've seen in the U.S.—including Carlsbad Caverns in New Mexico and the Cave of the Winds complex in Colorado—for its sheer size, voluminous rooms, and huge variety of stunning formations. As with other Guizhou caves, Zhijin is well set up for tourists, with lighting, paths, handrails in some spots, and guides if you want them. While I prefer caves in their natural state, the lighting does enable you to see the full depth and texture of the cave, and the paths keep people away from the more delicate formations.

We also had an opportunity to go rafting on the Luobei River, which is a couple of hours' drive from Guiyang. For many miles, the river huddles next to a stunning cliff face that must be at least 1,200 feet high. While the rapids didn't get much above Class III, I was assured that the high-water season produces much more exciting times. The forest leaned over parts of the river and gave it a feeling of being untouched by the inroads of civilization. The water itself was clear, cold, and inviting, although I was informed that no one usually swims in it. If only it weren't March. The rafts were exciting all by themselves, being built for only two to four people. I had never seen such small rafts. They made even the Class III rapids pretty entertaining.

Amazingly, none of the things we had seen or done up to that point was what the province considers its crown jewel—the Huanguoshuo waterfalls. They are about a two-hour drive from Guiyang and well worth the trip. The falls themselves are truly spectacular. They are 70 feet higher than Niagara Falls, though not as wide. While they may not rival Niagara in overall size, they certainly do in beauty and power. A footpath winds around the falls and actually goes into a 400+-foot cave behind them. We got a bit wet, as holes in the cave walls allowed us to see the falls from behind, while also allowing some water to splash in onto us. Apparently the falls are lit at night and the pictures I've seen of them are amazing…but we had other plans that evening and couldn't stay to check out the spectacle for ourselves.

This was the only time on our entire trip that we saw other Westerners—three Canadians who were teaching English nearby and had taken the day off to see the falls. There were also hordes of Chinese tourists. There are other interesting attractions in the vicinity, including a "garden" of odd-shaped, otherworldly pieces of stone and a small museum at a great archaeological site where full dinosaur skeletons (including the "Guizhou Dragon") have been unearthed.

Eight days in Guizhou was truly not enough. I have already been back for a second visit and intend to return again. For the adventure traveler who wishes to experience the beauty of nature, unspoiled cultures, interesting food, and fascinating music, Guizhou is an incredible place to visit. Get there before the crowds descend and change it forever.

WHY GO: China is and has always been a force to be reckoned with. With its booming middle class, enormous population, and strong culture, it will have a huge impact on the way the world will operate in the 21st century. China also contains some of the biggest tourist attractions in the world—the Great Wall, Summer Palace, Forbidden City, X'ian Warriors, and others.

This trip to Guizhou was about an entirely different experience. This is the China that many still imagine—the pastoral China with peasants still working the land, sharp dragon-clawed peaks jutting out of the mist, quiet back roads, and small, welcoming villages. Guizhou is also very unusual in that much of the population is not Han Chinese, the dominant ethnic group in most of the country, so the visitor gets a taste of culture—dress, food, customs, and language—that is literally not seen anywhere else on Earth. Since the province has so far largely missed the industrialization boat, it is a "throwback" to an earlier era and offers the tourist a completely unique experience.

SPECIAL ISSUES AND CHALLENGES: Accommodations in Guizhou are rustic, to say the least, and may not be to everyone's taste and comfort levels (e.g., thin mattresses, stark lighting, and bathroom maintenance that is not up to Western standards). The tourism infrastructure is still very basic, and not much English is spoken. This trip would be very difficult for most people without a guide/driver/interpreter.

Since this is a region that has had little contact with Western tourists, some Western customs might be out of place or even destructive. This is particularly the case with respect to tipping and monetary donations. The significance of this issue was brought home to us when we stayed in the Dong village. We found out that our host's darling little three-year-old girl was not actually theirs. They found her in a box as an infant one morning when tending to their fields. Moved by their love and compassion, we asked our guide if we could help out financially, as it was obvious that it is not easy to raise an unexpected child when you are earning less than $300 a year. Our guide suggested that we leave a $2 tip in our $3 a night room. This didn't seem like nearly enough, but our guide pointed out the potential problems that can result from large donations by well-intentioned Western tourists. When more money than the locals can even dream of is spent, thrown around, flashed, or even given in generosity, it can be a shock to the local community. Clearly, this issue has to be approached very carefully by visitors. View spending like a fire. Keep it in the fireplace where it belongs and it keeps everyone warm...but too much fire can be destructive.

VARIATIONS AND OPTIONS: Talk to a specialist about what interests you the most. If culture is your thing, with more than 50,000 villages in the province, Guizhou is so rich and full that you literally could not come close to running out of interesting places to visit. If outdoor activities are of more interest, the climbing, caving, trekking, and rafting are stellar. Since this is adventure travel, building a custom itinerary will serve you well.

RESOURCES AND INFORMATION: Book your trip with a Guizhou specialist. I recommend the following agencies:

China Professional
3300 Holcomb Bridge Road, Suite 23
Norcross (Atlanta), GA 30092, USA
Tel: 770-849-0300 / 800-25-CHINA
Email: *cptt@chinaprofessional.com*

China Travel Service
Main Office
119 South Atlantic Boulevard, Suite 303
Monterey Park, CA 91754
Tel: 800-890-8818, 626-457-8668
Email: *info@chinatravelservice.com*

San Francisco Office
930 Montgomery Street, Suite 501
San Francisco, CA 94133
Tel: 800-899-8618, 415-352-0388

FROM THE BRAHMAPUTRA RIVER TO THE MALABAR COAST (INDIA)

CHRISTINA HEYNIGER

One of the things that impresses me most about Christina is her willingness to dig below the surface of a destination and go beyond its familiar images and attractions—even when it's uncomfortable and off the beaten track. More than most people I know, she can uncover and immerse herself in the real, everyday life of a place and create a picture that is very different and much richer than what is seen in tourist brochures. I am always intrigued by her descriptions of her trips, but probably none have affected me as much as her trips to India. She is one of those rare writers who not only makes you imagine a place, but also makes you imagine yourself there. —Shannon Stowell

TRIP DESCRIPTION

Tinged with yellow, the tall green grasses gave off the fresh wet smell of the previous night's showers. The ground was marshy, and every step was accompanied by the sound of gentle suction and the rustling of grass. I tasted moisture in the air and also the faint residue of musky animal. Looking over the grasses and across the wide valley, I considered how easy it would be to get lost here in the breathy morning mist and hush, in these grasses so tall that, had I not been sitting on the back of an elephant for this early morning walk, I would have been easily engulfed by them.

It was an early November morning in the Kaziranga National Park of Assam, a state in India's far northeast. I had been invited here to learn about the state's adventure tourism resources as part of my consulting work before continuing my journey south to Kerala, a state located along India's far southwestern coast known for its own particular brand of nature and ecotourism. I had been to Kerala on a previous trip just a few months before, but only briefly, and I knew there was more to explore there. These two states, at opposite corners of the country, bracket much of what India has to offer the adventurous traveler willing to explore off the beaten tourist track. In these states, you can get away from India's teeming cities and image-making monuments like the famous Taj Mahal and simply enjoy the amazing diversity of India's scenery, cultures, and everyday life.

ASSAM

Despite the gorgeous landscape and its rich cultural heritage, Assam is largely overlooked by international travelers (fewer than 8,000 visited in 2005, according to Assam's state tourism department). Assam and its neighboring states, Meghalaya and Arunachal Pradesh in particular, are draws for adventurous travelers who like the thrill of exploration and don't mind a few bumpy roads and less-than-gleaming toilets along the way.

Kaziranga National Park is famous the world over as a UNESCO World Heritage site and for its success in protecting the rare one-horned rhinoceros. Although 60 percent of the world's population of these rhinos is thought to live in Kaziranga park, they can also be found in other parks in Assam— the Orange Reserve, the Laokhowa Reserve, the Pabitara Reserve, and the Manas Sanctuary.

On the elephant, I felt that I was almost part of the scenery in the expansive park. The many rhinos we saw that day were unflustered by our presence; even a mother with her calf continued munching grass without paying us much attention. I had been on game drives before in Tanzania, but had never been so close to rhinos or able to observe them from above. As I peered over the bristly-whiskered head of our elephant, I was able to make out the details of the leathery gray folds of the rhinos' skin, their prehistoric protective armor.

We also saw many birds, swamp deer, and monkeys—capped langurs, rhesus macaques—and kept our eyes peeled for monitor lizards and Royal Bengal tigers. Although many wildlife lovers are drawn by the dream of seeing one of these rare and glorious tigers, the rhinos and other animals I sighted more than made up for missing the shy, elusive Bengals.

THE BRAHMAPUTRA RIVER

Besides the rare one-horned rhinoceros, Assam is also known for the wide Brahmaputra River, affectionately known as "Baba Brahmaputra" ("Father" Brahmaputra) by proud Assamese. The river flows past fresh, undulating hills framed by the green and blue, often snowcapped, sub-Himalayan ranges that loom over Assam's northern border. The river enters Assam from the north, having already coursed for miles over the Tibetan Plateau and rushed through the narrow gorges of Arunachal Pradesh. Here it flows broadly and majestically on its way south into Bangladesh, where it empties into the Ganges-Brahmaputra delta.

It was a cloudy day when my two colleagues and our hosts in Assam took our trip on this powerful river, sitting side by side in a creaking wooden boat with peeling paint. Like most everything else I saw in Assam, nothing about this excursion felt even remotely like it had been manufactured for tourists. We found our boatman and his skeleton crew along a muddy shore and climbed aboard, everyone all smiles in the gulf between our languages.

As we set off up the river, which looked dense and thick and impenetrable, we had high hopes of seeing Ganges River dolphins. These unusual dolphins are an endangered species found only in the freshwater river systems in Bangladesh and India. We were sitting quietly on the chilly boat, bundled against the wind and splattering rain, when our boatman shouted excitedly—a group of dolphins was splashing in the river ahead of us. The next 40 minutes passed quickly while we witnessed a circus of these long-beaked dolphins playfully leaping up and out of the water. I experienced a sense of absurd joy seeing such a bizarre and unexpected display in the middle of a river, while I hunched against the rain on the deck of a wooden boat. Such wild, wild life exists out here in the middle of this river! When I saw two dolphins simultaneously break the surface of the wide flat river right in front of me, I really did wonder if perhaps there was a stage master lurking somewhere along the shoreline amid the frames of the delicate-looking Chinese fishing nets.

TEA AND SILK

Assam is green and lush with huge tea plantations that thrive in its cool air and warm sunshine. Sixty percent of the world's tea is grown in this state, and multiple generations of planters proudly pass the legacy of their work on to their children.

My base of operations in Assam was on one of these tea estates. I was lucky enough to stay at the Wild Mahseer Lodge (named for the large gape-mouthed golden fish endemic to the region) snugly tucked away within the confines of the Balipara Tea Plantation in Addabari. On the plantation, I stayed in the "Main British Assam Heritage Bungalow." In India, the term "bungalow" is used to describe luxurious and spacious accommodations, and this one surely lived up to this description. It has three bedrooms, each larger than my first 600-square-foot studio apartment, and beautifully appointed sitting rooms, a library, and a dining room. My two colleagues and I were each given our own rooms in the bungalow Attention has been paid to every detail here: the lighting is subtle and warm, Asian antiques are carefully placed, and everything is beautifully maintained. I felt like I had been invited to stay with very gracious and cosmopolitan friends for a few days.

We spent one morning wandering through the neat rows of tea in a gentle rain. As I walked, I exchanged looks of curiosity with the tea pickers, all women, as they methodically moved through the neatly squared off and groomed tea trees, plucking the leaves and depositing them in the long woven baskets they carried on their backs. They wore cheerful smiles, big aprons, and flip-flop sandals on their bare feet. Their toes were girlishly polished with red varnish. After drifting quietly through the fields for a couple of hours, we toured the processing plant, and then took part in our first tea tasting. Maybe it was the setting or perhaps it was the intimate hours spent watching the women pick the tea, but it was the best tea—strong and full, but with no bitterness—I have ever tasted.

If I'd never thought so much about tea before this experience, I'll probably never feel or look at silk in quite the same way, either, after my exposure to handwoven Assamese silk. Beautiful textiles and weavings are easy to find throughout Asia, and of course I've done my share of shopping on past excursions to Thailand, Cambodia, Bhutan, and Nepal, but the *muga* silk of Assam is indeed something special. Rare for its texture and shimmering warm color, the muga silk is highly prized in Assamese tribal culture. While people have tried to nurture the unusual silk worm (*Aantheraea asamenisis*) responsible for Assam's fine muga silk in Japan and other places around the world, the only place they continue to thrive is northeast India, in Assam and its bordering states.

KERALA

On my first trip to Kerala, I rarely strayed far from the beach. Like most everything in India, Kerala's beach scene ranges from the sublime to the surprising. One morning I sat in the sand on Lighthouse Beach in Kovalam, a natural bay on the Arabian Sea coast, sipping from a small plastic cup of warm chai (cost: three rupees—about ten cents U.S.—from the man with a container mounted on the back of his cycle cart). As I sipped, I looked out at the placid Arabian Sea, then shifted my gaze to the beach to take in the day's early, increasingly frenetic scene. Fishermen gathered on the crowded shoreline for the ritual hauling in of nets and pushing out of the heavy wooden boats. Dressed only in their brightly colored *lungis* and headwraps in the early mist, they chanted as they pulled, wedging their heels into the sand and agreeably adjusting their lineup for the lone tourist who wanted to pitch in and help.

The day was to end even more raucously, with a Kali festival. I have had several opportunities to appreciate Indians' love of firecrackers in the many festivals that give explosive voice to their adoration of the gods. On this night, drowsy from a day lazing at the beach, the jolt of the Kali celebration came like a direct shot of adrenalin straight into my bloodstream. Sipping my tropical cocktail and gazing out at the moonlit sea, I was startled to life as I watched a crowd dressed in red carrying a figure of the goddess on a palanquin up the beach. They accompanied their procession with crashing drums, banging cymbals, and of course firecrackers, sending an incredible amount of noise pulsing through the humid night air.

In addition to the allure of the ocean and its many beautiful beaches, Kerala also boasts an extensive network of backwater canals. An afternoon or a week's stay on a houseboat can be arranged with very little trouble. A Canadian friend and I spent an afternoon in the backwaters and found a quiet and peaceful contrast to the chaos of Lighthouse Beach. Resting under a thatch canopy with a cracked-open coconut on my lap, I sagged limply in my chair as our boatman slowly poled the boat through the labyrinth of canals. At sunset, the birds were busy and active, their tropical colors zinging along the surface of the water or posing perfectly on the extended branch of a tree.

TOO MUCH VADA!

Many people in the West are beginning to learn more about Ayurveda, an ancient Eastern healing discipline, and Kerala, famous as the birthplace of the discipline, is densely populated with luxury resorts and spas touting therapeutic Ayurvedic treatments. In Ayurvedic philosophy, all living organisms are made up of five elements, or *Panchamahabhutas*: space, air, water, fire, and earth. Each element corresponds to a bodily part, function, or process. When these five constantly fluctuating elements are in harmony, a body is thought to be in a state of good health.

Given Kerala's Ayurvedic reputation, I made it a point to find time for a short consultation. Instead of going to a commercial spa, I followed a friend's recommendation and sought out a true Indian experience by choosing a doctor practicing in his own small local clinic. My doctor was the warm and charismatic Dr. Vinoy Vighneswar. Operating out of a simple office and series of massage rooms steps from Lighthouse Beach, "Doc," as he is known, diagnoses me as having "too much air." He asks whether I grew up in a cold and dry climate (I did—Alaska!) and through a series of other questions and examinations of my skin, hair, and body shape, develops a plan for my treatment. The treatment took place over the course of five days—hot oil massages and a diet that avoided overly spicy foods and favored "heavy" fruits like bananas to help balance my "too much air" with "more earth." Although I was a bit skeptical at first, there's no denying I felt great after a week of this regime. The trick, of course, would be to keep the discipline and maintain the diet after I came home.

MEGALITHS

On my return visit to Kerala after my working trip to Assam, I resolved to leave the beach and explore inland and north. On a drive one morning to the small town of Marayoor from Munnar, a hill station in the Western Ghats, I watched in amazement as a new kind of rolling ocean—not water this time, but tea plantations—gradually gave way to towering sandalwood forests as we descended a winding road into a broad valley. Munnar's Kanan Devan hills are shocking in their cultivated expanse. Looking in any direction for miles, all I saw were steep hillsides carefully planted with brilliant green tea trees. The air here felt clear and crisp, and the colors seemed more brilliant in the fragrant sunshine. The effect of these hilly plantations is very different from the flat ones of Assam; here the contours of the deep valleys and hills have been laid bare with the clearing of the natural forest to make space for the tea trees. And while one part of my heart lamented the loss of the natural forest, the other reveled in the cultivated beauty of the hills of tea before me.

From a ranger's station in the sandalwood forest, we drove and hiked a short distance over bare stone hills and underbrush, eventually coming to a rocky outcropping overlooking vast fields of flowering sugarcane adjacent to a small jaggery factory. Just steps away from the thatched-roofed factory where I'd watched an old man tend a massive metal basin of boiling sugar, I found myself now peering into the stony cold silence of several ancient "dolmenoid cists," megalithic burial chambers.

These megaliths are thought to have been created between 4500 and 1500 B.C. Each one is made of four thick stones several feet long placed on edge and covered by a fifth, like a roof, known as the capstone. Chambers like these have been discovered in many places throughout Europe; on the Indian peninsula, more than a thousand have been identified. The megaliths of Marayoor are unmarked and unassumingly scattered about the hillside, somewhat obscured by weeds and earth, earning little attention from the locals or tourists. Roaming quietly among them, I felt awed and vaguely overwhelmed, trying to comprehend how they were constructed and how they have survived through the ages.

A TALE OF TWO VILLAGES

I love the way Indians seem to live in the ancient past and the modern present simultaneously. This is especially apparent in the South Indian district of Pathanamthitta, a couple of hours inland from Kovalam, where I visited the village of Aranmula. Here I strolled narrow dirt lanes past thatched-roofed and cement houses, some with satellite dishes positioned in the yards, others with chickens and goats. Cars and motorbikes sped along the main paved road, while down the side lanes people walked barefoot with large baskets balanced on their heads.

I was lodging at the well-known Vijnana Kala Vedi Cultural Center, founded in 1977 by Louba Schild, a Frenchwoman with a passion for India. The center has gained a global reputation for offering foreign students of all ages a rare opportunity to actively experience village life as participants, not observers, while learning native Indian cultural arts. Students stay in a scattering of houses located throughout the village and mix regularly with local people while going about their daily activities. They are also welcome to participate in local performances and gatherings.

First-time students as well as serious practitioners can develop their skills in everything from language (Malayalam, the primary language of Kerala, as well as Hindi and Sanskrit); Kathakali, a 17th-century style of dance-theater; Mohiniattam, a classical dance first performed by women in temples over a thousand years ago as an offering to God; Hatha yoga; Karnatic vocal music; wood carving; mural painting; and Kalarippayat or Kerala martial arts, one of the most ancient martial arts in the world.

In contrast to the villagers of Aranmula in Kerala's interior, the people in the gorgeous seaside village of Kumbalanghi near the major Indian port of Cochin share an entirely different lifestyle with visitors. People typically arrive at the village by canoe and stay in one- or two-night homestays. These homestays, in sparkling neat and tidy rooms in some of the village's newer homes, give guests the chance to take their time quietly exploring without being part of a structured program. The fact that a village such as Kumbalanghi still exists in such close proximity to Cochin, where you'll see billboards advertising IT training as you speed along a multilane divided highway, is testament to the concerted effort the people of Kerala are making to preserve their cultural heritage even as they embrace the modern world.

At Kumbalanghi, I relaxed with the view of the tranquil backwaters and delicate Chinese fishing nets and devoured a delicious lunch of fresh shrimp-and-fish curry and tapioca made from dried cassava. And although the name "Model Tourist Village" may cause some adventurers to shrink away with an expectation of performance-like faux representations of village life, nothing could be further from the truth at Kumbalanghi. The presence of tourists does not get in the way of the local people going about their regular business—fishing, crabbing, shrimping, harvesting clams, and making coir, a fiber fashioned from coconut husks that is woven into rugs, rope, and mats.

My visit to these two villages underscored the reasons why I had come to India. I have been curious and interested in the country for many years, but I knew I wanted to learn more than just what a visit to the Taj Mahal or a ride on a camel could teach me. I wanted to see something of the "real" India. The glimpses of rural India I had in these villages, and throughout Assam and Kerala in general, are not only foreign and "exotic" but also authentic, something deeper than simple sideshow attractions. As India moves rapidly forward into the future, it offers visitors a chance to experience the real life of its people—one in which ancient tradition frequently collides with modern technology and global attitudes.

WHY GO: India's power as a country with influence over global commerce, politics, and culture is rising. And where else in the world will you see such diversity, in its politics, wildlife, mountains, sea, and especially its surprising mix of cultures? It is the world's largest democracy, populated by Christians (including Baptists and Catholics), Hindus, Muslims, Sikhs, and Buddhists whose influences all bring their unique contributions to the traveler's experience. While these groups have their history of conflict, they often manage to transcend their differences. For example, in the elections of 2004, a leader of Roman Catholic background (Sonia Gandhi) gave way to a Sikh (Manmohan Singh), who was sworn in as prime minister by a Muslim (President Abdul Kalam)—and all of this in a country that is 81 percent Hindu!

This is an exciting, engaging time to visit. Travelers who go now will see a vibrant country in the midst of transformation, Also, many people speak English, especially in Kerala and Assam where education is excellent, simplifying travel for those who do not speak Hindi.

SPECIAL ISSUES AND CHALLENGES: In my experience, the issues for travelers in India stem mainly from the frequent Western desire to have trips carefully planned. India is a busy, busy place, and plans are always changing for one reason or another. But the people here are open, tolerant, and overwhelmingly welcoming to visitors. Whether you are traveling on your own or as part of a group, the biggest challenge you will have to overcome is yourself—your own fears of the unknown and your personal habits relative to planning and a desire for predictability.

People considering a course of Ayurveda should research their doctors well—even some of the high-end resorts in the area market Ayurveda spa packages but employ people as "therapists" who are not doctors. If you are serious about following a course of treatment, take your doctor's advice to avoid the sun and ocean, as pores opened daily through heavy oil massages may absorb too much salt and additional moisture from the ocean and salt air.

It is also important to note that a number of insurgent groups operate in Assam. Over the years, there have been terrorist attacks throughout the state, but most of the problems have been confined to remote areas that few tourists visit. That said, travelers should inquire locally about conditions that might put them at risk and plan accordingly.

VARIATIONS AND OPTIONS: India is so vast, diverse, and complex that the variations and options are almost limitless. You can easily tailor a tour based on wildlife, temples, cities, or mountains—or whatever your particular interest might be. Consult any of the excellent guidebooks on India published by National Geographic, Lonely Planet, and others for ideas, suggested itineraries, and detailed information on where to go and what to see.

RESOURCES AND INFORMATION: Although the travel program and experiences related in this chapter were not part of a planned tour supported from start to finish by a tour operator, its outlines and the people who brought it to life are readily accessible—as long as you're ready to strike out in regions of this majestic country where tourism has yet to become commonplace.

Do it yourself by contacting the guides I used—you'll get a complete education and have the freedom to modify your trip as you wish—or contact an established and reputable adventure tour operator.

How to Do It: Krishna Varier is the guide I used in Kerala. He can be reached at *mrkvarier@gmail.com*. If you want the experience of riding around in the classic Indian Ambassador, you can ask Varier that Ganga be your driver. For guides in Assam, inquire at Wild Mahseer. The tour operator Myths and Mountains *(www.mythsandmountains.com)* can also arrange tours throughout India.

Where to Stay: The website for Wild Mahseer is *www.nivalink.com/wild mahaseer/index.html*. For Wild Grass Lodge, where I stayed in Kaziranga, Assam, see *www.nivalink.com/wildgrass/index.html*. For a homestay in Kumbalanghi, I recommend Kallanchery Retreat *(www.kallancheryretreat .com)*. In Kovolam, I enjoyed the small, simple Subeesh Bhavan hotel *(www .subeeshbhavan.com)*; ask for Ambika. For luxury retreats, contact Mala Barua, founder of Mystic Asia *(www.mystic-asia.in)*, at *mala.barua@gmail.com*.

Other: For Ayurveda in Kerala, visit Dr. Vinoy Vighneswar's website at *drvighneswar@yahoo.com*. Information on the Vijnana Kala Vedi Cultural Center, can be found at *www.vijnanakalavedi.org* or by emailing *louba @vijnanakalavedi.org*. For the Kumbalanghi Model Tourism Development Society, see *www.kumbalangitourism.org* or email *info@kumbalanhitourism .org* or *kumbalanghitourismsociety@yahoo.co.in*.

OCEANIA &
ANTARCTICA

———✺———

VISITING THE JUNGLE TRIBES
OF PAPUA NEW GUINEA

MARTIN RICHTER

Marty and his wife, Carol, retired educators in their late 60s and early 70s, travel to more exotic destinations than anyone I know. They have been all over the world—e.g., Borneo, Alaska, Brazil, Iceland, India, Turkey, and Australia, to name just a few of the places they have visited in the last few years. They first began traveling to see birds, but the farther they went, the more interested they became in other wildlife as well as in experiencing exotic cultures and seeing beautiful scenery in remote destinations. This trip to Papua New Guinea is a perfect example of their broadening interests. Visiting the tribes of the jungle highlands before they became too much a part of the modern world ended up being one of the most interesting trips these seasoned travelers have ever taken. —Don Mankin

TRIP DESCRIPTION

We left the plane hesitantly and with some anxiety looked at the hundreds of villagers staring at us through the high fence that surrounded the small airfield. Behind the fence were men, women, and children standing motionless, just staring at our tourist group of 40, plus our two guides. We had been to other places where being totally surrounded by local people was unsettling—for example Kenya, Jamaica, and especially cities in northern India—but no place with as violent a history as that of the people of the jungle highlands of Papua New Guinea (PNG).

Until fairly recently, in modern terms, many of the highland tribes were locked in almost constant warfare with each other, warfare that was often marked by such terrifying ritual practices as headhunting. Although the

European powers that took control of the country in the middle of the last century banned this tribal fighting, disputes and conflict still erupt from time to time. Fortunately, these conflicts are more contained and less bloody than in the past. Nonetheless, this fierce history was the backdrop for our arrival in the tribal highlands of the island.

We left the airplane with trepidation, but it wasn't long before we noticed that the crowd was well behaved. Most striking, especially compared to our experiences in other countries, no one was begging or trying to sell us anything. Eventually, several men in ceremonial dress came through the fence and, again without asking for or even saying anything, posed for pictures for anyone who was interested. And they were exotically dressed indeed, with brightly painted faces and bodies, decorations made from bird feathers and plants, strings of pig tails around their waists, and most impressively, large wigs, also brightly decorated. One of the men appeared quite fierce, though after looking more closely, I detected the hint of a smile on his face as he twirled the stick that pierced his nose. This impressed me, but most of the members of our group grimaced while uttering exclamations of revulsion like "yech" for emphasis.

So went our bizarre introduction to the highland people of Papua New Guinea. New Guinea is the second largest island in the world, and Papua New Guinea is the nation comprising the eastern half. It is an extremely mountainous country, which makes travel difficult. There are not many roads, and only 4 percent of those are paved. Hence most of our travel was by small plane and boat. There are modern towns and cities, but the primary purpose of our tour was to see the people who still live in traditional ways in the small villages and clans in the highland valleys. There are about 700 such villages, each with its own governance structure and language. Our visit with these people over the next several days was almost like stepping back in time.

WIGMEN AND WILDLIFE

After a spine-jarring two-hour drive in a Land Rover over one of the worst roads I have ever seen, we arrived at our first destination, Ambua Lodge, a spectacular resort in the highlands. Listed in the book *1,000 Places to See Before You Die*, the lodge is situated at 7,000 feet on the border of a rain forest. It includes individual cottages with 180-degree glass windows opening onto river and forest views, set in beautifully kept grounds and gardens.

As we sat on the veranda, we watched the "wigmen" on the grounds of the lodge put on their makeup and decorations for a performance later that day. The wigmen are adult males who grow their hair long after entering adolescence, then cut it off to weave into wigs decorated with feathers, sticks, and other decorative objects. These wigs are then handed down from generation to generation, often being enhanced and elaborated in the process. At dusk later that day, on a hilltop overlooking a sharp drop into a valley with more mountains beyond—a truly spectacular location for a performance—the dressed-up wigmen did a sing-sing for us.

Sing-sings were initiated by the Europeans to take the place of tribal wars and give the men a substitute for their traditional warrior roles. Many clans and tribes participate in these events, which feature chant-like singing, drum playing, and dancing. The men decorate themselves and perform together to foster cooperation and friendships, though they still compete for prizes given to the winning groups. (We should note that our guides believed that the villages still fight, but the combatants keep quiet about it.)

The participants made themselves available for photographs throughout the sing-sings. The decorated wigmen looked fierce and intimidating, no doubt intentionally, but with us they always appeared gentle and cooperative. Though some could speak English quite well, they seldom spoke with us or even among themselves.

The animals in the area keep themselves well hidden, and our wildlife viewing suffered as a result. As long-time birders, we were especially disappointed we did not see more birds, particularly the spectacular and aptly named birds of paradise, which are more plentiful in New Guinea than anywhere else in the world. The popularity of the sing-sings may be the reason they were scarce, as the feathers from these spectacular birds are used for ornamentation. Although we saw the long feathers of hundreds of these birds adorning the heads of the villagers during the sing-sings, we spotted only five of the 13 species of this bird that are found in PNG (though sighting five species is actually considered quite good).

The flying foxes were a high point of our wildlife viewing. These huge fruit bats, unlike their smaller cousins elsewhere, roost outside during the day. At one of our resorts, they could be seen hanging head-down high in the trees all around the restaurant. Their squabbling and screeching could be heard even during the day, but toward dusk they are awesome, wheeling overhead, with their five-foot wingspans.

ON THE SEPIK RIVER

After a few days at Ambua Lodge, we flew to Madang on the coast for our boat trip up the Sepik River, the longest river in New Guinea (another entry in *1,000 Places to See Before You Die*). This boat would be our home for the next five nights as we cruised up the river to visit tribal villages in the highlands. We selected a small, inexpensive cabin with no windows, but it was perfectly serviceable since we used it only for sleeping.

We rose early to see the dawn and the beautiful world enfolding before us as we made our way up the river, past the lush and mysterious jungle shrouded in mist. We usually traveled at night, docking near the village we would visit the next morning. As the sun came up, we could see the kids, with few if any clothes, come out to play by the riverbank and start the day with an early swim. The men also came down to the river to prepare their dugout canoes, often with outriggers for stability, to fish on the river. At one point a man and a child passed close to our ship in a canoe. One of my most compelling memories from the trip is the image of the early morning sun bathing them in sunlight, while the water simultaneously caught their reflection and that of the shimmering green jungle on the opposite bank.

We visited at least one village each day, sometimes two or even three. Typical houses had walls and roofs made of palm leaves and bark, sometimes in neatly woven mats, and most all were perched on wooden stilts several feet above the ground. The stilts allowed cooling breezes to waft through the house and provided protection against flooding.

Each village welcomed us with a sing-sing performed by fully decorated villagers, both men and women, or with a skit. In one skit, two men who had stolen fruit from another man's trees were punished by an enchanted stick that lodged itself painfully between their legs. As they danced around yelling from the pain, the children in the audience laughed and squealed in delight. The most ambitious skits we saw, apparently sponsored by the Catholic Church, focused on violence toward women and the consequences of unsafe sex. In the latter, two men with large fake penises danced as an accompanying band repeatedly sang "HIV."

The people in all these performances were dressed in traditional garb (not much garb, actually), with woven fabrics garnished with lots of plant parts and bird feathers. However, some of the villagers in the audience wore more modern dress, including T-shirts and similar Western clothing, reminding us that these traditional people will inevitably be transformed by their increased contact with the outside world. We were grateful we could experience their world before the more drastic changes to come.

We were allowed to go anywhere in the village we wanted and to look at and photograph anything. Everyone posed if we indicated we wanted to take their picture, and sometimes even when we did not. One member of our group brought a Polaroid camera and took hundreds of pictures of villagers, which she handed out to the subjects. This was a wonderful idea. She was always surrounded by enthusiastic crowds and was often the last person to return to the boat. Another of our group was very popular with the children, running after them making faces and noises. The children seemed as curious about us as we were about them; at one village, a cluster of kids stayed partially hidden behind a hedge while peeking out at us during our visit.

LOW-PRESSURE SALES TACTICS

Each village also set out souvenirs for sale, usually just a line of blankets, wood carvings, gourds, and other items on the ground. There was no hard sell. In fact, the artisans did not say anything at all or even beckon to anyone to examine their wares. There was bargaining, of course. We were told by our guides to ask for a "second" price and to stop there. Some in our group bragged that they had bargained the price for an item from about $30 down to about $2, but we were not inclined to do that. Our most expensive purchase was a carved and painted wooden dish with crocodiles curved around the outside. Thirty dollars was the initial price; the second price was $20. We were more than satisfied with the second price; the dish was certainly worth that much to us and would go for much more than that if imported into the U.S.

The differing artistic styles in the villages enticed us to buy more than we had planned. In addition to the dish (now on our living room table), we bought six carved and painted masks (keeping three for our own mask collection), two carved wall hangings, a sculpture, a densely woven basket, and two penis shields, all for less than $100 and all welcomed as gifts by friends and family, especially the penis shields. People in our group generally bought even more than that, often big and impressive things that could not be carried back. Most had their souvenirs shipped at considerable expense, but we limited ourselves to what we could fit in our luggage. Fortunately, the memory of the gentle friendliness of these fierce-looking warriors hawking goods like any modern entrepreneur, one of our most important "souvenirs," took up no space at all.

As comfortable as we felt among these exotic people, we did not get to talk to them much—but when the opportunity arose it was always interesting. One day we met a man standing outside a Catholic church. Most of the population of Papua New Guinea is Catholic, but he was a Seventh-Day Adventist. He told us that he wanted to build a church for his religion, too. After letting that sink in for a moment, he mentioned that one problem was that there were only two other Seventh-Day Adventists in the area.

SING-SING AT GOROKA

Our tour concluded with two days in the highland town of Goroka for its annual sing-sing, the largest and most famous one in the country (the third New Guinea entry in *1,000 Places to See Before You Die*). It was a great way to conclude our journey, and one of the highlights of our travels anywhere. Saturday, the first of the two days we attended, was a practice day for the groups, with Sunday the actual day of competition.

The show was spectacular. The participants, roughly 70 groups of maybe 15 to 40 individuals, change the color of their skins with pigments ranging from darkest black to reddish tan. They reserve the brightest colors for their faces—mostly reds with some whites, yellows, and blues—and adorn themselves with shells, parts of plants, feathers from the exotic birds of paradise, and cut-off pig tails around their waists. They wear few clothes; their genitals are covered but most of the women are topless. Many groups carry banners and other large decorations. The groups enter what looks like a large football field one at a time through a gate, dancing and chanting as they continue to the other end of the field to their assigned place. This continues until more than half the field is filled with bobbing and chanting people with brightly painted faces and elaborately decorated bodies. The only thing I can compare this to is the Mummers Parade in Philadelphia on New Year's Day, but this is far more spectacular (perhaps because it was so different).

Only the paying spectators like us were allowed inside the field with the participants. There were covered bleachers for us at the end of the field, but we were also allowed on the field and could circulate freely among the groups, looking and taking pictures of anything we wished. Several times I was almost run over by different groups as they marched to their locations. They paid us no notice whatsoever except to pose for pictures. Most of the spectators stayed in the bleachers out of the sun, but I spent hours on the field, so high from the experience that I stayed until I became dehydrated and had to retreat to the bleachers for some water and shade.

The only sour note was the riot that broke out at the end of the first day. It gave us a bit of a scare, reminding us of the area's violent and not too distant past. After most of the participants had left the field, music was still playing over the loudspeakers. The people in the crowd outside the fence apparently wanted to get in to dance but were barred from entering, so they began throwing stones onto the field. Our worried guides herded us back onto our buses, parked in the middle of the field out of range of the rocks. The "professional" security force inside the field with us did not make us feel very secure when they just ran around shouting at the rock throwers and then started picking up the rocks and throwing them back! Finally the buses made a run for it out of a side exit away from the rock-throwing crowd. The incident did not deter us from returning for the second day of the sing-sing, which came off without a repeat of the previous day's ruckus.

WHY GO: Papua New Guinea provides a unique opportunity to comfortably visit people who are still relatively untouched by modern civilization. Discover this unspoiled gem for yourself before it is changed forever by designer T-shirts, TVs, and hordes of tourists. The spectacle of the sing-sing at Goroka is itself reason enough to go. We had seen suggestions in guidebooks to go to other sing-sings because the one at Goroka is so well known and crowded with tourists, but we found this to be not at all true. The few hundred tourists who were there were easily lost in the tumult of the far more numerous participants.

SPECIAL ISSUES AND CHALLENGES: Physically, this was not a difficult trip. Travel is by plane and boat with only a moderate amount of walking. However, Papua New Guinea is not yet well prepared for tourism. Our guides worked especially hard to make sure we would get where we were supposed to go because they were unsure that commitments would be fulfilled. Be prepared for problems with transportation and lost luggage—something on the order of 17 bags in two locations were (temporarily) lost on our tour alone. Our tour company advised us to just stay cool and that becoming angry and demanding would probably be counterproductive.

Packing is challenging: the small planes allow only one checked bag, not exceeding 22 pounds, per person. You must be able to tolerate frequent plane flights—there were eight internal flights on relatively small planes and 17 flights in all.

VARIATIONS AND OPTIONS: The operator for our trip, International Expeditions (IE), often offers additional options on its tours, but these vary from year to year.

RESOURCES AND INFORMATION: In 2007, IE *(www.ietravel.com)* charged about $7,700 per person, not including international airfare, for a 19-day trip in the least expensive cabin on the boat. It can also book your international flights. Other companies offering versions of this trip include Abercrombie & Kent *(www.abercrombiekent.com)*, which started offering a 16-day trip in 2007 for about $8,000 (not including airfare).

SAILING IN THE
KINGDOM OF TONGA

HAZEL CAPER FURST AND CHARLES FURST

S ailing is Hazel and Charlie's first love, with the possible exception of each other and their kids. Both of them came to sailing relatively late in life—Charlie was 50 when they bought their first boat—and they haven't stopped since. Besides the waters off Southern California, they have sailed in the Pacific Northwest, the Caribbean, and Mexico, as well as a rousing 1,200-mile open-water crossing taken by Charlie to deliver a boat from St. Martin to Newport, Rhode Island. Nowadays, they can often be found on the *Reprise,* their 46-foot Kelly-Peterson, cruising the coast of Mexico. A few years ago they chartered a boat in Tonga, where their cultural adventures were as much fun as the sailing. —Don Mankin

TRIP DESCRIPTION

The world starts its day in Tonga. Located on the international date line, this group of islands in the South Pacific is the first place where the sun comes up. We wanted to celebrate that unique distinction by being the very first people on Earth to see the sun rise one morning. Before dawn, we were in the cockpit of our boat—looking east across the water to the horizon. And sure enough, the sun rose magnificently, right on schedule—just for us. It was delightful to take advantage of being in just the right place at just the right time to do something we could never do anywhere else in the world. Then, feeling very special indeed, we went below to make coffee and plan our day.

After several years of chartering sailboats for vacations in the cold waters of the Pacific Northwest and the crowded waters of the Caribbean, we wanted to try sailing in a remote tropical paradise. A friend recommended Tonga. He had spent some time in the South Pacific and considered Tonga to be the most unspoiled of the South Pacific islands. Looking at the map, we could see that Tonga was remote, far away not only from the U.S. but also from just about anywhere else. Its geographical position ensured that it was tropical. And when we got there, we found out that it was indeed a paradise.

ABOUT TONGA

The Kingdom of Tonga is one of the last true kingdoms—i.e., the government is run entirely by a hereditary king and a council of nobles, not by an elected legislative authority. Captain Cook called Tonga the "Friendly Islands" when he first landed on its shores in the 18th century. They have changed little since then. This is especially true of the northernmost island group, Vava'u.

Vava'u is everyone's fantasy of a South Pacific paradise: tropical islands, deserted beaches, pristine coral reefs, and warm trade winds. It's an archipelago consisting of 40 islands, 21 of them uninhabited, covering an area of about 30 miles by 20. Sitting behind a barrier reef, the islands of Vava'u enjoy protection from the South Pacific swells.

Outside of Neiafu, the capital of Vava'u, there are only small villages, sometimes just one per island. Villages consist of a meetinghouse/church and several small thatched-roof houses called *fales* made from mostly local raw materials. Most houses have a pig or two roaming around, often a dog, and some chickens. By law, each Tongan family is granted a plot of land on which to grow their own vegetables. The land is quite fertile; one definition of the word *tonga* is garden. Since Vava'u has only about 20,000 people spread among the various islands, overcrowding is not an issue. The natural world, especially the sea, dominates here, not buildings or other man-made structures.

Tongans are Polynesians and Melanesians and are among the largest and heaviest people in the world. They are very friendly to outsiders, especially in Vava'u, where contact with tourists has been limited. Tongan custom emphasizes hospitality and sharing. The Western concept of strict individualism is antithetical to the community and familial spirit that governs Tongan life.

The only way to access the vast majority of islands of Vava'u is by small, private boat. There are no cruise ships or commercial passenger vessels. Except on the main island, there are no cars, shops, office buildings, hotels, restaurants, bars, or discos. It is just the people who live there, along with the very occasional travelers on private or chartered boats, like us.

The beaches and water activities are excellent. You can cruise the island group and anchor in a series of tropical coves with unspoiled white sand, coral reefs, and friendly locals. The distances between islands are short, and the trade winds make for dependable sailing. Since the waters are protected, the conditions are generally benign and the seas relatively flat. The water is crystal clear, and the coral reefs are unspoiled. Colorful species of fish, turtles, rays, and dolphins abound, and humpback whales occasionally pass by on their annual migration. Gemlike tiny islets with lagoons beckon to be explored.

SAILING AND EXPLORING

After a 125-mile flight from the Tongan capital city of Nuku'alofa, we spent the first night at our hotel in Neiafu. Neiafu has a population of approximately 6,000 and is the only real town in Vava'u (complete with streets, cars, government offices, commercial buildings, etc.)

We took possession of our boat the next day. We chose to have it provisioned by the charter company, which supplied all the food and drink and stowed it away for us before we came aboard. We also decided to hire a captain for the first two days to accustom us to the boat and the sailing conditions in the area. It alleviated a lot of stress to have a guide who was familiar with the peculiarities of that particular boat and also knew the reefs and prevailing sailing conditions.

Our boat, a Beneteau 38, sailed beautifully in light wind and was easily reefed (sails shortened) for heavier blows. She was well equipped, with two cabins, two heads with showers, and the latest sailing gear. We towed a dinghy with an outboard motor to explore the anchorages.

Our captain, Lua, was large and beefy like most Tongans, but remarkably nimble around the boat. He was more than happy to let us do as much of the sailing work as we wanted, which in our case turned out to be most of it. We relied on him to keep us away from the reefs and to tell us about local wind and other conditions. Lua was also a very good cook, not only preparing the scallops we gathered by the reef while trying out our snorkel gear on our first day but also treating us to his specialty, garlic potatoes.

Most days would start with an early morning swim off the boat, then we would haul in the anchor and sail a short distance to another island. Afternoons found us snorkeling on unspoiled tropical reefs in water with extraordinary visibility, exploring deserted beaches and underwater caves, or just following the shoreline in our dinghy. We visited small villages, walked through lush vegetation, and investigated tide pools. Sometimes we just sat in the cockpit reading and staring off at tropical seascapes. At night we were lulled to sleep by the gentle rocking of the boat and the sound of crickets drifting across the water.

We had most of the anchorages to ourselves (well, us and a few fruit bats). When there were others in the anchorage, more often than not they were friendly Aussies or Kiwis living full-time aboard their own boats. If you felt like socializing, it was easy to find company for the cocktail hour at sundown.

Overall, we spent two weeks in Tonga, ten days of which were on the boat. We visited many islands and anchorages, some for the night and others for just a few hours. Each had its own unique charms. The coral gardens at Nuapapu were resplendent with incredible colors, textures, and shapes; the turquoise waters of Nuku were picture-postcard perfect; and for amazing shells, there was Ofu. One of the smallest inhabited islands, Taunga, was tantalizingly beautiful, lush, vibrant, and sparkling, but the wind was up and unfavorable so we were not able to land. We just stayed as close as we safely could and savored it before sailing off to a more protected spot.

This wasn't the only time weather interfered with our plans; it was a factor throughout our trip. A stationary low brought rain and caused higher-than-usual winds and swells. We had looked forward to exploring Swallow's Cave on the northwest tip of Kapa, which is said to rival the iridescent colors of Italy's Blue Grotto when the sun is out, but conditions were dicey when we got there. The only access is by dinghy and it requires favorable seas. Since the water is 250 feet deep and anchoring is impossible, one of us had to stay on board, circling around for an hour or so while the other took the dinghy over to explore the cave. By the time Charlie got back to the boat after his excursion into the cave, the swells were too big for Hazel to go, so she missed out.

GOING TO CHURCH, TONGAN STYLE

On one of the first mornings, we awakened to the sound of roosters greeting the dawn from a small village across the anchorage. The local radio station played Polynesian music. The sounds were exotic and soothing.

It was Sunday. We had heard that the church services in Tonga featured beautiful singing and that outsiders were welcome. Tonga has a long history of contact with missionaries from the Methodist Church, and the people are devout Christians. While Lua stayed aboard, we landed our dinghy on the beach and walked a short distance to the island's village of Falevai. The village has a few houses and a wooden one-room church with a porch in the South Pacific style.

The church services had started, and we could hear this beautiful chorus of hymns in Tongan. We sat in the back and could see that everyone, absolutely everyone, in the congregation was singing, and singing full out. About 30 people were there, and the bare surfaces of the walls rang with the resonance of their voices. While we couldn't understand the words, the singing was so beautiful and heartfelt that it brought tears to our eyes.

People were dressed in their Sunday finery, which for the men consisted of jacket, dress shirt, tie, and *ta'ovala,* a woven grass mat that is wrapped around the waist over a cloth skirt or pair of pants. The ta'ovala is a very important part of Tongan tradition and is worn by men at all formal occasions, much like a tie in Western cultures. The women had ankle-length garments also secured around the waist with a ta'ovala.

We were lucky to be there on a day when a visiting noble, a chief from another village, as well as a guest minister were in attendance. The visit was an occasion for a big feast. We were the only *palangis* (foreigners) there, and we inferred from our pretrip research that it would have been an insult to the villagers if we had not stayed for the feast. This was not a commercial event staged for tourists, it was an honest-to-goodness feast in the age-old Tongan tradition and we were awed to be a part of it.

After the service, we retired to the community hall, a palm-thatched large open room, where we sat cross-legged on grass mats and were regaled with copious dishes of pork (cooked luau-style), different kinds of fish, potatoes, yams, watermelons, bananas, sweet fruit wrapped in leaves, cellophane noodles, hash, sausage, a tray of sweets and apples, and much more. There were also small "trees" made out of driftwood hung with prized victuals, such as cans of Spam (Spam is prized throughout the South Pacific), displayed as decoration and as a symbol of richness and plenty.

Following the meal, the men gathered on one side of the hall to drink *kava,* a strong intoxicating tea brewed from a plant found throughout the South Pacific. They invited Charlie to join them (it was for men only); he took his place in the circle and shared the brew that was passed around again and again. Being a polite guest, and a man who has been known to share a brewski or two with his buddies, he fit right in.

Throughout the feast and the drinking of the kava, people took turns telling stories. They spoke in Tongan, so we couldn't understand what they were saying. Each rendition was only five minutes or so in length and was punctuated with laughter or tears, often both. We thought they must be eulogizing a recently departed family member, especially since many of the speakers held black articles of clothing as they spoke. But upon checking this theory with Lua later that day, it turned out that the stories were from the Bible, sometimes personalized and embellished. Their sincere expressions of emotion were for people who had died at least 2,000 years ago, but that did not prevent them from feeling a genuine personal connection with the stories and the people.

Lua's explanation for the fervor and emotion of the storytellers, as well as for the way they welcomed us into their world, was, "It's important for one's heart to be open." We took that to mean being open to other people and empathizing with their lives, their travails, and their stories, biblical or otherwise. There is no better description of the typical Tongan—big, open-hearted, outgoing, and warm. Most important from our perspective is the wholehearted welcome they extend to the occasional traveler who has the good fortune to pass their way.

WHY GO: *Why* is easy; *when* is a bit more complicated. May to November, the Tongan winter, is high cruising season. Southeast trade winds blow at 15–25 knots, but seas are flat. The climate is pleasant, but a bit cooler than what you might associate with the tropics, the temperature rarely rising above 80°F. In the Tongan summer, December through April, breezes are lighter, typically 10–20 knots, and it's warmer and more humid. The average maximum temperature in summer is closer to 90°F. The summer is also the rainy season, so most people prefer to visit in winter.

SPECIAL ISSUES AND CHALLENGES: Activities for this trip are well suited for older travelers. By chartering a boat with a crew, the physical demands are entirely optional and you can choose how much sailing, anchoring, rowing, and swimming you want to do. In addition, a boat is a good place to relax if you become tired or sore.

The water temperature is cooler than normal for this latitude (around 75°F most of the year), so be sure to take a lightweight wetsuit or at least a vest and hood if you want to spend a lot of time in the water.

If you are prone to motion sickness, it often helps to take antiseasickness medications for a day before you get on the boat and for a day or two after that. By the second day, in these protected waters, you'll probably have your sea legs.

When visiting villages in the islands of Vava'u, it is a good idea to bring along gifts for the local children, such as ballpoint pens, balls, flashlights, or other inexpensive articles. These can be donated to the local school.

Education is highly valued in Tonga and the literacy rate is 98 percent, so school supplies are always welcome. We also brought several yards of cotton cloth to give as gifts. We donated our first aid supplies—bandages, antibiotics, and other medications—to the local hospital before we returned home. Everything was gratefully accepted.

In addition to our regular camera, we brought along a Polaroid. This was a big hit. We took pictures of the people of the village posing with the visiting nobles. We also took photos of kids, and for many parents, it was their first picture of their children.

VARIATIONS AND OPTIONS: The trip described here does not require any previous knowledge of boats or sailing. We are experienced sailors, so we chose to do most of the trip with no crew. For those who are not as proficient, though, or who just don't want to do all that work, crewed charters are available. A family or group of up to four couples can charter a boat for a week or longer. Depending upon the size of the boat and the number of passengers, a one- or two-person crew can pilot the boat, cook all the meals, and allow you to just enjoy the many pleasures of the region hassle-free. Or you can help out as much as you want and use the opportunity to improve your sailing skills.

If hanging out and exploring is not enough activity for you, kayaks, surfboards, and fishing, diving, and windsurfing equipment are also available for rent.

Not everyone gets to participate in a genuine traditional Tongan feast honoring a visiting noble, but there is a commercial Tongan feast available for visiting yachts on Aisea's Beach, on the island of Pangaimotu, featuring good food and traditional song and dance.

RESOURCES AND INFORMATION:

Getting There: The trip to Vava'u is a long one. It's remote—that's why it's interesting. You need to fly into Nuku'alofa, the Tongan capital on the main island of Tongatapu. Two airlines fly from Los Angeles to Tongatapu, Air New Zealand (one nonstop flight and others that connect through Auckland) and Air Pacific (connecting through Fiji). Peau Vava'u Airlines or Airlines Tonga (operated by Air Fiji) fly the last 125-mile segment from Nuku'alofa to Neiafu, the largest town in the Vava'u island group, where the local sailboat charter companies are based.

How to Do It: There are two sailboat charter companies in Neiafu: Footloose Charters/Tonga *(www.footloosecharters.com)* and The Moorings *(www .tongasailing.com)*. Sail Connections *(www.sailconnections.com)* can connect sailors with private boats for lease.

Where to Stay: We stayed at the International Dateline Hotel *(www.dateline hotel.com)* for our first night in Tongatapu. Its main advantage is that it is right in the heart of things in Nuku'alofa. There are more resort-like hotels outside of town with more amenities and ambience if convenience is not your main consideration. In Neiafu, we stayed at the Paradise International Hotel (no hotel website available; check with on-line travel sites such as Travelocity, TripAdvisor.com, etc.).

HANGING OUT IN ANTARCTICA

DON MANKIN

hortly before my 60th birthday, I received a call from an old friend to tell me about a very special present he was giving me to mark the event. A successful consultant and corporate speaker, he had arranged a trade with one of his clients, a large travel company offering high-end trips throughout the world: a day of his services in exchange for the trip of my choice from their wide-ranging catalog.

After I picked myself off the floor and finished blubbering my gratitude, I went to the company's website to start looking for a trip that would appropriately celebrate the transition to my golden years. After scanning through the luxurious safaris, river cruises, and archaeological expeditions, my eyes fell on their Antarctica offerings—not the typical cruise along the Antarctic Peninsula, but a flight into the interior on a converted Russian cargo plane to spend eight days in a tent on the ice. I knew immediately that this was it! Despite some bumps along the way, this trip fulfilled all my expectations and more and is still one the most memorable trips of my life.

TRIP DESCRIPTION

As usual I was the first to wake up. I didn't know the time, since I wasn't wearing my watch and was once again in one of those distant places where the sun never sets. It was the middle of summer, but there was a fresh layer of snow covering my tent and everything else as far as I could see—which was very, very far in the frozen interior of the world's coldest, driest, and most barren and surreal continent.

I tried not to wake up my tentmate as I slid out of my warm sleeping bag, put on the many layers of clothes that make life possible in this frozen corner of the world, and crawled out of the tent onto the cold, silent "beach" where we had set up camp the day before. No one else was up. "Perfect!" I thought, as I looked for the faint edge between the gravel moraine at the base of the hills behind our camp and the ocean of ice that curved off in waves toward the horizon—except that there was no horizon. The snow was still blowing, and if it weren't for our colorful tents and the vague silhouette of the hills and the "shoreline," it would have been a total whiteout. I scanned the line of the shore into the distance where it disappeared behind a hill. "If I follow the edge, I can't get lost," I told myself.

Getting lost would be bad news. There were only 11 of us in our temporary overnight camp, another 20 or so in the semipermanent base camp at least 10 miles away, and then it was hours by air (more about that shortly) to the nearest city, Punta Arenas, at the southern tip of Chile. Trying to find a lost camper here would be futile and dangerous. "But I can't get lost," I nervously repeated to myself with less then total conviction. Besides, I would never have another opportunity like this. What would it feel like to be so totally alone and so completely out of touch, in this, the most remote and weirdly beautiful place on Earth?

I had spent most of my life dreaming about visiting other worlds and other planets, reading science fiction voraciously as a preteen, studying engineering as a college student in the hopes of becoming an astronaut, and after finally realizing that I did not have the "right stuff," using my vacations to seek out some of the most otherworldly places on our own planet. This was the closest I would ever get to fulfilling that near impossible childhood dream. How could I pass it up?

I started to walk, or more accurately shuffle, through the fresh snow. In a few minutes, the camp was a mere handful of dots in the distance, and a few minutes after that, I was around the bend and out of visual contact with the only connection I had to the human world. All I could hear was the rush of blood in my temples as my heart raced in fear. Or was it excitement? I couldn't tell. I stopped and sat on a rock and stared out at the vast expanse of ice before me. All I could see was white on white in the soft sunlight. I had never felt so insignificant. There was no wind, so the only sound I could hear, besides the pounding of my heart, was the flutter of snowflakes falling on the ground. I took a few deep breaths, stopped thinking, and just stared into the vastness, in splendid solitude, trying to take it all in. My mind became as empty as my surroundings. In the words of those who have spent lots of time on the ice, I was having an "Antarctic moment."

After a few minutes of this, I can't say that I had had enough, but my sense of survival started to reemerge. Besides, I was getting cold. I sighed, arose from the rock and began to make my way back along the visual lifeline to the hot coffee and breakfast that was waiting for me at camp.

THE MOTHER OF ALL WEATHER DELAYS

This otherworldly shuffle was the highlight of a trip full of highlights. It seemed as if everything that had gone before built up to that transcendent moment. Given how the trip began, I was more than a little surprised that I had managed to make it to that rock behind the hills at the end of the world.

The trip actually began in Punta Arenas at the bottom of the Western Hemisphere on the fabled Strait of Magellan. After flying into Punta Arenas, my wife, Katherine, and I spent the week and a half prior to the Antarctic trip exploring southern Patagonia, especially the iconic granite towers of Torres del Paine National Park (see p. 274).

We returned to Punta Arenas for the orientation meeting that marked the official kick-off to the Antarctic trip. Of the 50 or so people at the meeting who would be flying into Antarctica on the next, approximately weekly flight, there were only a handful like me, curious travelers simply hanging out in Antarctica for a few days. The rest were an assortment of hard-core adventurers: mountain climbers there to climb Mount Vinson, the tallest mountain on the continent; cross-country skiers planning on skiing the last degree to the South Pole on a two- to three-week journey; and two crazy but charming Irishmen on an expedition to travel the almost 700 miles from the South Pole to our camp at Patriot Hills in two kite-powered sleds (see *www.icekites.com /home.htm* for more information on their expedition).

At the meeting, we learned that weather had indefinitely delayed our flight. Snow had covered the natural blue-ice landing strip at the base of Patriot Hills where the camp was located. The strip is usually kept clear by the winds sweeping down from the hills, but there had been too much snow and not enough wind over the last few days. We had to wait for the winds to pick up again and do their work, aided by the minimal snow removal equipment at the camp. The irony was that if the winds were *too* strong, we wouldn't be able to land. We had to wait until the conditions were just right. These delays were fairly typical and warnings to that effect were prominent in the information packets we were all sent, but I guess no one wanted to believe it would actually happen.

We were stuck in Punta Arenas until further notice. Since Katherine was scheduled to leave the next day, I faced the prospect of losing not only her companionship but also her language skills—she was the only one between us who spoke any Spanish. For the next few days, I had to get by with *gracias, agua,* and *cerveza* and little else. I quickly ran out of ways to amuse myself as one idle day stretched into the next. Fortunately, I made fast friends with the ice kite Irishmen and passed the time drinking with them in the local pubs and swapping stories.

We finally got the word at our impromptu Christmas Eve dinner that things were looking up and we might be able to leave in a couple of days. We stayed close to our hotels until we were told to get ready, and then we were finally on our way.

A FLIGHT LIKE NO OTHER

The adventure began with the flight, on a former cargo plane with a pallet of passenger seats bolted into the frame. There were no windows at the seats and only a few portholes. Most of the flight was over water, so there wasn't a lot to see, anyway. But as we approached the continent, we caught a glimpse of some icebergs through the portholes. A chill went up and down my spine at my first sight of Antarctica.

Landing was the true adventure. There was no control tower, only a handful of staff on the ground with a radio, wind sock, and signal mirrors to flash at the pilot so he could align the plane with the runway and see where it began and ended. With no windows, we couldn't tell what was going on. As we started our approach, we just sat and waited anxiously for the first bump and bounce of the landing, then hung on for dear life as the plane continued to bump and bounce down the runway for what seemed a lifetime. It took a while to come to a stop since only engine braking is used to slow the plane, not wheel brakes so that it doesn't do 360-degree circles on the ice runway.

When the plane finally came to a stop, we all put on our heavy down parkas, the cargo hold door dropped down, and we filed out onto the ice for our first breathtaking, heart-stopping view of Antarctica at ground level. The ice sparkled in the incandescent light and did not end until it reached the sky.

After looking around in wonderment for a moment or two, we shuffled off to the camp a mile away, to be greeted by the staff with cups of hot soup and by the departing clients eager to get on the plane for their long-overdue return to civilization and warm beds. After finishing our soup, we were taken to our large insulated tents, each with wooden floors, two cots with mattresses and box springs, a chair, and two bedside tables. I unpacked my sleeping bag, took off only those clothes I had to, and crawled in for my first night on the ice.

THE CAMP

Patriot Hills Camp is located at the base of the hills and in close proximity to the mountains that make up the Independence Range. It is run by Antarctic

Logistics and Expeditions, the only private company allowed to operate in the interior of Antarctica for commercial purposes, that is, tourism and expedition support. The camp is about 670 miles from the South Pole and can hold up to 60 people at a time, including staff. During my visit, there were on average 25 guests (including the mountain climbers, skiers, and other people on expeditions that would pass through) and 20 or so staff. The camp is open from early November through January and shuts down the rest of the year due to the perpetual dark.

The dining and cook tent was the center of activity and, with 24 hours of daylight, the activity occurred around the clock. The tent was fairly warm and there were always high-carbohydrate snacks available to keep us energized. The camp employed two chefs, and the food was quite good. There was also a maintenance tent for the snowmobiles and Sno-Cat that are essential for exploring the area, and a radio tent for monitoring the weather and keeping in touch with expeditions, the main office back in Punta Arenas, and the planes, including the four located at the edge of the camp.

These planes—a Cessna, a single-engine Otter, a Twin Otter, and a modified turbine DC-3—are used to take people to various points of interest on the continent, including the South Pole, the Vinson Massif, and the penguin colony. They all take off and land on skis and use a different runway—a patch of snow-covered ice alongside the camp marked by black trash bags—than the one used for the "international" flights to and from Punta Arenas.

Two of the most important facilities, and the ones that inspired the most comments and jokes, were the urinal and the aptly named "ice toilet." Without going into much detail, all waste, including human waste, is shipped back frozen to Punta Arenas in the rear cargo hold on each return flight. So, for obvious reasons, the facilities were not heated. As you might imagine, we soon learned how to get in and out as quickly as possible.

There were a couple of other tents—a wash tent and a library—but that was pretty much it. It was enough. Not luxurious accommodations by any stretch of the imagination, but it did provide for a modicum of comfort and security in a place where one might expect neither.

LIFE ON THE ICE

Our days were surprisingly full, given the obvious restrictions on our movements and activities. The first was spent orienting us to our environment via an informal but riveting presentation on how to avoid serious injury (e.g., frostbite, hypothermia) and a tour of the area around the camp on cross-country skis. On the second day, we were taken on snowmobiles to the base of the hills, where we explored the pools of ice formed from the runoff of melted ice and snow from the hills. The ice in these pools had crystallized in a variety of patterns that were best observed, believe it or not, by lying face-down and peering deep into the ice pools for several minutes.

On the third day, we rode on the camp's Sno-Cat over a pass to the other side of the hills to explore other ice pools, ridges of rock, and the expanse of ice between them. In some places, the rocks in the ice, warmed from the sun's rays, had melted holes large enough to crawl into, which of course we did to create some very amusing and bizarre photo ops. We finished off the day by sledding back down the pass in a long, uninterrupted run that was one of the most exciting rides on ice I have ever taken without getting hurt.

The overnight camping trip, where I had my "Antarctic moment," took place on the fourth and fifth days. We rode the snowmobiles for several miles under overcast skies to our campsite for the night. The quality of the light and the way it played off the ice was unlike anything I had ever seen before or since. Long waves of deep blue ice rolled away from the base of the mountains. The sparkle of the muted sunlight reflecting off the indentations on the ice surface looked almost like white-capped waves on the ocean. The experience was similar, I imagine, to being on another planet.

We climbed up into the hills on the sixth day for an incredible view of the infinite expanse of ice before us. The featured activity on the seventh day was a five-mile cross-country ski trip to view a DC-6 that had crash-landed in 1993 (everyone survived). Since then, blowing and falling snow has covered all but the tail, which sticks above the flat white plane of the ice like a surrealistic monument. That afternoon, each of us had a chance to go up in the Cessna for a 45-minute tour of the surroundings by air.

On day 8, we had the choice of returning to Punta Arenas on the plane bringing in the next group or taking our chances on the next flight a week later. I would have liked a couple more days on the ice, but I wasn't sure that another week, or possibly even more if the weather turned bad, wouldn't have been too much of a great thing. I packed my gear, climbed up the loading ramp of the plane, and filed past the drums of frozen waste in the cargo area to get as close to the front as possible, in case their contents began to melt before we landed.

WHY GO: Of course, the main reason for going is the truly unique experience. As Adm. Richard Byrd described his winter on the ice in 1934, it was "something that I had not fully possessed before: appreciation of the sheer beauty and miracle of being alive."[*]

Another plus was the knowledge we gained about the natural history and geology of the continent—and, by extension, the natural forces that have shaped our world—from the camp staff and the National Science Foundation scientists camped a mile or so away who dropped by from time to time. We also learned a great deal about the threat of global warming. Not that you can actually observe the effects as you go about your daily business, but just being embedded in the environment and in daily contact with people whose lives are inextricably linked to the phenomenon is an eye-opener. There is also much to be learned from the expeditions that pass through or end at Patriot Hills. Expedition members made presentations about their adventures and were available to discuss their experiences at most any time.

The social dimension of this trip was an unexpected plus. The group—staff, guests, and expedition members—included people from Canada, Chile, England, Scotland, Ireland, Belgium, Northern Ireland, New Zealand, and the U.S. I made several good friends on the ice, including one of the ice kite Irishmen, Brian Cunningham, and a couple from New York whose input was very helpful in writing this chapter, Mariquita and Matt Blumberg (see the trip description on their website, *http://home.nyc.rr.com/blumbergs*).

Those enthralled by the penguins in the movie *March of the Penguins* may be disappointed by the lack of wildlife. The interior is too harsh to support indigenous plants, birds, or mammals. All of the wildlife is along the coast. The tour company also runs trips to the emperor penguin colonies a couple hundred miles away (see p. 270).

SPECIAL ISSUES AND CHALLENGES: Clearly, this trip is not for everyone. Most people will be deterred by the prospect of cold, communal toilets, and the ever-present danger of slipping on the ice. However, it wasn't as cold as I expected. The air temperature usually ranged between 15° to 25°F, but with the almost constant sun and warm clothes, it sometimes felt almost balmy when the wind wasn't blowing. In fact, the biggest problem I had was overdressing and sweating from the exertion of skiing and hiking

---

[*] Byrd, Richard E., *Alone*, G. P. Putnam, New York, 1938.

in the hills. This can be dangerous in polar climates, so I spent a lot of time thinking about what I was wearing, what I should take off, and when. The temperature in the tent was bearable, if not toasty, getting up to as high as 50–55°. As my New York friends note on their website, "When we woke up in the morning, everything was warm except for those things that weren't in our sleeping bags—noses and ears."

The camp was also not as peaceful and quiet as I would have liked. The tent rattled in the wind, and the 24 hours of daylight plus the warmth of the dining tent, which was only a few yards away from our tents, encouraged people to hang out and talk at all times of the day and "night."

Despite the potential hardships, a healthy traveler of almost any age can do this trip. One of the guests on our trip was 80 years old. It was not always easy for her, but she felt that the opportunity to fulfill her life-long dream of visiting the South Pole was well worth the inconveniences. The staff was very solicitous and attentive to her needs and even put a portable toilet in her tent to make things easier for her.

VARIATIONS AND OPTIONS: Antarctic Logistics and Expeditions charged $16,950 for this trip in 2006–07. The trip described here can be supplemented with a flight to the South Pole for an additional $16,000–17,000. Two-week trips to visit the emperor penguin colonies cost more than $38,000. The company runs a number of other Antarctic trips, ranging from $15,000 to run a marathon on the ice to $59,000 for a 50-day ski trip all the way from Patriot Hills to the South Pole.

An increasingly popular option for those who don't relish the idea of sleeping in a tent on the ice is one of the many expedition cruises that visit the Antarctic Peninsula, as well as South Georgia Island and the Falklands (e.g., see *www.zeco.com*).

RESOURCES AND INFORMATION: Antarctic Logistics and Expeditions is the only company that offers private, nonresearch trips into the interior of Antarctica. See its website for more information (*www.adventure-network .com*) or contact them at *general@adventure-network.com* or 801-266-1592. The company provides detailed information on how to get to Punta Arenas, where to stay, where to eat, and so forth.

TWENTY-SIX ADDITIONAL TRIPS, IN BRIEF

———《》———

I n January 2007, we conducted a survey through the Adventure Travel
Trade Association *(www.adventuretravel.biz)* of several hundred tour
operators around the world, asking them to recommend trips especially
suited for seasoned travelers. The respondents suggested a number of very
exciting and unusual trips that are included in this chapter. The descriptions
here are brief, but like the preceding chapters, they cover a wide range of
destinations, levels of difficulty, and activities. Check the websites for prices
and other details.

NORTH AMERICA

POLAR BEAR TUNDRA LODGE
ADVENTURE (MANITOBA)
Natural Habitat Adventures (www.nathab.com)
Observe polar bears up close and in their natural environment for seven
or eight days on the shores of Hudson Bay in northern Canada. Travelers
view polar bears on daily excursions in special protected vehicles as well
as from the Tundra Lodge, a rolling hotel located on the subarctic tundra
outside the small Canadian outpost of Churchill, Manitoba. Dogsledding
excursions, helicopter flights, and presentations by indigenous people are
also available.

WHY GO: The focus on nature and local culture makes this a particularly
interesting destination for people who are curious about this fascinating
corner of the globe and concerned about our environment, especially the polar
bear, one of the first large mammals to be impacted by global warming.

SPECIAL ISSUES AND CHALLENGES: The trip is not physically demanding.
There is very little walking, and because of the almost constant presence
of polar bears, guests spend most of their time inside the lodge or the
tundra vehicles.

WOLVES AND WILDLIFE OF YELLOWSTONE (WYOMING)

Natural Habitat Adventures (www.nathab.com)

On this seven-day safari, travelers will track wolves, moose, elk, bears, and other wildlife amid the awesome peaks of the Grand Tetons and the snowy valleys of Yellowstone National Park. This trip also features excursions by snowcoach to Old Faithful to watch geysers erupt against the snow, as well as by sleigh across the National Elk Refuge to see the vast winter herds up close.

WHY GO: This adventure gives people the chance to experience the incredible beauty of Yellowstone in wintertime and to explore areas where typical tourists never go. Guides keep in constant communication with scientists studying the wolves to give guests the best opportunity to see them in their natural environment.

SPECIAL ISSUES AND CHALLENGES: Conditions are snowy, icy, and/or wet, and it can get very cold. However, hikes are moderate in physical exertion and a good amount of wildlife viewing takes place from the vehicles. Travelers can opt to not go on particular excursions.

ALASKA INDULGENCE PACKAGE

Alaska Railroad (www.akrr.com/arrc1000.html)

This 12-day trip visits Denali, Talkeetna, Anchorage, Seward, Kenai Fjords National Park, and other highlights of the state of Alaska by train, bus, and floatplane. Activities include rafting, hiking, and fishing, as well as visits to museums and galleries.

WHY GO: The trip enables travelers to experience the beautiful scenery and wildlife of Alaska while staying in rustic but comfortable backcountry lodges. Travel is by floatplane and first-class rail service.

SPECIAL ISSUES AND CHALLENGES: The trip does not involve any overly strenuous or risky activities. Travelers must be able to climb in and out of small aircraft.

OREGON: LAKES, LOOKOUTS, AND SHAKESPEARE

Austin-Lehman Adventures (www.austinlehman.com)

Crater Lake National Park and its surrounding area are the locations for this six-day trip. Activities include rafting on the wild Class II–IV Rogue River, hiking on park trails, and biking along the crater rim. An additional feature is a visit to the town of Ashland for a performance of classic Shakespearean theater under the stars at the renowned Oregon Shakespeare Festival.

WHY GO: This is an active adventure to one of the least visited national parks in the U.S., blended with local culture, cuisine, and VIP seating at an internationally acclaimed festival. The level of accommodations is upscale.

SPECIAL ISSUES AND CHALLENGES: This is an active and multisport trip, but it also provides ample options to reduce (or increase, if desired) the level of difficulty and exertion. The rafting is Class II–IV with the option of walking around the largest of rapids. Van support adds flexibility to the biking and hiking.

LATIN AMERICA AND CARIBBEAN

AMAZON EXPLORER (BRAZIL)

G.A.P Adventures (www.gapadventures.com)

Cruise down the Amazon for nine days on a first-class, 19th-century-style riverboat. The trip includes daily excursions to view the diverse wildlife of the Amazon such as sloths, egrets, macaws, capuchins, squirrel monkeys, toucans, pink dolphins, and more. The excursions also provide an opportunity to meet the local people, including a shaman who will explain traditional use of medicinal plants.

WHY GO: The Amazon is one of the most biologically diverse habitats on Earth. This trip provides an opportunity to experience this endangered place while it is still relatively undeveloped, and to experience it in comfort.

SPECIAL ISSUES AND CHALLENGES: The trip involves light walking and hiking that is suitable for most fitness levels.

HIKING THE GALAPAGOS (ECUADOR)

Adventure Life Journeys (www.adventure-life.com)

Hike through the archipelago's remarkably surreal landscape on this unique, nine-day, land-based Galapagos adventure. Travelers will explore some of the islands' most remarkable areas via hikes through El Chato Tortoise Reserve and to the rim of the Sierra Negra volcano, and will snorkel in waters rich in marine life in Tortuga Bay, El Junco Lagoon, and other locations.

WHY GO: This is a more active, intimate alternative to the traditional Galapagos cruise. This trip visits areas on the islands where most cruises cannot go and offers an up-close look at the rich and diverse wildlife for which these islands are famous—rays, sea turtles, sharks, sea lions, tortoises, iguanas, and thousands of seabirds.

SPECIAL ISSUES AND CHALLENGES: The Galapagos are volcanic islands, so trails are often uneven and rocky. Travelers should be prepared for long walks and easy-to-moderate hikes.

END OF THE WORLD TOUR (SOUTHERN PATAGONIA IN ARGENTINA AND CHILE)

Adventure Life Journeys (www.adventure-life.com)

This 11-day trip combines a land-based tour of Los Glaciares National Park in Argentina and Torres del Paine National Park in Chile with a five-day small-ship expedition through the Strait of Magellan. Daily Zodiac trips allow exploration of the remote landscape and its animals and flora.

WHY GO: This tour visits remote and secluded regions that are widely celebrated but not so easily visited. It is designed to allow travelers to experience the wilds of Patagonia without sacrificing comfort. For example, accommodations for part of the trip are at the exclusive EcoCamp, which is designed to protect the beauty of Torres del Paine and enable travelers to learn about and experience sustainable tourism. The five-day expedition cruise follows ancient explorers' routes to remote regions accessible only by sea.

SPECIAL ISSUES AND CHALLENGES: Because of its remoteness, the transfer in and out of Torres del Paine National Park is quite lengthy and involves a bumpy ride on dirt roads. There is quite a bit of hiking/walking involved, so travelers should be moderately fit and prepared to venture on foot.

TREASURES OF TRINIDAD AND TOBAGO

Paria Springs Eco-Community (www.pariasprings.com)

The aim of this seven-day trip is to see the best that Trinidad and Tobago have to offer. It includes three days at the world-famous Asa Wright Nature Centre, two on Trinidad's North Coast to see nesting leatherback turtles, and two in Tobago's scenic Speyside for snorkeling, scuba diving, and kayaking. The tour also includes hikes to see red howler monkeys and scarlet ibis and to Tamana Cave for a close encounter with thousands of bats.

WHY GO: This trip showcases the natural wonders and culture of Trinidad and Tobago. Travelers visit both world-famous and off-the-beaten-path locales. It is a custom, not a group trip, so it can be modified to meet the needs of individual travelers.

SPECIAL ISSUES AND CHALLENGES: There are no technical or exceedingly tough hikes, though for some the climb to Tamana Cave can be challenging. Assistance is available to help individuals manage difficult portions of the trails, and there are other options for those who cannot do a particular component of the tour.

FIBER ARTS OF THE
OAXACA SOUTH COAST (MEXICO)

Traditions Mexico Hands-On Tours (www.traditionsmexico.com)
This is a nine-day pioneering tour of the remote Oaxaca coast of Mexico, one of the most traditional indigenous areas in Mexico. Through a focus on fiber arts (traditional weaving, cotton spinning, and natural dyeing), travelers gain special access to villages and households and meet traditional artisans for a peek into this unique world.

WHY GO: This is a trip for people who are curious about culture and history and who want to expand their knowledge of this unique part of Mexico. Although the region's beautiful textiles are the focus of the trip, it's the window into the traditional way of life of the indigenous people that makes this tour so special.

SPECIAL ISSUES AND CHALLENGES: While this trip is not at all physically demanding, it does require the traveler to deal with some heat and humidity, funky bathrooms on home visits, and walking on uneven surfaces in the homes and on the beaches.

EUROPE

A LAND BEFORE TIME (ICELAND)

Scott Walking Adventures (www.scottwalking.com)
This is a six-night, seven-day hiking adventure through the dramatic, otherworldly landscape of Iceland, featuring volcanoes, glaciers, geysers, hot springs, lava fields, and rugged coastlines. Highlights include visits to the Blue Lagoon, the Hidden Waterfall, and the Great Geyser.

WHY GO: Besides the incredible and unique natural beauty of Iceland, the country is also noted for its progressive and innovative culture, especially in the use of sustainable energy and development of ecofriendly lifestyles.

SPECIAL ISSUES AND CHALLENGES: The trip is suitable for all travelers able to walk on rugged terrain (e.g., on lava fields, but not up mountains).

INN-TO-INN SEA KAYAKING AND HIKING (CRETE)

Northwest Passage (www.nwpassage.com)

The location for this eight-day, seven-night hiking and warm-water sea kayaking trip is the remote south coast of Crete and its magnificent mountains, Minoan ruins, and small, picturesque villages.

WHY GO: Most tourists in Crete stay on the north coast, leaving the south coast still quite undeveloped and remote. Two towns visited on this trip are accessible only by water. The trip also includes visits to ruins and other historical sites. Guests stay in small, family-owned, seaside inns.

SPECIAL ISSUES AND CHALLENGES: The trip is van-supported, so participants have multiple options to paddle or hike as much or as little as they want each day. Previous kayaking experience is not required. Most hotels do not have elevators but arrangements can be made to accommodate those who are mobility challenged.

CROATIA'S DALMATIAN COAST

Classic Journeys (www.classicjourneys.com)

Explore Dubrovnik, the Peljesac Peninsula, and the island of Hvar on this seven-day, six-night cultural and walking adventure. The tour combines easygoing walks with activities and visits designed to immerse travelers in the culture and history of Croatia.

WHY GO: Croatia was not open to tourists for almost a decade, due to its war with Serbia. The country is not the usual first place that people visit in Europe, and is often only discovered after the more classic European destinations. Croatia appeals to the seasoned traveler looking for a slightly more exotic experience.

SPECIAL ISSUES AND CHALLENGES: This tour blends three to four hours of walking each day with visits to cultural and historic sites. The tempo is active but casually paced. The terrain varies, with easy-to-moderate walks along the coastline, inland, and on peninsulas and islands.

THE ARCTIC: SPITSBERGEN EXPLORATION CRUISES (NORWAY)

Hurtigruten, formerly Norwegian Coastal Voyage (www.hurtigruten.us)

Travelers can choose among three different cruises, ranging from nine to 16 days, exploring the Svalbard Islands in the High Arctic, north of mainland

Norway. This is the last wilderness of Europe, rich in unspoiled nature and wildlife with enormous glaciers, polar bears, whales, seals, abundant birdlife, and rare Arctic flowers.

WHY GO: This region of the Arctic is unknown to much of the world. The cruises are in expedition-size boats that are small enough to negotiate fjords that larger vessels cannot enter. Small landing boats also take guests ashore for closer explorations. Visits to local communities and onboard lectures provide further knowledge about the natural and cultural history of the region.

SPECIAL ISSUES AND CHALLENGES: Ships are not equipped for people in wheelchairs. Most of the landings (once or twice a day) are by Zodiac or PolarCirkel boats, and the terrain on shore may be fairly rugged. Guests need to be able to get in and out of the boats and be reasonably surefooted.

SELF-GUIDED CYCLING IN THE LOIRE VALLEY OF FRANCE
Pure Adventures (www.pure-adventures.com)
Cycle through the heart of the scenic Loire River Valley on an eight-day self-guided trip. The region is known for its colorful vineyards and orchards and magnificent castles. The flat-to-rolling terrain is perfect for cycling.

WHY GO: The trip goes through countryside and villages and to places rarely visited by mainstream tourists. It includes cultural sites and one-to-one experiences with local people. The trip is more appropriate for people with some travel experience who are independent and comfortable sorting out their own activities during the day. Accommodations are in historic, three- to four-star chateaus. The cost of this self-guided trip is less than guided group tours.

SPECIAL ISSUES AND CHALLENGES: There are few constraints for those in good health who exercise regularly. Riding is on average 25–28 miles per day over flat to slightly rolling countryside. The cycling routes have little traffic and are safe. The weather is pleasant during the main season, May through September.

AUSTRIAN ADVENTURE
Euro-Bike and Walking Tours (www.eurobike.com)
This seven-day bike tour in the beautiful and pristine Tyrol and Salzburg areas of Austria features majestic waterfalls, fantasy caves, and endless vistas of fortress-topped hills. The trip also includes optional opportunities

for hiking, glacier skiing, paragliding, and visits to castles, scenic villages, and the region made famous by *The Sound of Music.*

WHY GO: In addition to the beautiful countryside, the region is rich with history and culture.

SPECIAL ISSUES AND CHALLENGES: This is an easy to moderately easy bike tour. There are some hills, but nothing extremely challenging. A support van is available to offer a lift to those who prefer to stick to the flat parts of the tour. Clients should spend at least a few hours a week biking before the trip, even though the cycling can be made very easy for those who ride occasionally in the van.

AFRICA

ULTIMATE SEYCHELLES WITH ALDABRA ATOLL

Zegrahm & Eco Expeditions (www.zeco.com)

This is a 14-day small-ship expedition cruise aboard the three-masted French sailing vessel *Le Ponant* through the Seychelles Islands to Aldabra Atoll, which is known for its giant Indian Ocean tortoises and endemic bird species. The itinerary focuses on birding, snorkeling, diving, and natural history.

WHY GO: This cruise gives passengers the chance to learn more about the natural history and biology of the region, as well as the opportunity to enjoy white sand beaches and coral reefs. The flora and fauna are rich in diversity and often unique to the region.

SPECIAL ISSUES AND CHALLENGES: This is a moderately active but not strenuous trip, involving snorkeling and walking along beaches and on short, level trails.

ETHIOPIAN EXPLORATIONS

The Fazendin Portfolio (www.FazendinPortfolio.com)

Several options are available for exploring the rich history, culture, and unique terrain of Ethiopia. One is a 12-day tour of the northern part of the country to visit Bahir Dar, Gondar, Lalibela, and Axum, famous for 17th-century castles, 12th-century rock-hewn churches, and gigantic obelisks over 2,500 years old. More adventurous travelers can opt for an 11-day trip to the Danakil Depression in the Afar region, a "cradle of mankind" known for the large number of hominid remains that have been found there. This extremely remote area along the Great Rift is also one of the lowest and hottest places on Earth. Only the Afar people have been able to inhabit this difficult region, and continue to live today as nomads, tending to their livestock, as they have for centuries.

WHY GO: While Ethiopia is still off the beaten path, the destination is growing increasingly popular. Travelers can still walk through uncrowded centuries-old churches, talk with priests, and touch ancient manuscripts (though this practice may well be discontinued soon).

SPECIAL ISSUES AND CHALLENGES: The tourism infrastructure in Ethiopia is relatively undeveloped. Hotels are clean and comfortable but very basic. The Danakil Depression adventure involves camping and travel through extreme environments.

ON FOOT IN THE SERENGETI (TANZANIA)

KE Adventure Travel (www.keadventure.com)

The highlight of this ten-day trip across the Serengeti is a three-day walking safari led by seven-foot Masai guides. The trip features visits to Tarengire and Serengeti national parks, Ngorongoro Crater, and Olduvai Gorge, camping out under the African sky, plus an optional ascent of Lengai Volcano.

WHY GO: This is one of the best opportunities to see the "big five" of African game viewing—elephant, rhino, leopard, lion, and buffalo—in the heart of the Masai countryside. It is a much more intimate experience than game viewing in four-wheel-drive vehicles.

SPECIAL ISSUES AND CHALLENGES: For the most part the trekking is easy and fully supported and is suitable for anyone who enjoys walking. The drive to the volcano is very rough, however, and the optional hike up is quite difficult.

MOROCCO: FROM FEZ TO MARRAKECH

Country Walkers (www.countrywalkers.com)

Experience the diverse landscape of Morocco via a 12-day walking tour of the unspoiled trails of the Atlas Mountains, the pink sands of Morocco's highest dunes, and the vibrant souks of Marrakech. During the trip, participants have considerable contact with the indigenous Berbers and the off-the-beaten-path history and culture of the region.

WHY GO: This Morocco tour provides an in-depth perspective on this rich and multifaceted area by traversing the country—venturing from ancient city to remote villages—and experiencing a range of natural climates. The trip exposes parts of Morocco not readily visited and offers such unique features as interaction with the Berbers, an overnight stay in a luxury desert tent camp, and cultural encounters with musicians, weavers, potters, and other artisans.

SPECIAL ISSUES AND CHALLENGES: This tour incorporates rugged walking on trails (3–7 miles per day, with options on some days) on uneven rolling terrain, unpaved paths, and trails with exposed roots, rubble, and rocks, plus ascents and descents of up to 1,000 feet. Travelers need to be steady of foot and must prepare for this terrain. As with all travel, the change of diet presents the potential for discomfort, although the food is exceptionally healthy and fresh.

ASIA

THE PEPY RIDE (CAMBODIA)

PEPY (www.pepyride.org)

This multiweek educational bicycle trip across Cambodia mixes volunteer opportunities with visits to traditional tour locations, ranging from the spectacular ruins of Angkor Wat to the beaches of Sihanoukville.

WHY GO: The trip features travel on off-the-beaten-track dirt roads to schools and rural communities where participants are sometimes the first foreigners to visit. Along the way, riders will learn about Cambodia from PEPY's partner organizations, teach environmental lessons at local schools, and experience the beautiful rural landscape of Cambodia.

SPECIAL ISSUES AND CHALLENGES: All participants must be very physically fit. Some roads are very rough, and some days are quite long (60 miles). This trip would be ideal for avid cyclists.

SECRETS OF SIAM (THAILAND)

Journeys International (www.journeys-intl.com)

This eight-day journey explores the Golden Triangle—the wild frontier where Thailand, Laos, Myanmar, and China meet—a region infamous for both legal and illicit commerce. Among the available options are visits to exotic markets and temples, hikes to lush rain forest waterfalls and hot springs, elephant rides, treks to mountain tribe villages, and a Thai cooking class.

WHY GO: This exploration of northern Thailand enables travelers to experience local traditions and immerse themselves in a culture very different from their own. The Golden Triangle is a place where people from four nations meet in the markets to bargain as they have for centuries. It is an area that is largely unknown to tourists. Accommodations are in ecolodges and nature resorts including a lodge above the Mekong River with views of the borders of Myanmar, Laos, and Thailand.

SPECIAL ISSUES AND CHALLENGES: This trip mainly involves easy walking. The optional biking and full-day treks to the rain forest waterfalls and hot springs are more difficult. Guests should be in good shape for these optional activities.

MONGOLIA: LAND OF THE NOMADS

Boundless Journeys (www.boundlessjourneys.com)

This 15-day trip ranges from the Gobi Desert to Lake Hovsgal, Mongolia's largest lake. For most of the trip, travelers stay in authentic *gers* (yurts) to experience the Mongolian nomadic way of life. They will also visit Kharakhorum, the 13th-century capital of the Mongol Empire created by Genghis Khan, and Erdene Zuu, Mongolia's largest Buddhist monastery. Optional hiking and horseback and camel riding are also available.

WHY GO: This trip offers a rare glimpse into the last unspoiled wilderness in Asia and an ancient culture of nomadic horsemen and traditions dating to the time of Genghis Khan. Relatively unchanged for centuries, Mongolia has one of the last remaining horse-based, nomadic cultures in the world.

SPECIAL ISSUES AND CHALLENGES: The trip involves long drives on some days, primitive (but authentic) accommodations on several nights, and walks and optional daylong horseback riding.

JOURNEY THROUGH CENTRAL ASIA: THE FIVE STANS

MIR Corporation (www.mircorp.com)

On this 21-day tour, participants form a modern-day caravan for an epic journey to the independent Central Asian countries of Kazakhstan, Kyrgyzstan, Uzbekistan, Tajikistan, and Turkmenistan. In addition to the natural beauty of Central Asia, this in-depth visit also offers a rare view of the cultural personality of each country through their energetic cities, alleyways lined with breathtaking blue-tiled mosques and madrassas, teeming bazaars, and Silk Road oases.

WHY GO: This tour is perfectly suited for seasoned travelers, as it goes beneath the surface and beyond the ordinary to places often considered off-limits to outsiders, while maintaining a moderate pace. What sets it apart from other tours of the area is the level of accommodations: Western-style four- to five-star properties are used throughout the tour.

SPECIAL ISSUES AND CHALLENGES: This trip is moderately active due to the daily walking involved, and travelers may encounter unpaved sidewalks. Flexibility, a sense of humor, the ability to walk at least a mile a day, and tolerance for the shortcomings of developing nations' tourism infrastructures are essential for the enjoyment of this trip.

FROM THE GREAT WALL TO RED SQUARE: A TRANS-SIBERIAN RAILWAY ADVENTURE

MIR Corporation (www.mircorp.com)

This 18-day tour travels by second-class rail to provide maximum contact with local people. The highlights are the cross-cultural opportunities: meeting Chinese, Mongols, Buryats, and Russians as the tour crosses three countries and thousands of miles, tracing the old tea route from Beijing to Moscow.

WHY GO: With a maximum group size of ten, this interactive cross-cultural journey is especially suited for the seasoned traveler who has "been there, done that." Participants will go beyond the usual tourist stops to meet the locals and experience their lives.

SPECIAL ISSUES AND CHALLENGES: This trip is moderately active and fast paced, covering substantial distances with extensive walking and stair climbing. It requires flexibility and a willingness to accept local standards of amenities and services. Accommodations vary from superior tourist-class hotels to very basic and simple facilities including *ger* camps in Mongolia (with shared shower and toilet facilities), a rustic lodge at Lake Baikal (with outhouse-style facilities; no indoor plumbing), and berths on overnight trains (shared toilet but no bath facilities). Although services are improving in the region, travelers will most likely encounter problems with plumbing, bureaucratic constraints, road conditions, unpaved sidewalks, uneven surfaces and steps, and a lack of public restrooms.

INSIDER'S VIETNAM BY RIVER, RAIL, BIKE, AND TRAIL

Asia Transpacific Journeys (www.asiatranspacific.com)

On this 17-day trip, travelers will first visit Vietnam's major cities for an introduction to this fascinating country, then journey to the countryside for biking, trekking, and kayaking.

WHY GO: This trip features a variety of activities that are designed to help travelers soak in the flavor of specific locations—for example, trekking and biking in remote hill tribe villages and kayaking among the dramatic limestone formations of Halong Bay. Active days of planned activities are balanced with free days for personal exploration and relaxation. Accommodations are all five-star with amenities.

SPECIAL ISSUES AND CHALLENGES: Participants on this trip should be in good shape and comfortable with biking (intermediate level—flat terrain/touring bikes), kayaking (beginning level), and hiking (intermediate level).

OCEANIA

THE BEST OF NEW ZEALAND HIKING

Mountain Travel Sobek (www.mtsobek.com)

This 11-day trip takes travelers on the best of New Zealand's world-class hiking trails, including a four-day hike along the acclaimed Milford Track. This adventure also includes hiking at Mount Cook National Park, part of a spectacular World Heritage site where most of New Zealand's highest mountains and largest glaciers are found; a hike into a remote alpine valley in Mount Aspiring National Park; and an optional glacier walk accessed by helicopter.

WHY GO: The best way to see New Zealand is on foot, especially with experienced Kiwi guides who are passionate about their country and very keen on showing it to visitors. Accommodations throughout are in comfortable and casual hotels and lodges.

SPECIAL ISSUES AND CHALLENGES: The hikes are moderate in nature and suitable for any fit, healthy person, although the Milford Track may offer a bit more of a challenge. Travelers will carry a day pack large enough to contain their personal belongings (clothes, toiletries, etc.) for the entire four-day excursion (food, sleeping bags, and the like are all provided at the lodges). The trails vary dramatically, from well-groomed paths to steep rocky declines, climbs over rocks and tree roots, and the occasional fording of a river after a heavy rain. Hikes will last between six to eight hours a day.

We could have included many more trips in this chapter. As access opens up to different parts of the world—and probably, more important, as our imaginations soar—the possibilities are limitless. Consider this very brief sampling of trips you may have never even imagined:

- Learn to be a game ranger in South Africa. This 28-day trip includes subjects like handling snakebites, how to approach wildlife, and more *(www .fazendinportfolio.com)*.
- Flyfish for the world's largest salmon. Mongolia's taimen is larger than Alaska's king salmon *(www.mongoliantravel.com)*.
- Tour the vibrant *favelas* (slums) of Rio de Janeiro with an experienced guide to see the complexity of Brazilian society and how tourists can make a difference *(www.favelatour.com.br)*.
- Trek across the Taklimakan Desert in China along a portion of the legendary Silk Road *(www.trekchina-tour.com)*.

If you can dream it up, it probably exists. If it doesn't, perhaps you have an idea for a new adventure travel business. Let us know. Maybe we can include it in our next edition.

WHAT'S NEXT IN ADVENTURE TRAVEL

===≈≈≈===

I n 30 years, the adventure travel industry has morphed from nearly no industry at all to thousands of organizations, large and small. These organizations offer a wide variety of trips throughout the world and a growing range of products and services, from clothing and equipment to insurance and Internet search engines.

Like any dynamic industry, adventure travel is constantly being shaped by changing trends—unfamiliar destinations are discovered, different activities gain favor, new issues and concerns emerge. Some of these trends may soon affect where you go and what you choose to do with your time and money. Understanding these trends and making informed, responsible decisions is the key to adventure travel experiences that will not only meet your needs and provide you with a more enriching trip but also help sustain our world.

Three issues will shape adventure travel in the years to come. One is sustainable tourism, which includes ecotourism, green tourism, and geotourism. This is not a future trend, it is a current reality. As more and more travelers visit isolated, out-of-the-way places, the challenge is how to keep these places authentic and healthy and to protect rather than overwhelm the sensitive, fragile environments and cultures we discover and visit. In the next section, we describe a number of "best practices" travelers should look for to make informed and responsible choices about the tour operators they use to arrange and conduct their trips.

The second issue is "voluntourism." Many travelers want to do more than just have fun and experience something different—they also want to contribute to the health and welfare of the locations and communities they visit. Adventure travelers are increasingly looking for opportunities to donate their time and effort, in addition to their tourist dollars, to deliver medical supplies to remote areas, teach English, help clean up after disasters, build sanitation systems, and the like. But many programs are not well thought out and, despite their good intentions, some may even do a disservice to the communities they try to support. Voluntourists need to evaluate the effectiveness of the available options. We offer a number of recommendations for how to do that.

The third issue has to do with the ongoing search for the cutting-edge travel destinations of the near-, medium-, and long-term future. For the pioneers among us who want to beat the crowds to the next, hot, off-the-radar destination and get there before highly developed tourism infrastructures leach the adventure from the experience, we offer a few hints about where to look and what to look for in your search for new places to go.

SUSTAINABLE TOURISM

The expression sustainable tourism—along with the kindred expressions, ecotourism and green tourism—has recently entered the everyday lexicon of tour operators, environmentalists, community leaders, and aware travelers throughout the world. The National Geographic Center for Sustainable Destinations uses the expression "geotourism" to encompass the various meanings of all of the terms.

Geotourism is defined as "tourism that sustains or enhances the geographical character of a place—its environment, culture, aesthetics, heritage, and the well-being of its residents." As the Center puts it, "Geotourism incorporates the concept of sustainable tourism—that destinations should remain unspoiled for future generations—while allowing for enhancement that protects the character of the locale. Geotourism also adopts a principle from its cousin, ecotourism—that tourism revenue can promote conservation—and extends that principle beyond nature travel to encompass culture and history as well: all distinctive assets of a place."* In short, spend your travel dollars in ways that support those assets.

Here we offer a list of questions that travelers can ask tour operators to make sure that they are protecting, not destroying, the destinations they visit. The questions are adapted from "A Practical Guide to Good Practice" and its accompanying "Self-Assessment Checklist," both published by Conservation International and the United Nations Environment Programme (UNEP). Although the guide and the checklist are specifically aimed at managing the environmental and social impacts of mountain tourism, many of the principles and questions can be applied to adventure trips across any environment and culture.

---

* See *www.nationalgeographic.com/travel/sustainable/about_geotourism.html.*

VISITOR EDUCATION AND INTERPRETATION

The assumption underlying the first set of questions is that being knowledgeable about the places you visit will make you a more responsible traveler who will respect the natural environment and culture.

- Does the trip include educational activities designed to increase the travelers' awareness, understanding, and appreciation of the natural environment and local culture?
- Is the program presented by trained guides? How were they trained?
- Does the program include information on local laws, customs, and appropriate behavior (including photography)?

MANAGING THE IMPACT ON LOCAL COMMUNITIES

Adventure travelers want to experience the local culture up close. But this interaction can have a negative impact on the local community. It can change the culture and customs in undesired ways, distort the economy, and provide temptations and opportunities for crime. Responsible tour operators try as much as possible to ensure that their presence and impact help the community rather than damage it.

- Does the tour operator consult with the community to make sure that the tour activities interfere as little as possible with daily routines and lifestyle?
- Are routes and sites chosen to avoid sensitive or private community areas and activities?
- Does the tour operator employ local residents, use local suppliers, and include stops at local businesses and markets?
- Does the tour operator help develop their guides' language and guiding skills—for example, through courses and other training programs?
- Is the tour operator involved in any projects to improve community living conditions, such as providing health care, sanitation, or access to food and clean water?

ENVIRONMENTAL PRACTICES

For trips to destinations with fragile or sensitive environments, it is critical that tour operators do what they can to preserve the local habitat for future visitors, as well as for the communities that live there. They need to manage their interactions with wildlife and dispose of waste responsibly, conserve energy and other resources, and support local conservation initiatives.

- Does the tour operator have policies about feeding and handling wildlife and how to act in animals' presence (e.g., avoiding loud noises and sudden movements)? How do they communicate these policies to their clients?
- What do they do to minimize energy consumption?
- How do they handle human waste?
- Does the operator support any local conservation programs? Are these activities incorporated into tour activities?

This is only a sampling of the many issues addressed by the Conservation International/UNEP report, but it does give you a good idea of the kinds of questions you can ask to determine whether tour operators are doing what they can to protect and enhance the character of the places they visit. We are not suggesting that you extensively grill each and every tour operator, but we do recommend that you examine what is in their promotional materials and trip documents, ask probing questions, and weigh this information in the choices you make about trips and tour operators. By voting with your dollars, you can play a major role in encouraging tour operators to adopt sustainable practices.

VOLUNTEER ADVENTURE TOURISM

In the past, volunteer travel required a significant investment of time, with volunteers spending several weeks or months on a project. Now there are many options for people interested in mixing some volunteering with their holiday travel. The key question for many would-be voluntourists is how to find good volunteer travel programs and how to evaluate the various options that are available.*

FINDING A VOLUNTEER TRIP

Given the range of possibilities, scouting your ideal trip will involve a fair amount of Internet searching. The process can be broken down into two primary steps.

STEP 1: ASSESS YOUR INTERESTS. Before you go crazy on Google, honestly assess your interests: Do you want to spend more time volunteering or more

---

* This section is adapted from the article "The Complete Guide to Volunteer Tourism" by Christina Heyniger, published in the online travel magazine, *Brave New Traveler*, July 23, 2007 (*www.bravenewtraveler.com/2007/07/23/the-complete-guide-to-volunteer-tourism*).

time touring? In other words, do you want volunteer activities to compose the main dish or the seasoning of your holiday meal? This first decision will be crucial to how you conduct your search and select a program.

STEP 2: START YOUR SEARCH. An online search is the best way to size up the vast universe of volunteer opportunities. Depending on whether you want mostly vacation or mostly volunteerism there are two approaches to searching through the options.

If you want mostly holiday with a little volunteering thrown in, you can start your search by simply identifying trips that interest you or look for recommendations on websites like Off the Radar *(www.traveloffheradar .com)*, which occasionally reviews trips that blend volunteer service with adventure travel. From your short list of possible experiences, contact the tour operators and ask whether they have any volunteer opportunities available on their trips. Many adventure tour operators have volunteer options, but because it's not their primary focus, they often do not advertise them.

If you want volunteering to be a primary focus of the trip, you can check the following resources for more volunteer-focused travel opportunities:

- Transitions Abroad *(www.transitionsabroad.com)* is a magazine dedicated to volunteering and working abroad.
- Idealist.org *(www.idealist.org)*, with its vast and growing database of more than 61,000 nonprofit and community organizations in 165 countries, is another excellent resource.
- Peter Greenberg's travel site *(www.petergreenberg.com)* has a good section on voluntourism with links to several larger voluntourism organizations.
- Voluntourism International *(www.voluntourism.org)* is a nonprofit organization dedicated to disseminating information about volunteer travel.

Several books also offer useful ideas and information:
- *Volunteer: A Traveler's Guide to Making a Difference Around the World*, by Charlotte Hindle, Nate Cavalieri, Rachel Collinson, and Korina Miller (Oakland: Lonely Planet, 2007).
- *Volunteer Vacations: Short-Term Adventures That Will Benefit You and Others*, by Bill McMillon, Doug Cutchins, Anne Geissinger, and Ed Asner (Chicago: Chicago Review Press, 2006).
- *The 100 Best Worldwide Vacations to Enrich Your Life*, by Pam Grout (Washington, D.C.: National Geographic, 2008).

EVALUATING A VOLUNTEER PROJECT OR TRIP: HOW TO TELL THE GOOD ONES FROM THE SCAMS

Once you have identified various options, the next question is how to evaluate the substance of the programs you'll be supporting with your time and money. Although volunteer travel can be extremely beneficial to local communities, there are instances where well-meaning tour operators or nongovernmental organizations (NGO) have initiated poorly designed and researched programs that do more harm than good.

In addition to all of the standard questions about fees, accommodations, time spent volunteering, and nature of the work (e.g., manual labor to build or fix something, teaching English, etc.), we recommend asking the program manager specific questions about the nature of the program and its impact on the community. Here are some questions you can ask to determine whether the tour operator or NGO you plan to volunteer with is worthy of your time and effort:

- *How long has the organization been supporting humanitarian or environmental projects in the country you'll be visiting?* If the tour operator or NGO has little experience in the region, it doesn't mean it's not worthy of your support, but you should at least know that you may be volunteering with a new, untested project.
- *Does the organization have a regular presence in the community?* Tour operators that do not have a continuing presence in the area but just periodically pass through may make the local communities dependent on services or materials they cannot support over the long term.
- *Do they understand the local language?* Organizations can interact well and understand the social undercurrents in local communities only if they speak the language and can establish trust. This may be especially challenging in countries where local people speak a variety of dialects.
- *How is the project need determined?* Did the operator simply cruise through the village one day and say, "Looks like these people need more tennis shoes, windbreakers, and blankets. I'll bring some through on my next tour!" Or did it take a collaborative approach and work with local people to ask them what they need and then determine whether and how to support those needs?
- *How involved is the local community in planning and managing volunteer service projects?* Is the community in full receive mode or are they making some contribution of time and/or money as well? Unless local

communities are invested in the projects, they will not value or maintain them over the long term.

- *How self-empowering is the project?* Local communities may become permanently dependent on the support of foreign volunteers. Programs aimed at self-empowerment are best, so it's good to ask about the organization's long-term goals and what it is doing to help communities eventually manage projects themselves with minimal or no foreign support. The goal should be "a hand up, not a hand out."
- *How do they measure results? Do the results indicate success?* Ask directly whether and how they measure the results of their program. If an organization can show measurable improvements over time, it's a pretty fair bet that its contributions and efforts are achieving their objectives.
- *How do they deal with corruption?* Sometimes tour operators may not even know when their financial or material contributions are being mismanaged. For example, they may take travelers to visit and volunteer at an orphanage, but not know until too late that the orphanage is "hiring" kids to pose as orphans in order to encourage donations. Ask them whether they've had to face issues of corruption. They should be candid and willing to share their experiences and tell you what they have learned from these experiences and the modifications they have made to address these issues.

Since you may be investing a fair amount of time and effort on the volunteer project, as well as some money, you should probably be more compulsive about asking these questions than is the case with the questions in the previous section. An unsatisfactory answer on any one of these questions could mean that you might at a minimum be wasting your time and effort, or in the worst case scenario, be in for a frustrating and unpleasant experience.

WHERE TO GO NEXT

Travelers, especially adventure travelers, are always on the lookout for new destinations not yet sullied by hordes of tourists. In this final section, we give you our recommendations for next trips after you have sampled a few described in this book.

The region that we believe offers the most value, exotic destinations, friendly people, and comfortable accommodations is Southeast Asia. If you haven't already been there, go now. It is fast becoming one of the most popular travel destinations in the world. Although the more familiar destinations—the beaches of Thailand, the spectacular ruins of Angkor Wat in Cambodia, and now the major cities of Vietnam—are overrun with Western tourists and won't offer you a pristine adventure experience, don't let that stop you from visiting. There are plenty of destinations within easy reach that will still feel very remote and exotic. For example, visit Laos (see p. 217) or any other location in Cambodia after Angkor Wat (which is indeed a must-see). After zoning out on the beaches of southern Thailand, head north to Chiang Mai and beyond to tour the countryside, villages, and historic sites of northern and northeastern Thailand. Skip the hill tribe treks in Thailand and do them in Laos and southern China, instead. After a week or so in Hanoi and environs, including Halong Bay, visit the remote mountains of northwestern Vietnam along the border with China. Southeast Asia is well represented by several of the trips included in this book (see pp. 217, 280, and 282).

Another region on the rise is Central Asia, especially the five "Stans"—Kazakhstan, Kyrgyzstan, Uzbekistan, Tajikistan, and Turkmenistan (see p. 281). In the minds of most people, these countries share the dour image of the former Soviet Union, of which they were once part, or the unrest of the other Stans, Afghanistan and Pakistan. Those impressions keep many tourists away—which is one of the reasons why they are such great destinations for adventure travelers. The other reasons have to do with their natural beauty, cultural treasures, and a history that goes back to Alexander the Great, Genghis Khan, and Marco Polo.

The emergence of the Stans as a travel destination suggests an axiom that might serve as a guide for those who want to look farther down the road for the adventure travel destinations of tomorrow. A few years ago, hardly anyone would have anticipated that we would now be talking about Uzbekistan, for example, as a tourist destination. A few years before that, we might have said the same of Croatia, one of the fastest-rising travel hotspots in Europe, or of Vietnam, which is booming with tourists from North America. Today's war zone or trouble spot is often tomorrow's adventure travel destination. Think about the stunning scenery of Afghanistan, which we see way too often on the evening news in a far less positive context. Think about the fabled antiquities of Iraq, the cradle of civilization and the ancient site of Babylon. It may take quite a while before peace comes to these regions and they are safe for tourists, but recent history does suggest that their time will eventually come.

We also recommend keeping your eyes on Colombia, Iran, Libya, Myanmar (Burma), northern Iraq (Kurdistan), and Israel and the Palestinian Territories. Cartegena in Colombia is booming with tourists, some companies already offer adventure travel trips in Iran and Libya, and Myanmar has been open to tourism for some time, although many people will want to defer their visit until the political conditions improve. As for Israel and the Palestinian Territories, just imagine what peace would do for tourism in the Middle East. It would make it possible, for example, to travel easily and safely within and among all the countries of the region and to see the antiquities and sites that tell the story of the birth of Western civilization.

Global warming, for all of the difficulties it creates, will also open up destinations now deemed too inhospitable for most travelers. For example, the Northwest Passage across the top of North America is rapidly becoming fully navigable in summer, opening up a region that until recently has been virtually inaccessible to all but the most adventurous. The sad irony is that it also diminishes one of the primary reasons for making this journey, the unique wildlife of the Far North, particularly polar bears. Climate change will also change other destinations—moving premier wine-growing regions farther north, for example, and making others too hot to visit comfortably.

For the ultimate adventure travel destinations, look to the depths of the ocean and into space. Tycoons and oligarchs can train like cosmonauts and fly in a Russian spaceship to the International Space Station for around $20 million. Virgin Galactic is planning on bringing suborbital space travel to the masses—sort of—for a mere $200,000 or so. In time, maybe the rest of us will also get a chance to go.

Skeptical? Good. This shows a healthy respect for danger and an appropriate sense of place in the universe. However, many psychologists, philosophers, and theologians agree that the need for adventure is intrinsic to the human spirit. It has driven us to leave our caves, move across continents, sail across oceans, fly into space, and go to the moon. Explorers go first, then the rest follow in their footsteps. Some of us, the adventure travelers, will follow sooner than others. It's just a matter of time, maybe not for us, but possibly for our children, surely for our grandchildren. As this book so clearly demonstrates, the spirit of adventure endures even as we grow older. It may morph a bit—for instance, we may want more comfortable accommodations and low-impact activities—but it's still there, throbbing in our hearts, pulsing in our veins, ready to take us for ride down the Hulahula all the way to the Arctic Ocean.

ACKNOWLEDGMENTS

We would like to thank several people who have made this book possible. Carol Mann, our agent, helped us shape our ideas as we worked through several different concepts and approaches, then connected us with the publisher of our dreams. Elizabeth Newhouse, Director of Travel Publishing at National Geographic Books, took it from there, shaping our ideas even further before handing us off to our editor, Larry Porges, who helped us turn these ideas into an actual book.

Don would also like to extend a special thanks to Ken Dychtwald, who inspired him to pursue his passion, and to his wife, Katherine, who provided the encouragement and support to make it possible. And he is especially grateful to his partner and collaborator, Shannon Stowell. Without him, this would still be just a fantasy, an adventure imagined but yet to be taken.

Shannon would also like to thank Don, whose tenacity and apparently limitless patience managing the process made this exciting project come together. Great creations always require somebody to go through the oft painful exercise of keeping everyone on track, and Don did just that. Shannon would also like to thank Chris Doyle, Chris Chesak, Christina Heyniger, Murray Bartholomew, Jason Reckers, Amber Silvey, and Quannah Reekers for helping make the ATTA what it is today. Shannon is also extremely grateful to his wife, Shelly, a godsend and an incredible support in this writing process.

CONTRIBUTING
AUTHORS

—⟨⟨⟨⟩⟩⟩—

HAZEL CAPER FURST is a psychologist who lives in Pacific Palisades, California. Her favorite song when growing up in Boston during the 1940s and 1950s was "Don't Fence Me In." Her husband, **CHARLES FURST**, is a neuropsychologist in his mid-60s. Though still working, he is able to spend a third of his time cruising in Mexico on his sailboat, *Reprise.*

CHRISTINA HEYNIGER is in her mid-30s and lives in Santa Fe, New Mexico. She is the founder and CEO of Xola Consulting, Inc., which works closely with adventure tour operators and government tourism boards around the world to develop and promote sustainable tourism practices for the benefit of local communities and the environment. Her adventures began with her childhood in Alaska and have since taken her through many countries in Africa, China, Southeast Asia, and Europe (see *www.xolaconsulting.com* and *www.traveloofftheradar.com*).

DENNIS HICKS is in his mid-60s and lives in Venice, California, with his wife and coauthor, **STEPHANIE WAXMAN**. He is a psychotherapist and has recently published his first novel, *Camera Obscura (www.dennishicks .net)*. Stephanie is in her early 60s and the author of three books, *A Helping Handbook: When a Loved One Is Critically Ill, Growing Up Feeling Good,* and *What Is a Girl? What Is a Boy?,* as well as a collection of short stories, *Sex and Death.* Her fiction has also appeared in numerous publications, including W. W. Norton's anthology *New Sudden Fiction* (see *www.stephanie waxman.com*).

DALE A. JOHNSTON is a humanities professor and former university president and **ELSA P. PAULEY** is a retired clinical psychologist. They are in their mid-60s and live in Los Angeles. They travel widely and regularly in Europe and South America. When not traveling, they write, garden, cook, and spend considerable time with their seven grandchildren.

THOMAS KRAMER is currently chair of the Department of Professional and Community Leadership at the University of West Florida in Pensacola. Tom and his wife, Mary, have traveled extensively in Europe and, more recently, Australia and New Zealand. On their vacation trips they enjoy cycling, playing golf, and finding new and exciting wines to sample. Tom is in his early 60s.

KATHERINE BRAUN MANKIN is in her early 60s and well into her third career as an attorney for a federal government agency. She lives in Venice, California, with Don, one of the authors of this book.

JOAN MERRICK, in her early 60s, is a former New Yorker who has lived in rural Alaska for more than ten years. She has been a nurse practitioner for more than 30 years, including five working in the bush at fly-in villages, mostly on the Yukon River and in the Pribilof Islands.

SUSAN MUNRO, who turned 60 the same year that she traveled to Greenland, works as an independent strategic planning, development, and communications consultant to nonprofit organizations. A mother and grandmother, she lives in Evanston, Illinois, with her husband, Bruce, and small dog, Gozo.

MARTIN RICHTER is in his early 70s and lives with his wife, Carol, in eastern Pennsylvania. He is a retired university professor who, in addition to traveling to remote and exotic places with his wife, enjoys walking, gardening, reading, and volunteering as a classical music disc jockey for a local public radio station.

DEBORAH VANDRUFF (aka Koala) is a 50-something baby boomer, born in the San Francisco Bay Area to parents who loved to travel. She moved to Alaska in the 1970s and, after many other jobs and careers, now works nights as a registered nurse, which provides the flexible schedule she needs for extended travel. A good trip for her usually involves several types of public transport, learning or sharing a skill or service, and a hammock under a palm tree.

INDEX